The Papal Council
and the Gospel

The Papal Council and the Gospel

*Protestant Theologians Evaluate
the Coming Vatican Council*

EDITED BY

KRISTEN E. SKYDSGAARD

Professor of Theology, University of Copenhagen

AUGSBURG PUBLISHING HOUSE

Minneapolis, Minnesota

THE PAPAL COUNCIL AND THE GOSPEL
Copyright © 1961 Augsburg Publishing House
Library of Congress Catalog Card No. 61-17915

A German edition is being published simultaneously by
Vandenhoeck & Ruprecht Verlag, Göttingen, under the title
*Konzil und Evangelium, Lutherische Stimmen zum kom-
menden Römisch-Katholischen Konzil.*

Scripture quotations are from the Revised Standard Version
of the Bible, copyright 1946 and 1952 by the Division of
Christian Education of the National Council of Churches.

MANUFACTURED IN THE UNITED STATES OF AMERICA

FOREWORD

The announcement by Pope John XXIII of his intention to convoke an ecumenical council has already produced a great quantity of literature. This indicates the extraordinary interest this step has aroused and the great importance that is attached to it, primarily in the Roman Catholic Church but also in the rest of Christendom. A host of questions are being asked by theologians and laymen: What is an ecumenical council? What was the attitude of the Reformation toward the idea of a council? Why is a council being convened at this particular time? What is going to happen there? All these questions focus upon the one central question which we consider essential: Does this council concern *us* as evangelical Lutheran Christians? What position should *we* take with regard to it? In authoritative Catholic quarters the coming council is being quite consciously described as a step on the road to the unity of Christians. This prompts us, too, to give fresh thought to the unity of the church of God and the questions and problems related to it.

This book was written in order to make a contribution toward the answering of these questions. *The Special Commission on Interconfessional Research* of the Lutheran World Federation—whose chairman is Bishop Dietzfelbinger from München, Bishop of Bavaria, and whose Director of Research is the undersigned—has regarded it as its task to provide factual orientation and to speak a word to clarify and state our position. What happens in the Roman Catholic Church cannot be unimportant for evangelical Christians. The time of isolation is past. More than earlier generations we are aware today that we must live with one another and also that we cannot live without one another. The ecumenical movement has opened our eyes to others and impressed upon our hearts anew the pain of the divided state of Christendom.

Everything we do in the church must be done as a ministry of the Good News of the Kingdom of God, the Gospel. No theology, no denomination can have a sole lease on the Gospel. But we can and we must help one another to see to it that all we do is done in the light of this one Gospel and that it can stand in that light. The authors are conscious of the fact that this book is not the last word on the subject. Their opinions are not closed but rather open to further insights. Among the many voices which are being heard this year with regard to the council, they have a concern that probably also has a right to be heard not only in the evangelical Lutheran churches and congregations but also in the Roman Catholic Church.

The contributions here assembled are naturally expressions of the personal convictions and knowledge of the individual authors. The discerning reader may note certain differences in the authors' points of view. Nevertheless, behind all the contributions there is a fundamental theological and spiritual attitude which is shared by all the collaborators on the book. This book was not written in order to magnify the difference between the confessions, but rather to contribute to mutual understanding. More and more there is a growing conviction on both sides that this will be possible only if we try to get a clear comprehension of the difficulties and openly express our viewpoints in a spirit of brotherliness. This way is not an easy one, but it is the only way if we honestly desire to end our isolation and enter into a real dialogue with each other.

Kristen E. Skydsgaard

Copenhagen, July, 1961

CONTENTS

Translators of the German text are John Doberstein,
Max Steuer, and David Granskou.

Chapter I

The Ecumenical Responsibility
of the Reformation Churches

"The whole Christian church on earth," of which Luther speaks in his explanation to the Third Article of the Apostles' Creed, is very naturally the context in which the Reformer moves in his thinking and preaching. The belief in the Spirit of God who "calls, gathers, enlightens, and sanctifies the whole Christian Church on earth, and preserves it in union with Jesus Christ in the one true faith," has an ecumenical horizon. In this respect the Reformation is very modern—as modern, by the way, as the New Testament, which always has the entire world of God in view, and also as modern as the whole of Christendom is today compelled to be in its thinking and believing. In these days politicians, military strategists, and business men realize that one must do business and make plans on a world-wide basis. To no less a degree—because indeed it has a Lord who has said, "All authority in heaven and on earth has been given to me. Go therefore . . ." (Matt. 28:18f)—Christianity dare not lose its global perspective.

For us, as Lutherans, the Reformation does not take its position alongside of, but rather within Christendom. It is ultimately because of this understanding that evangelical Lutheran Christianity in its

1

theology and church affairs does not shun the many-sided confrontation with the Roman Catholic Church in which it both raises questions and allows itself to be questioned. Precisely for that reason we do not take a detached view of the projected council of the Roman Catholic Church, but rather feel obligated to make a witness in accord with the Reformation to that which is happening, without, however, being thereby caught up in an alien sphere of influence.

The ecumenical significance and responsibility of the Reformation has too often been ignored and too long forgotten. The protest of the conscience bound to God's Word not infrequently evaporated into an individualistic, anti-Catholic defensive mentality, and in the historical narrowness of the era of the *Landeskirchen* it lost the originally wide perspective which encompassed the world. In the generation of the ecumenical movement we ourselves must therefore reflect anew on the ecumenical responsibility of the Reformation. Our first task is to consider the Reformation's charge to direct a witness to the whole world. Beyond this, we must become more conscious that this mission, if it is to be a true witness to Christ, must be made in the form of service or *diakonia*. Finally, the ecumenical horizon may become still clearer to us by our considering our mission as an aspect of *leiturgia,* or worship, i.e., in prayerful conversation with God.

I

It is most clear to the followers of Luther that the ecumenical responsibility of the Reformation is first of all the responsibility of a truly evangelical witness. What happened in the Reformation was that one single man was gripped by the question concerning the salvation of his soul in the presence of God. The answer which he found in Holy Scripture was the message of the justification of the sinner by grace alone through faith in Jesus Christ. The answer of this single man is, however, at the same time the ecumenical answer, the answer for the whole of Christendom, indeed for all men in the world. In this respect Luther proclaimed, as a matter of course, that the Gospel had been relit again for everybody, "*Dear Chris-*

tians, one and *all* rejoice. . . ." What had been found was not just a theological discovery which belonged in a corner. Is it not true that on each page of the New as well as the Old Testament one confronts precisely that God who, by grace alone, in his great faithfulness saves the godless and the distant ones for the sake of Jesus Christ? In his contemplation, struggle, and preaching, Luther, as it were, witnessed this justifying activity of God. And what he has learned by seeing and hearing the hands, words, and of course the heart of God—all this he attempted to incorporate into his message of justification. Because it is nothing else but the central word of Jesus Christ who "was put to death for our trespasses and raised for our justification" (Rom. 4:25), it follows that it has universal comprehensiveness, and therefore he coined the phrase *"hominem justificari fide"*[1] as the most significant description of man, which means that whoever would understand what man is must see him in the light of justification.

It is unthinkable to have a stronger motivation for all the tasks in the world than the message of justification. What drove the Apostle Paul from city to city and country to country was the certainty that "the Gospel . . . is the power of God for salvation to every one who has faith" (Rom. 1:16). The former Norwegian mission director and now Bishop of Stavanger, F. Birkeli, has expressed how compellingly relevant this message can be in our day: "The *sola fide* and the *sola gratia* must be proclaimed anew to the men of Asia and Africa in modern terminology. When one speaks of the message of the Reformation in the new world of Asia and Africa, then one sees plainly that justification through faith and not through works has a variety of important connotations for the millions in Asia when this word is taken to heart. In addition, the redemption on the cross, not the countless human work sacrifices, has an even greater impact for the Africans when this truth brings them to freedom."[2]

It is, therefore, not a new church which is founded with this central message, but rather, "the old church here brought to light" (Luther). Also, therefore, from a historical point of view, the Reformation thinks ecumenically. It does not renounce the history of the church from the first Pentecost until the year 1517. Rather, it shares in the church's blessings and burdens, and rejoices wherever in its history the Gospel of Jesus Christ is expressed in word or deed. We do not in any way deny that even in Christendom before the Reformation, the justifying proclamation was again and again breaking forth into life. On the contrary, we thank the Spirit of God that he never has deserted his church. The distinction between a true and a false church—which came into prominence because of the Reformation—cannot be made as though the two churches exist side by side. On the contrary, it belongs to the mission and the power of the Gospel to bring about this distinction within Christendom itself in each new situation. As a living room must be tidied up when its furniture has been taken from its place, so the Reformation had to reorganize the confused perspective on salvation and the church, bring the mediation of Jesus Christ again into the center, and allow the Word of God to have its course as the source of revelation. The Reformation at the same time brought the proper standards back into the life of the church, namely, *sola scriptura, sola gratia, solus Christus.* It is, after all, the norm of "seek first his kingdom and his righteousness, and all these things shall be yours as well" (Matt. 6:33). It appears to me that this ecumenical responsibility of the Reformation must be taken as seriously today as in the other times—especially in confrontation with the Roman Catholic Church. Already at the time of the Reformation the Roman Catholic Church was renewed by Luther himself, even though it excommunicated him, and we do not err today if we thank God for the living, ever continuing work of his Reformation. I am referring here to the many movements which can be observed even today in German and middle-European Catholicism which would approach the evangelical faith and life, such as the singing of evangelical chorales in Catholic churches, or the increase of Bible reading.

II

In addition we certainly have to learn anew that this ecumenical responsibility of a true witness will be taken seriously, not in the form of a false pretense, but in the form of *diakonia.* When Paul wished to describe the essence of the mission given him to proclaim the justifying Gospel to the whole world, he used this profound term, *diakonia.* "All this is from God, who through Christ reconciled us to himself and gave us the ministry of reconciliation . . . but as servants of God we commend ourselves in every way" (II Cor. 5:18–6:10). It cannot be otherwise, i.e., the witness of the Gospel must go forth in the garb of Christian service *(diakonia):* "through great endurance, in afflictions, hardships, calamities, beatings, imprisonments, tumults, labors, watching, hunger." It is, nevertheless, Jesus Christ himself who, being preached by them, is "among you as one who serves" (Luke 22:27). After all, the Son of Man has himself "come, not to be served, but to serve, and to give his life as a ransom for many" (Mark 10:45). Until the end of the world, the servant *(diakon)* Jesus has a concern for the world and his congregations and seeks men who, with him, will continue to have this same concern (Luke 22:26). In addition, everything which he does in and through his church for the salvation of the world is also *diakonia.* Baptism, through which he brings men into his fellowship through the forgiveness of sins, is to be so understood; *diakonia* is the Holy Communion, in which he gives himself into our mouth and inner being; *diakonia* is the Holy Scriptures in which he confronts us—not according to his power but because of our weakness, not according to his omniscience but because of our folly, not according to his glory but for our salvation. Can his congregation make its ecumenical witness in any other way than that of the *diakonia* of Christ-service? In the competition between the confessions the decisive factor will not be the question of power, influence, or self-assertion, but rather that of the *diakonia* of the Word of God.

In the present world situation the religions of man have been pushed very close together. It also appears that a new phase is developing in the confrontation of the Christian faith with the world religions, both theistic and atheistic. In New Delhi, 1961, and elsewhere, this confrontation will find its place as a new variation to the main theme, "Christianity and the world religions." How would that appear if the theme "Jesus Christ—the Light of the World" were raised as a demand? It will not be a demand, rather it must be a service. Already in the theme this must be clarified.

We must no longer say, "Christianity and the world religions," but rather, "Jesus Christ and the world religions"; or better still, "Jesus Christ and the people of other religions." It is therefore most important that we do not speak ourselves but rather listen to the words of Jesus Christ, "I am the light of the world." It is even more imperative that our western Christianity is not raised to the level of an absolute demand, as has already been done a thousand times. Rather, Jesus Christ himself should say, "I am the light of the world," and should do so both with humility and nearness (see John 4), and also with majesty and Savior-like authority. When this happens, then the understanding breaks through, that wherever he comes to a man, no matter in what part of the world the man is, there Jesus Christ comes in his own uniqueness regardless of whether this man is white, black, or brown.

The evangelical witness cannot occur in any other way than by Christians mutually witnessing to the truth. We must confess that in such a joint witness to the Gospel the attitude of service can often be pushed to the background and be replaced by a self-justifying pretentiousness, or self-assertive confessionalism. This cannot mean that we should suppress or efface the truth. The point is that we must not witness to *our* truth, but to the truth of Jesus Christ. "Among the main reasons for church heresies, schisms, and divisions is the lack of the inner power of mutual service, of mutual inter-dependent existence. The greatest sin of the people of God is that they have neglected to perceive the theological, vertical dimensions of *diakonia* in the ecclesiological, horizontal one." So said Nikos A. Nissiotis in his memorable lecture, "Diakonie der Kirchen untereinander," delivered in Nyborg, Denmark, in 1960. The churches of the Reformation will have to confess this neglect, too, in order to become free for their responsibility. They know full well that the people of God continue to live in the world solely because of the service and ministry of their Lord. We lose this life itself unless we pass it on in willing service. This undoubtedly is the meaning of the plea which W. Elert once made to the various Lutheran churches, namely, to return to their own ecumenical origins and in this way to make the work of the Reformation profitable for the whole of Christendom, for we "also deprive

Christianity as a whole of the message which the Lord of the church has specifically commissioned us to deliver to all men."[3]

Today we can, very gladly, refer to the new and better climate which is making itself felt in the discussions between the confessions. We are thankful for the decrease of intolerant polemics, of charge and countercharge. Any true reduction of prejudice can also be classed as *diakonia*. However, it is much more than a better climate. *Diakonia* keeps both truth and love in view. Many times it will have to cause pain though maintaining love. It will also have to cut sharply and still do so with the intention of helping. It must concern itself with the best possible organizational efficiency and still have the individual in view. It realistically sees the human frailties of men, but cannot simply ignore them, because Jesus does not do this. It suffers for them, and is concerned for them—in the hope that Jesus Christ himself has for us. *Diakonia* cannot overlook the others, as if they were not in existence. It therefore goes out in such a way that others are helped, helped with the truth. It must see all men as created by God even when their skin has another color or they wear different clothes.

How can the message of the Reformation be so witnessed that it is at once *diakonia* and also recognized as *diakonia*? The trumpet call of the Reformation should not become uncertain. The freedom which broke forth in the Reformation concerning the concept of the church, the enthusiasm for the Word of God, the joyful tension of faith in the Sacrament of the Altar, must be clearly witnessed to. However, this must most certainly be done after the manner of *diakonia*.

It will often not be able to bypass or resolve the conflict between truth and love, but *diakonia* does cleanse itself from egotism, belligerence, and dogmatism (Eph. 4:1, 2). It bears with the divisions, and allows the different varieties of discipleship to find expression as the Lord himself bore the variety of the apostles and their strife. The ecumenical responsibility of the Reformation can be taken seriously, not in ambiguity or softness, but rather in cheerful sincerity which is at the same time tempered by sorrow and repentance. There are many indications that today God is carrying his Reformation far beyond the confines of the evangelical Lutheran church, even into many sections of the Roman Catholic Church. However, he is not acknowledging us, but rather his reformation. He can even acknowledge this reformation in such a way that we thereby are made small. He does not carry on his work for the purpose of glorifying the church to which we belong; on the contrary it often develops to our embarrassment. It is not *our* triumph that is at stake but God's; "thanks be to God, who in Christ always leads us in triumph" (2 Cor. 2:14). *Diakonia* can in this way affirm the contemporary course of the Reformation, even when it develops in ways other than what we would wish. "Only that in every way . . . Christ is proclaimed; and in that I rejoice" (Phil. 1:18).

III

This approach (stressing service in the witness to the truth of the Gospel) can be truly affirmed only when a congregation at the same time acknowledges its ecumenical responsibility in worship, that is, as it stands in the presence of God. There is no better, appropriate, true, or promising way to meet a man than to pray with him and for him. There is no better or responsible witness in or for the church of Christ than that made when one speaks to God in the church and for it. Here we know of its unity in spite of all the appearances to the contrary. Here we learn to entrust God with everything and see our own work and activity in the proper perspective. Martin Luther was certain of the one church of Jesus Christ, but the struggle between the true church and the false church within Christendom troubled him sorely. There are many indications that he himself was often embittered by it. Beyond that he, more than anyone else, has been charged with the guilt for the division of Christendom. Also, when one reflects on the sharpness of his polemics, one is sooner or later tempted to question whether he had all too often allowed the concept of *diakonia* to fall into the background of the Reformation's witness of the Gospel. However, in addition to this we must insist that through his belief in the Holy Spirit he never lost sight of the one church, even if he acknowledged that we must in bitter conflict for it "await the righteous judge" (WA 51, 524, 20). And we also remember in this respect that he also witnessed to the unity of all Christendom in his prayers:

"O eternal and merciful God, you are a God of peace, love, and unity, not of division and variety. We acknowledge that this world has forsaken you, who alone can create and sustain unity and has fallen from you out of love for its own truth. We also acknowledge that with your righteous judgment you have allowed this world (especially those parts entrusted with the preservation of your divine truth and holiness) to be divided and split that, on account of their supposed wisdom, they may be brought to nothing and return to you, O lover of unity. O Father, you desire through the Holy Spirit to bring the scattered together, and to unite and make whole the divided. We poor sinners, whom you have most graciously acknowledged, implore and beseech you to so guide us that we return to your unity, seek your one eternal truth, avoid all dissention, become one in understanding, will, knowledge, soul, and mind, which ought to be turned towards Jesus Christ. We pray for this so that, in a calm unity, we will with one voice praise and glorify you, O heavenly Father of our Lord Jesus Christ." (WA 10, II, 477).

Ecumenical responsibility implies at all times and before all things a responsibility in prayer. It is precisely in prayer that the one church comes to the fore with its concerns and with its hidden glory. Its very life is to be in prayer. The oft cited prayer of Jesus, "that they may all be one" (John 17:21), is not only (as often interpreted) an expression of yearning but rather (if we reflect on the fact that Jesus himself is praying for his own) a point of certitude in the middle of travail over the one church. The Lord's Prayer, which is universally prayed in Christendom, is, as it were, a living surety of the hidden unity of Christendom. Whenever it is recited in the ecumenical movement it will do two things. On the one hand, it will remind us of our painful divisions, which even make it difficult to understand each other's way of speaking. On the other hand, it is still the prayer which "encompasses the world," and holds Christendom together. Whoever has recited the prayer petition by petition with the whole of Christendom in mind will also have caught wonderful insights and received new impetus for ecumenical responsibility. As we pray, "Our Father," we place our trust in the fact that, in spite of all its divisions, Christianity is one. As we pray, "who art in heaven," we lay on him the concern for the one church and are put to the test to take these concerns into human administration.

Especially when it is made for the gathering of his congregation from the ends and corners of the world, this prayer must be the source of our activity, just as it is for all affairs throughout the church. Here God's honor is likewise at stake. Of course, he cannot allow to remain unfinished the work most dear to his heart, his "most cherished thoughts of love in which he allows his love of men and the love of his Son to manifest itself with a veiled face" (W. Lohe). Whoever prays to this God receives in this activity a new perspective on human affairs. On the other hand, prayer is simply service in the certainty that Jesus, the *diakonos,* carries on his decisive ministry. Prayer is also the hope of the glory of his church (Col. 1:27). Therefore, the certainty which waits for things to happen through the working of God ought not to fail in spite of the struggles and disappointments connected with the establishment of the one church. Whoever would observe the contemporary movements in Christendom, will most properly first direct his gaze to the Lord, for while the human factor can be seen in all of these movements, the activity of the Spirit of God has also been made manifest in them. One can therefore pray:

> *Behold, as the eyes of servants*
> *look to the hand of their master,*
> *as the eyes of a maid*
> *to the hand of her mistress,*
> *so our eyes look to the Lord our God,*
> *till he have mercy upon us* (Psalm 123:2).

Because the division of Christendom frequently came about through the fault of men, it is not probable that the unity of Christianity will be carried very far forward through the ability and the wisdom of men. Because of this it is imperative for us to be even more diligent in paying attention to God and his Word during those times when human longing and plans for one visible church are on the increase. So we should pray, "That thy way may be known upon all the earth, thy saving power among all the nations" (Ps. 67:2).

At many times in the past, the church of the Reformation was in an outspoken way a praying church. Today this aspect of its power

seems to be falling into the background. In general our churches
are now going through a crisis in regard to the practice of piety.
Also the prayer for one church is prayed more frequently and with
more zeal in circles other than our own. Therefore the ecumenical
responsibility of the Reformation drives us to pray anew with
greater earnestness that God himself will bring the scattered together through the attestation of his truth. In addition, the prayer
for the gathering together of Christendom ought to be certain, as
all prayers in his name, that he is waiting for it and hears it, for

> *He who scattered Israel will gather him,*
> *and will keep him as a shepherd keeps his flock* (Jer. 31:10).

Notes

1. *Disputatio de homine* 1536/WA 39 I, 1757.
2. *Die neue Welt Asiens und Afrikas als Frage an unsere Kirchen im Abend-
land,* 1959.
3. Cited by Ernst Kinder, "Evangelische Katholizität," *Kerygma und Dogma,*
1960, p. 81, note 54.

Chapter II

Will the Council
Be Ecumenical?

I

The Church Council announced by Pope John XXIII for the first time in January, 1959, is to be an *"ecumenical* council." So we read in the papal encyclical "Ad Petri Cathedram" of June 29, 1959, in connection with the quotation of John 10:16, "So there shall be one flock, one shepherd": "And indeed, this fondly cherished hope has now led us and strongly impelled us to publish that intention of ours of summoning an ecumenical council for which the bishops from all over the world will assemble to deal with the important issues of religion."[1]

The term "ecumenical" in connection with a council, according to official Roman Catholic usage, is firmly established and is to be understood in a particular sense which has developed in the course of history[2] and is strictly defined in canonical law of the Roman Catholic Church.[3] "Ecumenical" is to be understood in distinction from regional and denotes a church assembly, representing and concerning the *entire* Roman Catholic Church and not only parts of it. Eichmann-Moersdorf defines it as "an assembly of the bishops of the entire Catholic world and of other prelates summoned and presided over by the pope" (p. 359). This "ecumenical council,"

12

according to Canon 228, 1, "exercises the highest governing power over the entire church." Here the entire Roman Catholic Church is, therefore, validly and authoritatively represented—that is, by its bishops and prelates.[4] Only these have the right to vote at an "ecumenical council" (Canon 223, 1). The decisions of this council are binding for the entire Roman Catholic Church. Whether at this council bishops not belonging to the Roman Catholic Church, say those of the Orthodox Church, who, as is known, according to Roman Catholic views are legitimate bishops, can participate in the decisions—this is an open question. Decisive for an "ecumenical council" is, in every case, its *absolute obligation to the pope*. "The ecumenical council is possible only in connection with the pope," says Eichmann-Moersdorf (p. 359). He alone can convene it and without his summons it is not an "ecumenical council." "There can be no ecumenical council that has not been summoned by the pope" (Canon 222, 1).[5] Moreover, the pope alone is entitled to preside at an "ecumenical council" either in person or through a substitute, as also to determine the subjects to be considered at the council, to lay down the rules governing the transactions, to remove it to another location, to adjourn it, or to dissolve it" (Canon 222, 2).[6] Furthermore, "the resolutions of a council receive their binding force only after they have been ratified by the pope and have been published by his authorization" (Canon 227).[7] Finally, Canon 228, 2 stipulates that against an assertion of the pope there can be no appeal to an "ecumenical council." A penalty for this is expressly laid down in Canon 233, 2. The moot question whether the "ecumenical council," according to Roman Catholic interpretation, is to be ranked under or beside the pope is not to be discussed here. Eichmann-Moersdorf speaks of a ranking that is in principle "beside" the pope.[8] But according to the stipulations of the Codex Juris Canonici it is actually viewed as being *under* the pope.[9] In every case this is what matters, that an "ecumenical council" is absolutely obligated to the pope and dependent on him.

But by this circumstance this "ecumenical council" is limited to the church that is subject to the pope. This absolute obligation to the pope makes an "ecumenical council" in the sense of the Codex Juris Canonici, viewed legally, a matter exclusively of the Roman

Catholic Church, representing this church alone and valid for it alone. Although the council of the Roman Catholic Church now approaching, in an indirect way and by virtue of its "radiations," will certainly in some way bear some significance beyond the bounds of the Roman church and for Christendom as a whole, it must be clearly seen that directly and immediately it is valid for this church alone. This was unmistakably and distinctly expressed in correction of some misunderstandings and false hopes entertained shortly after the publication of the summons of this council by Archbishop Dr. Lorenz Jaeger in his article entitled: "The Ecumenical Council. The Church and Christendom. Heritage and Charge," p. 7, where we read: "The coming council will not be a union council like the one held at Ferrara-Florence, which in the year 1437 brought about a reunion of the oriental Greek church with Rome. It will, accordingly, not be a church assembly which would deal with authorized representatives of the non-Catholic Christian groups concerning an eventual union with the Roman Catholic Church. Even though Pope John XXIII brings his plan of the council into connection with the great matter of the separated brethren, the fact remains that the coming council is a matter concerning the Catholic Church, and that it will deal with this church's interests."

Strictly speaking, one should not speak of an *ecumenical council* but of a *general council of the Roman Catholic Church.* Some of the misunderstandings concerning this "ecumenical council" which arose shortly after it was first announced as well as some of the hopes and expectations of the same that were in part pitched too high, were probably based on the fact that the word "ecumenical" had in the meantime—that is, in the period after the last "ecumenical council" of the Roman Catholic Church, the Vatican Council of 1869-1870—been revived in its original sense—namely, in the sense of "universal," [10] applying to the entire inhabited earth and to Christianity and the church: "concerning Christendom as a whole and representing the same, aiming at *one* church of Jesus Christ, and seeking to present this one church anew in the common struggle of the different confessional churches." In *this* sense the term "ecumenical" is generally used today, as this may be expressed by the designation "ecumenical movement," the movement in which different confessional churches are participating in order to wrestle *jointly* for the proper presentation of the *essential* unity of the church of Jesus Christ now hidden under the existing schisms. Many Roman Catholic Christians also use the term "ecumenical" to designate *interconfessional* discussions extending far beyond the realm of the Roman Catholic Church, debates and efforts in behalf of the church's unity. Thus we can understand how some to whom this concept in its traditionally official force was not familiar, when the pope announced a new "ecumenical council," instinctively and with sentiment put something of the meaning of "ecumenical" current in our day into it.

Moreover, this council, as we have seen, from the time of its first announcement by the pope, is brought into relation with the matter of the reunion of divided Christendom. This, however, touches a matter which in our day "is in the air" everywhere in Christendom. All Christendom on earth is today possessed with the urgent longing for a greater manifestation of the unity of the church of Christ. This is the deeper reason for the general spreading abroad of the term "ecumenical" in the dynamic sense suggested. In view of this urgent longing prevailing everywhere and with which the announcement of a coming "ecumenical council" was heard, we can understand how this announcement called forth such a strong movement also outsidē the Roman Catholic Church, and how the hope of the council could be too directly in line with *that* idea of ecumenicity with which it is uttered by every one and with which it lives in the hearts of all today. The coming council will doubtless also have some meaning for the efforts of all Christendom in behalf of the church's unity, though it be only in the indirect sense of a loosening up, of a manifestation of some new aspects, also in the sense of some new impulses, as also of some changes and improvements of the general "climate," etc. Since it is so, in whatever sense it may be understood, that this council is connected "with the great matter of the reunion of the separated brethren" (Archbishop Jaeger, *op. cit.*), we continue to take great interest in it, follow its manifold preparations, and look forward to it with considerable expectation. Especially the

creation of a secretariat for the unity of Christendom on the part
of the Vatican, which meanwhile has taken up its work vigorously
under the direction of Cardinal Bea, shows how earnestly the
leaders of the Roman Catholic Church are concerned with that
great matter in connection with the coming council.

It is, however, not in a *direct* or *immediate* way that this
council will meet the expectations, in part pitched too high, which
some circles outside the Roman Catholic Church cherished of it
at the beginning; and, considering its structure as determined in
the Codex Juris Canonici, it will not be able to meet them all.
We must soberly and realistically observe that the council cannot
be anything at all but a general council of the Roman Catholic
Church, which is simply directly concerned with *this* church. The
subject of the reunion will not be and cannot be in the foreground
of this council. In the foreground there will rather be the subject
of the renewal of the Roman Catholic Church in various respects,
though it be distinctly *with a view* to the questions and tasks of a
reunion. This distinction (and at the same time this mutual bearing) of a direct immediate goal and an indirect distant goal of the
work of the coming council is made vividly plain on the basis of
the aforementioned encyclical, "Ad Petri Cathedram," by Hans
Kueng in his impressive book *Konzil und Wiedervereinigung. Erneuerung als Ruf in the Einheit (The Council and Reunion. Renewal as a Call to Unity),* Vienna, Freiburg, Basel, 1960.

Ecumenical in the true sense the "ecumenical council" announced
by Pope John XXIII will therefore not be and cannot be because
it is strictly bound to a very particular confessional church and
on principle restricted to the same—namely, to that churchdom
which is characterized and restricted by the unconditional primacy
of the pope. Here we have a clash of *two different conceptions of
the term* "ecumenical"—namely, a universal and a particular conception; one referring to all Christendom on earth and the other
to the entire "Catholic globe" directed from Rome (Eichmann-
Moersdorf, *op. cit.*). In this connection one must, of course, know
that according to Roman Catholic Church consciousness the ecumenical in the sense of universal-Christian is positively embraced
by the ecumenical in the sense of the Codex Juris Canonici and that

this according to the Codex is exactly not to be understood in a particularistic sense, with confessional churches involved—namely, in so far as the Roman Catholic Church under the leadership of the pope advances the claim to be the only legitimate historical expression of *the* church of Jesus Christ and consequently is governed by the consciousness of validly representing the entire orthodox Christendom on earth. In view of this ecclesiastical self-conceit it is conceivable that a council that is so constituted as we have come to know it according to the Codex Juris Canonici is indeed considered to be an "ecumenical" council even in the fundamental sense of the word.

But if one does not share this ecclesiastical self-conceit but is rather compelled to consider it as being opposed to the true nature of the church of Jesus Christ because of its absolute claims, then one also cannot consider a council in the sense of the Codex Juris Canonici to be a council that is "ecumenical" in the true sense of the word. Though such a council should eventually have some *significance* that would be ecumenical in character—that is, in some way concern all Christendom, it still could not be ecumenically *valid*—that is, valid also for those parts of Christendom who on principle reject the Roman Catholic ecclesiastical self-conceit.

II

What would a *real* ecumenical council then be in distinction from that which we have just considered? Fundamentally viewed, the answer to this question is simply this: A real ecumenical council, as the name indicates, would actually and seriously have to include the entire orthodox Christendom on earth, so that *this* Christendom would be constituting it through authorized representatives and would be trying to speak with one consent in the name of the *one* church of Jesus Christ. Practically—in view of the actual situation of Christendom in our day—that would mean that a genuine ecumenical council, if it is to be truly ecumenical, would have to be composed of delegates from confessional churches that are still divided, and that it could not be the general coun-

cil of *one* definite confessional church which advances the absolute claim that its way of historically representing the church of
Jesus Christ is the only true "ecumenical" way. (Such an absolute
claim can be advanced directly and officially as it is advanced by
the Roman Catholic Church; but it can also be done indirectly
and implied—namely, in case one considers the specific principles
of one's own confession, as a matter of course, to be alone truly
ecumenical and imposes them as the ideal standard of ecumenicity.
Thus many "ecumenical" programs also outside the Roman Catholic
Church essentially amount to this: "Let all become like me, then
we shall be one!") But it is true, nevertheless, that none of the
various confessional churches that have arisen in the course of
the church's history can imagine itself as fully, "one hundred per
cent," congruent with the one church of Jesus Christ *and* consequently can consider the others as *altogether* pseudo churches or
false churches; that rather each one must recognize in other
churches at least elements of true Christianity and elements of the
church of Jesus Christ and must, therefore, grant that Christendom
and the church of Christ, on principle, extends beyond the realm
of its own historical churchdom.[11] In order to give expression to
this actual situation of Christendom in our day a Christian council today, if it is to be truly *ecumenical,* would have to break
through the bounds of a particular confessional church and include confessional churches that are separated from one another.

But if one should now want to take hold of this matter in a
concrete way one would encounter an array of problems plainly
showing what a risky undertaking a truly ecumenical council
rightly bearing this name must prove to be in the present situation
of Christendom. Heading all these problems would be the fundamental question concerning the proper ecumenical criterion: Who
and what is included in all that belongs to *true* "orthodox" Christendom? For it would evidently not be possible and also not prac-
ticable to include, without any boundary or norm, every one who
might call himself "Christian"! A council that is really ecumenical
cannot, and of course should not, be a veritable conglomeration
and platform for the most varied conceptions of Christianity imaginable, which could never be reduced to a common denomina-

tor but which would be assembled with fully equal rights and privileges. For the concept "ecumenical" doubtless bears a connotation in which the proper norm figures: we are engaged not only, in a qualitative sense, with the entire *true* Christendom. But what do we mean by *"true"?* According to what standard is that to be settled, inasmuch as we have such standards, for one thing, bound up only in definite confessions and not "over" them whereas a council which is truly ecumenical is to transcend the different confessions? In view of a truly ecumenical council we are, therefore, concerned with *the truly common Christian obligation,* which follows from the very fundamental nature of Christianity and by which we should have to determine who and what *rightly* bears the name "Christian" and who and what ultimately does not, and what, therefore, belongs to the utterly inalienable "esse" (nature) of Christianity and to the non-negotiable "notae verae ecclesiae" (marks of the true church). But this very matter is understood, in part, quite differently by the different Christian confessions, and there is no "neutral" supraconfessional "court of arbitration" for this matter. Generally recognized criteria for that which is truly "ecumenical" in the qualitative sense, the absolute "ecumenical obligation," are not objectively at hand although beginnings in that direction have been made, perhaps on the basis of past experiences and undertakings in the area of the ecumenical movement. Therefore the participants in an ecumenical council would, to begin with, have to wrestle with one another concerning generally recognized principles, criteria, and standards of unity, which the very nature of the church absolutely demands. Gaining these things would precisely constitute the most important task of a genuine ecumenical council and could not be presupposed as characterizing such a council!

Such being the case, mark you, we should not be concerned with producing a complete "ecumenical dogmatics of norms" or with the blue print giving all the details for a united world church! In some respects differences might positively remain without prejudice to the essential unity of the church of Jesus Christ. Not all the differences between the confessional churches are truly of such a nature as to cause divisions and necessitate breaking off church fellowship; a whole array of them are simply an expression of the manifold nature of the church and could by all means exist side by side.

But not all differences can be explained by the theory of the church's diversity. There are also differences in points which are central and decisive between the confessional churches which mutually exclude one another and which simply cannot exist side by side, especially where absolute claims are advanced in connection with the points concerned. In such cases church fellowship is simply impossible. Such points would have to be honestly and earnestly examined and dealt with in common by the participants in an ecumenical council. The goal striven and hoped for would not be this, that all the confessional churches would become alike in all respects and that a united world church would come into being. It would be a bleak and terrible vision of the future if the opinion were to prevail that the essential unity of the church of Jesus Christ must needs express itself in a unified church structure extending 'round the world. It is far better if *those* differences between the confessional churches which are an expression of lively diversity would continue to remain. Yet those differences of an exclusive nature should be clarified by joint striving for the common recognition of the "notae verae ecclesiae" which the very nature of the church establishes and requires in order that church fellowship between churchdoms (the fact of their being different gladly granted) may become possible. Such church fellowship seems to us to be the proper manner in which the essential unity of the church of Christ wants to come to be historically exhibited. To bring this about in deed and in truth should be the aim of an ecumenical council.

Apart from these fundamental problems, serious difficulties present themselves with the question concerning a real ecumenical council when the historical situation is taken into consideration. For one thing, there are no precedents or historical examples with which one could begin and which one could use as "models." Especially after the great schisms in the western half of the church since the sixteenth and seventeenth centuries, a council that is really ecumenical, from the point of view of church history, would be *something absolutely new;* one would be operating on virgin soil in the realm of church history.

In the material history of the church there were, and up to the present there are, no other "ecumenical councils" excepting those mentioned in the ancient church, which extend up to the eighth century and in addition at most the union councils of the fifteenth century, with delegates from the oriental and the occidental churches in attendance, at which attempts were made to overcome the schism between the two.[12] The rest of the councils, designated "ecumenical" by the Roman Catholic Church, cannot, as we have said, be regarded as really ecumenical but must rather be considered as the general councils of a particular church which has become principally "confessionalistic," which in an unwarranted manner claims absolute infallibility for its church principles, especially the papacy but also the governing and teaching office of the bishops.[13] In distinction from this the seven "ecumenical councils" of the ancient church, jointly accepted by the oriental and the occidental churches, can be accepted, in a certain sense, as really ecumenical, since they were indeed councils of a church which, as a whole, was still undivided. To be sure, this is true only in a certain sense, inasmuch as the compactness of the church of those centuries (and therefore also the councils representing it in its entirety) had been upheld to a considerable degree only by the strong arm of the state, with the result that the considerable schismatic bodies then already in existence had either been forcibly suppressed or dropped from view as nonexistent. A similar situation prevails in view of the union councils of the fifteenth century, whose resolutions, as we know, came about substantially under political pressure and the one-sided dictation of the Roman Catholic Church, so that afterward the oriental church never considered them to be ecumenically binding. For a genuine ecumenical council, fundamental *freedom* from political influence and freedom of self-determination on the part of the churches would be an absolutely necessary presupposition.

Absolutely free from the participation of "nontheological factors" a church council will probably never be. The thing that matters, however, is whether "in, with, and under" such factors, central

motives of the fundamental Christian issues, will after all prevail
as matters of common Christian "obligation." In this respect—
that is, in view of the substance of their doctrinal decisions—we
may indeed, as did the Reformation too, consider the resolutions of
at least the *first four* of the "ecumenical councils" of the ancient
church as really ecumenical; for in their christological decisions
fundamental aims of the revelation of salvation in Jesus Christ
actually prevailed as being binding for all of Christendom.[14] Yet
it is important to note what really makes them binding—namely,
not this that it was an ecumenical council which spoke but that the
content of its resolutions is upheld by the original canonical testimonies of Holy Scripture! This gives us a further important observation regarding a genuine ecumenical council: It is not entitled
a priori and purely formally to supreme authority in the church,
nor can its resolutions without further appeal be regarded as
being absolutely binding. Here Luther's assertion at the Leipzig
Disputation in 1519—namely, that councils can err, is fundamentally
valid—but they must rather *prove* to be true in *content* and therefore valid. A truly ecumenical council through which common
Christian matter is to find expression cannot and dare not be com-
pressed within itself and be sanctioned simply as an institution;
it is rather itself still subject to the norm and the final judgment of
Holy Scripture, the original canonical testimonies of God's revelation of salvation in Jesus Christ.[15] In reality it is always the case
that one cannot tell until afterward—that is, on the basis of its
content and its resolutions—whether a council has really been
ecumenical!

If, therefore, in the first four "ecumenical councils" of the ancient
church we have, in a certain sense, examples of what a really
ecumenical council is, this will still not help us directly and sufficiently in view of *this* situation in which we find Christendom
today—that is, in view of those schisms which have come about
in the western half of the church since the sixteenth century, above
all as a result of the rejection of papal primacy but also for other
reasons, especially the intrusion of spiritualism. It would be a fic-
tion and flight into the past if one were to think as, for instance,
George Calixt did, that the present ecumenical problems could

be mastered by simply going back of the schisms in the faith and
in the church since the sixteenth (also since the eleventh) century to the common ground floor of the "consensus quinquesaecu-
laris" (the doctrinal agreement of the first five centuries).[16] Thus
we should be deceiving ourselves concerning the true nature of the
schisms which came about in the meantime—and that on the level
and in view of this common possession—and mistakenly consider
them as bagatelles and of secondary nature. But such they are not;
in part they concern matters of central importance! Thus when we,
in view of these schisms, raise the question concerning a truly ecumenical council we are actually setting foot on pioneer soil in the
church's history, where all analogies that served us hitherto fail
us. Thus it is, too, that in view of the present situation of Christendom we can only set up a "dogmatical reflection" concerning the
question as to what a truly ecumenical council *would be*—that is,
saying something fundamental concerning it. That is still not
unimportant. Such a reflection might let us see that which matters
as our "obligation" and show us what steps are necessary for the
realization of our quest.

There is, by the way, a phenomenon in the church's history
which can serve as a point of contact for our deliberations regarding a genuine ecumenical council; that is the ecumenical movement of our own day. For here the first breaching of the wall of
separation was accomplished and the beginning was made to set
foot on pioneer soil in the church's history—namely, that of assembling together and of mutual striving on the part of different
confessions with a view to the essential unity of the church of Jesus
Christ. Moreover, this ecumenical movement is not something that
was planned in advance and started according to a definite program, but really a genuine, elemental movement, in which, one
may say, the very essential, original unity of the church of Jesus
Christ really maintains its rights anew as a spiritual reality by
virtue of its own power. (Without belief in the pre-existence and
the inherent right of the essential unity of the church of Jesus
Christ as a reality a dogmatical reflection on what a really ecumenical council would be in the face of the present situation of
Christendom as well as such a council itself would indeed be a

"Platonic" affair and like the fruitless efforts of squaring the circle!) To be sure, we shall not yet be able to designate the world conferences of churches which have hitherto resulted from the ecumenical movement as ecumenical councils,[17] as we shall see further on, and also the next conventions of the World Council of Churches probably cannot yet be considered as such. However, we can observe in the entire matter of setting up the aims of the ecumenical movement as also in the experiences and the operations of its history, now dating back fifty years, various important points of view, indications, and tendencies which we cannot ignore in our thinking as to what a truly ecumenical council would be today. We shall, therefore, at least make use of them in our dogmatical reflection.

III

In addition to the observations which we have made incidentally in the preceding chapter we shall now expressly set forth in five points what, in our conviction, would belong to a truly ecumenical council in view of the present situation of Christendom.

(1) A truly ecumenical council of our day would have to exhibit the venture of church bodies of different confessions, which might in certain important points be mutually exclusive, coming together for the purpose of jointly and earnestly studying the true essence of the one church of Jesus Christ and what, in view of this essence, is of necessity required if the unity of the church is to become visibly manifest as it should. An assembly of the different confessional churches at which the central and decisive questions concerning theological truth would not be earnestly brought into play, at which the participants would rather be enthusiastically content just with the mere experience of fellowship, or would be striving only for "unity" pragmatically by church politics, and would be satisfied with practical cooperation, would not be a truly ecumenical council and would really not get anywhere. A genuine ecumenical council must strive for unity with regard to the central and inalienable truth of salvation. (See point 4 on page 28.)

In the present state of Christendom this is a real venture, in which one must forego a priori institutional security, perhaps after the manner of the Codex Juris Canonici, if the truth which Christians have in common, which is binding on them and to be recognized by them, and which is generally to prevail is not to be prejudiced and curbed from the very beginning in the sense of a definite historical confession. Indeed, as matters stand today, there cannot be absolute security a priori with regard to dogmatics; for the criteria and the norms for that which in view of the true essence of the church is absolutely required for legitimate manifestation of the church's unity, are not generally established but they must first be discovered by joint effort as being generally accepted. Thus, as we have said above, the generally recognized standards for that which is ecumenical in the qualitatively valid sense are not a required presupposition for an ecumenical council but rather just its task and *aim!* It is just through this that an attempt must be made to bring about the consensus of the different confessional churches with regard to that which is absolutely necessary "ad veram unitatem ecclesiae" (for the true unity of the church) from the point of view of its essence. Thus an ecumenical council would finally also have to be defined according to this matter of setting up its aims.

We could by all means tie in with that which in the course of the work already done hitherto, say by the ecumenical movement for faith and order, the different confessional churches have already expressed concerning the essence of the church and the genuine visible manifestation of its unity.[18]

But it has now also become plain that the church bodies assembling at an ecumenical council, even though they are not able to appear with a perfect consensus, yet should at least fulfil *certain* minimum prerequisites in order that they may participate in such a council and its earnest effort with some promise of success, and that the whole thing may not turn out to be a purely hypothetical and "Platonic" affair. Such a prerequisite could be complete readiness and openness, one's own confession fully brought into play,[19] to contend earnestly for agreement in central and decisive points concerning the truth of salvation with others who want to do likewise, the Holy Scriptures being the final arbiter. One might suggest also the joint recognition of the resolutions of the first four "ecumenical councils" of the ancient church—that is, in the sense described above. Moreover, one could also point to the World Council of Churches—namely, to its "Basis," which aims to set forth the requirements for a successful participation in the ecumenical effort,[20] as also the fourth part of the "Toronto Declaration," in which the obligations assumed by the member churches of the World Council are set forth. All this is presented only by way of example in order to illustrate fundamental points and to suggest matter for concrete consideration.

(2) In our deliberations concerning a really ecumenical council today we are concerned also with the question *by whom* the different church bodies which fulfill the prerequisites indicated under (1) and affirm the aims indicated there are to be represented in order that an adequate representation may be guaranteed. The fact that according to the Codex Juris Canonici only bishops and prelates are entitled to represent Christendom and the church with full rights and therefore also only they have the right to vote on resolutions of the council, corresponds specifically with the Roman Catholic conception of the church and of the office of the ministry and again amounts to a priori narrowing in the sense of a particular confession and therefore preventing what is truly ecumenical. This does not mean that the important truths—which cannot be surrendered—contained in Roman Catholic doctrine concerning the office of teaching and leadership in the church according to the New Testament are to be disputed as such in their relevancy for the formation of the church, but only in their absolute and exclusive claims which have been attached to them in the course of time. *This* must be considered as "confessionalistic" and cannot be viewed as an original and common Christian possession that would be genuinely ecumenical. Originally Christian and of common application is the proper mutual relation and coordination of the office and of the congregation in the structure of the church, and this must also find expression and become manifest at a genuine ecumenical council. This means that at such a council, in definite coordination with the representatives of the office in the church, also the responsible congregation, therefore also *lay-*

men, as representatives of the general priesthood of believers, must be represented with full rights in order that the church of Jesus Christ and not only a particular church confession may be adequately represented. A truly ecumenical council dare not be either a mere assembly of hierarchs or a democratic parliament of world Christendom (which would be equally out of line with the true nature of the church of Jesus Christ!). It must rather be a representation of the church suitable to its nature, and that means, concretely, a proper representation of the office and of the congregation in suitable mutual coordination.

(3) Furthermore, a genuine ecumenical council would have to be a council that is really free as Luther emphasized and demanded again and again. And that freedom would have to go beyond the freedom from political sponsorship and influence mentioned above: It must not be prejudiced by anything like a definite confession as is the case with an "ecumenical council" according to the Codex Juris Canonici by virtue of the absolute obligation to the pope. For this very reason such a council is of necessity no longer really *ecumenical,* but from the very beginning it is "confessionistically" directed! A council that is really ecumenical, on the contrary, if at its sessions the central truth of salvation itself in its own right is to prevail as binding on Christendom in its entirety, must present the genuine venture of entire, obedient *openness* to this truth. It actually presents a great *risk!* But the risk *must* be taken; and the risk *can* be taken—namely, with confidence in the inherent right of the "matter" concerned here and with obedience of willing subjection to *it.* It is just by reason of being absolutely bound by the revelation of salvation itself according to its original canonical testimonies in the Holy Scriptures that an ecumenical council can and must take the risk of being truly free. Naturally, if an ecumenical council is to come into concrete being at all, there must be certain restrictions of a "technical" and organizational character. Some authorized group or other will have to set up the program and make the preparations for the council, some authorized person or group will have to convene it, someone must preside at it, etc. But all that must really be a matter of rendering service, and no claim of superiority dare lurk in it and seek to maintain itself. All

this must give place to the inherent right of the "matter" and Churches dare not want to take it in charge.

Here again one might tie in with the experiences and rules issuing from the ecumenical movement, according to which the World Council of Churches itself plays the purely functional role of a servant and makes no claims of supremacy over the member churches whatsoever, in order that they, being bound by the truth of salvation itself alone, may jointly contend in freedom for genuine agreement with regard to this truth.[21]

The fundamental freedom which is necessary for a truly ecumenical council must finally also involve the inmost freedom of the council from itself—that is, that it does not compress itself within itself and consider itself as absolute, that it does not consider itself, on principle, as infallible but rather surrenders its resolutions to the final judgment of the Holy Scriptures, *by which* they must finally be approved (see above). This does not mean that they will be shaky or unstable—being tried and found sound by Holy Scripture, the resolutions of an ecumenical council are to be really valid and binding!—but they are not to be and cannot be *ipso facto* valid and binding *because* they were passed at an ecumenical council.

(4) An ecumenical council, to put it succinctly, must present a free theological striving on the part of different confessional churches under the jointly recognized truth in Christ, as originally testified by the apostles, for genuine agreement with reference to its central points, which are decisive for the church, and for its joint responsible expression, with the *aim* of making possible true church fellowship in which the essential unity of the church of Jesus Christ becomes manifest in the course of history. If it is to be a really ecumenical *council* it must also set itself *this* aim; and in pursuit of this aim there must also be earnest theological striving and responsible conduct on the part of the churches.

Because in the ecumenical movement this is not yet being done in sufficient measure and with sufficient earnestness and responsibility, because rather, on the side, too many tendencies of a different nature are at work seeking to present the unity of the church while evading the questions concerning the central theological truth (which in their place are also certainly important), therefore the global church conferences of the ecumenical movement, considered by themselves, cannot yet be what an ecumenical council would be; they are only in part of value as patterns for this. (Also for this reason they cannot present fully what an ecumenical council would be, that the Roman Catholic Church does not participate in them, but *without* the participation of this church, which represents fully one half of Christendom today, a council could not be called a really ecumenical council either! A truly ecumenical council would have to be more than merely a pan-Protestant, pan-Orthodox, or pan-Anglican council! It would have to seek earnestly to win the Roman Catholic Church for participation,[22] and this church would have to do what it could!) Neither the ecumenical movement as it is today nor the Roman Catholic Church as it is today can alone present a truly ecumenical council; they would have to come together, and each of them in its own way would have to become quite different in a number of respects if a truly ecumenical council were really to come about.

(5) Finally, a remark on the question as to how the resolutions of an ecumenical council are to become effective. According to the Codex Juris Canonici definite provision has been made through which alone the resolutions of an "ecumenical council" can become valid for the church—namely, the decision of the pope. But, taking everything into consideration, it is plain that neither this provision nor any other institutional fixing of the supreme authority can be allowed if the ecumenical council is not after all to be confined again within the structures of a definite confessional church and thereby robbed again of its ecumenicity. If this ecumenicity is to be preserved, we must have confidence in the resolutions of an ecumenical council, in the sense of our present sketch, to the extent that they will maintain themselves in the church and for the church by virtue of the truth and the validity inherent in them. Naturally, responsible agencies will be necessary to exercise the office of the watchman in the church also with regard to the resolutions of an ecumenical council which have proven themselves to be valid and binding with regard to their content. Yet these

agencies can never be vested with authority in a purely formal and institutional way, but their authority will always prevail only by virtue of the *content* of that for which they exercise responsibility.

———

In view of all that has been set forth here with reference to a real ecumenical council it has probably become clear to every reader that an ecumenical council, as matters now stand in Christendom, is not yet concretely possible today, and that it will also probably not yet be possible "tomorrow." Yet in spite of this a dogmatical reflection regarding this matter is not in vain and purely illusory. Above all, from the mere negation, it removes defense and criticism and allows the positive "obligation" and the constructive necessity to appear; and, furthermore, it shows what matters and what must be done if a true ecumenical council is ever to become possible. In view of the necessity of the "matter" it enables one to see what concrete steps in the direction of such a council should be taken now; and it challenges us to take these steps. Beginnings have indeed been made. But they must be taken advantage of much more and must be continued. The necessity is indeed present. But it alone will not yet give birth to the possibility and the concrete realization. In the direction of a real ecumenical council decisions should be made and resolutions passed by the confessional churches; to this end something should really be *done*.

Notes

1. "Quae quidem suavissima spes iam Nos duxit vehementerque excitavit ad propositum illud publice enuntiandum, Oecumenicum videlicet cogendi Concilium, ad quod sacrorum Antistites, de gravibus religionis rebus tractaturi, ex universo terrarum orbe convenient." (A.A.S. 51, 1959, 511).

2. Cf. Rubert Jedin, *Kleine Konziliengeschichte. Die 20 Oekumenischen Konzilien im Rahmen der Kirchengeschichte (Brief History of the Councils. The 20 Ecumenical Councils in the Frame of Church History).* Herder Buecherei, Band 51, Basel, Freiburg, Vienna. 1959.

3. Codex Juris Canonici, Canon 222 to 229.—Cf. Heribert Jone, *Gesetzbuch der lateinischen Kirche. Erklärung der Kanones (Book of Law of the Latin Church. Explanation of the Canons)* I, 2. Ed., Paderborn, 1950, p. 253 sq.; Eduard Eichmann-Klaus Moersdorf, *Lehrbuch des Kirchenrechts auf Grund des Codex Iuris Canonici (Textbook on Church Law on the Basis of the Codex . . .)* I, 9th Ed., Munich, Paderborn, Vienna, 1959, p. 359 sq.

4. The participants are exactly designated in Canon 223: 1 and 2: Cardinals, patriarchs, primates, archbishops, exempt abbots, and prelates, the provosts of certain orders, and certain titular bishops.

5. Cf. Eichmann-Moersdorf, *op. cit.*, p. 359: The pope is "the head of the general council . . . ; the reverse side of this is that the bishops have *no* independent right of assembly." See Canon 229, "If the pope dies during a convention of a general council, the council is automatically interrupted until the new pope orders its resumption and continuance."

6. Cf. Canon 226, "To the questions submitted by the pope the fathers of the council may add others, but only when they have been approved beforehand by the chairman of the council."

7. See Eichmann-Moersdorf, *op. cit.*, p. 359, "The resolutions of the council are not valid of themselves (episcopalism) but require the ratification of the pope, which customarily is pronounced either at the solemn closing session or in a papal bull. Besides, the resolutions of the council must be published by order of the pope. Statements concerning points of faith are binding immediately upon their proclamation; for resolutions of a different nature a later date may be set for their becoming effective."

8. *op. cit.*, p. 361: "The general council, in like manner as the pope, possesses the highest authority in the church. . . . The general council, according to its proper conception, is possible only *with* the pope; it stands *at the side* of the pope, not above him (as episcopalism would have it)."

9. Cf. also Eichmann-Moersdorf, *op. cit.*, p. 359: "Beside the pope and in subordination to him (!) are the bishops, 'appointed by the Holy Ghost to govern the church of God' (Acts 20:

28). This existence side by side of the two authorities, based on divine institution, comes to be an impressive cooperation at the general council." The pope is the "head of the general council." "An assembly of the bishops without the pope would be a *corpus sine capite* ('rump parliament')."

10. The concept "ecumenical" has taken on a variety of meanings in the course of its history: In pre-Christian ancient usage "Oikumene" signified the Hellenistic civilized world—that is, concretely, the people who were or were to be civilized and united in the Roman empire.—The New Testament continues this usage but adds the nuance: all of mankind as the mission field of the Christian Gospel.—In the second century, A.D., "ecumenical" (now an adjective) becomes an attribute of the church expressing its absolute universality (it is applied, without any limitations whatsoever, to the entire human race) as well as its pervasive inner unity in spite of its outer dispersion and diversity. In addition "ecumenical" assumes an ever more qualified and restricted meaning —namely, the *orthodox* church at large, which abides faithfully in the apostolic tradition, in distinction from the heretical separate "churches" or sects. This "ecumenicity" was protected by the emperor, so that "ecumenical" finally came to mean practically: representing the *church of the empire.* Thus we hear of "ecumenical synods" (councils) or of "ecumenical patriarchs" (of Constantinople) as also of "ecumenical church doctrines," which are authoritative for the orthodox church of the empire.—In the Middle Ages in the West the word "ecumenical" had already become a kind of rigid formula (already in the ancient church it was superseded more and more by the word "catholic," which originated

from the same connection); in the medieval occidental church the word "ecumenical" came to be used only as a stereotyped, traditional designation for the universally obligatory church councils.—That which was new in the usage of the Reformation is that the word "ecumenical" was used to designate the common Christian *creeds* —that is, those that are binding for all Christians, (as a common Christian "obligation")—namely, the Apostles' Creed, the Nicene, and the Athanasian Creeds, which from then on were called *"the three ecumenical symbols."* —Only from the middle of the nineteenth century on did "ecumenical" in the course of the world missionary and alliance movement come ever more to be a living general word with dynamic emotional connotation, partly in designation of the missionary task of Christianity (under an eschatological aspect), embracing all of humanity, partly in expression of the experience of Christian brotherhood transcending credal boundaries and of the longing and striving for a realization of true Christian unity in triumph over the schisms. Whereas the concept "ecumenical" in this lively sense at first grew rather out of a "kingdom-of-God" theology, it thereafter came to be applied more and more to the *church;* "ecumenical" came to designate all the efforts aiming at the expression of the essential unity of the church of Christ through overcoming the schisms and the isolations of the confessional churches. And that, hand in hand with its world missionary meaning, is in fact the original Christian sense of this word.

Literature on the history of the concept "ecumenical": J. Kaerst, *Die antike Idee der Ökumene (The Ancient Idea of the Oikumene),* 1903; W. Bauer, *Wörterbuch zum Neuen Testa-*

ment (Dictionary of the New Testament) οικονμεντ (Lit.); C. Fabricius, Art.: "Ökumenisch," RGG 2 IV, 638 sq. (Lit.); O. Michel, Art.: οικονμεντ *Theol. Wörterbuch zum Neuen Testament (Theol. Dictionary of the New Testament)* V, 159 sq. (Lit.); M. Paeslack, "Die Ökumene im Neuen Testament" *(The Oikumene in the New Testament),* in *Theologia Viatorum,* Berlin, 1950 (Lit.); A. Lehmann, "Mission und Ökumene" *(Missions and Oikumene),* Ev. Luth. Kirchenzeitung, 1953, Nr. 13, 193 *sq.;* W. A. Visser 't Hooft, *"The World 'Ecumenical' Movement, its History and Use,"* in Rouse-Neill, *History of the Ecumenical Movement,* 1954, Appendix I, p. 735 sq. (Lit.); The same author, *Der Sinn des Wortes 'ökumenisch' " (The Sense of the Word "Ecumenical"),* Stuttgart, 1954; the same author, Art., "Ökumenisch" *(Ecumenical),* RGG[3] IV, 1569 sq.; E. Kinder, "Der Gebrauch des Begriffs 'ökumenisch' im alteren Luthertum" *(The Use of the Concept "Ecumenical" in Older Lutheranism),* Kerygma u. Dogma, 1955 (Heft 3), 180 sq. (Lit.); E. Fascher, "Ökumenisch und katholisch. Zur Geschichte sweier, heute viel gebrauchter Begriffe" *(Ecumenical and Catholic. On the History of Two Concepts Widely Used in Our Day),* Theol. Lit. Zeitg. 1960, (Nr. 1) 7 sq.).

11. This idea is taken from the important "Toronto Declaration" of the World Council, 1950. I am here quoting Theses 3-5 of its Part IV: (3): "The member Churches recognize that the membership of the Church of Christ is more inclusive than the membership of their own Church body. They seek, therefore, to enter into living contact with those outside their own ranks who confess the Lordship of Christ. (4): "The member Churches of the World Council consider the

relationship of other Churches to the Holy Catholic Church which the Creeds profess as a subject of mutual consideration. Nevertheless, membership does not imply that each Church must regard the other member Churches as Churches in the true and full sense of the word." (5): "The member Churches of the World Council recognize in other Churches elements of the true Church. They think that this mutual recognition obliges them to enter into serious conversation with each other in the hope that these elements of truth will lead to the recognition of the full truth and to unity based on the full truth." —(In the interpretation of Thesis 3 we read: "All the Christian Churches, including the Church of Rome, hold that there is no complete identity between the membership of the Church Universal and the membership of their own Church. They recognize that there are Church members 'extra muros,' that these belong 'aliquo modo' to the Church . . . This recognition finds expression in the fact that with very few exceptions the Christian Churches accept the baptism administered by the other Churches as valid.")

At all events, the "Toronto Declaration" is significant as an expression of the present ecumenical situation with its accompanying points in common and its differences or separations. Cf. on this point Peter Brunner's "Pneumatischer Realismus. Bemerkungen zur theologischen Bedeutung der 'Toronto-Erklärung' " (*Pneumatic Realism. Remarks on the Theological Significance of the "Toronto Declaration"*), *Ev. Luth. Kirchenzeitung,* 1951 (Nr. 8), 122 sq.

12. We are concerned with the double council of Ferarra (1437-1438) and Florence (1439), at which the union with the Greek and the Armenian churches was consummated. On the Greek side this union was desired substantially by the emperor of Constantinople, who at that time was hard pressed by the Turks and was seeking help from the "western powers." The majority of the clergy and of the people of the oriental church rejected this union, so that, practically, it did not go into effect.

13. The inadmissible religious absolutism, in the first place, lies in the claim of infallibility on the part of the church's governing and teaching office and furthermore in the claim that the true church of Christ is present only in the body, including this hierarchical structure with the papal primate at its head. Apart from this absolutism with its unconditional religious emphasis (that this infallibility and this exclusiveness are "iure divino" valid and to be accepted as necessary for salvation) the episcopal office with its own important rights is not to be rejected. Luther was willing to accept even the papacy as he at times declared if only it were conceived of as having arisen "iure humano" in the course of history and as existing for practical reasons.—Also with a view to other confessional churches one must distinguish between historical necessity and fundamental religious and theological necessity. Thus, for instance, the evangelical Lutheran Church thinks that the confession of the Gospel which she represents is inseparable from the church but that her existence as a separate church together with all the forms that have developed in its interest is only a historical necessity conditioned by the situation of Christendom, which will no longer be absolutely necessary when it will no longer be necessary to maintain expressly and with empha-

sis this confession of the Gospel as a joint Christian "obligation." Cf. on this matter: Ernst Kinder, "Evangelische Katholizität. Zum ökumenischen Horizont der evangelisch-lutherischen Kirche" (*Evangelical Catholicity. On the Ecumenical Horizon of the Evangelical Lutheran Church*), *Kerygma u. Dogma*, 1960, p. 69 sq.

14. In view of the decisions of the first four "ecumenical councils" we must not dwell only on the contemporary political and ecclesiastical-political background or on their contemporary philosophical-theological forms of expression, but we must seek to grasp their fundamental doctrinal purposes. With respect to these Luther can say in his essay *On the Councils and the Church,* 1539 (WA 50, p. 591) that the "four great councils" of the ancient church really presented nothing new, but "as the supreme judge and the greatest bishop under Christ" they defended the old faith against new arrogance; "for this article (i.e., of Christ and the Trinity) prevailed in the church from the beginning and was not created by the council but was received from the Gospel or the Holy Scriptures."—The Nestorians and the Monophysites of our day must be asked where they stand with regard to this doctrinal purpose *as such,* apart from the political and church-political background of that time!

15. This is a matter of course for all the churches of the Reformation and of Protestantism. It is conceivable that also the Orthodox Church is fundamentally in agreement with this. At any rate, the Orthodox Church, which, as we know, abhors all priori and purely formal judicial fixation, also teaches that the resolutions of an "ecumenical council" really become "canonical" only after having obtained the inner assent of the or-

thodox church at large. Also according to this view, therefore, the authority of an "ecumenical council" is fundamentally a derived authority. Also according to the Roman Catholic conception the authority of an "ecumenical council," as the rejection of "conciliarism" on principle shows, is not an absolute authority but is likewise fundamentally subject to a standard, save that the standard to which the council is subject is the final decision of the pope.

16. This criticism applies also to the Orthodox conception, which in our day, for instance, is represented by George Florowsky—namely, that the true universal church must be sought in the time-dimension. Since the true unity of the church was really and fully present in its first, classic age, the criteria for the church's unity which are adequate for all times are to be found here. However much it may be in order to call attention to the "universal church in the time-dimension" over against a view which confines itself to the Christians living today (it is important that emphasis be laid on this that true unity of the church means also unity with the fathers!) and however right and important it may be to point to the "fundamental potential" common to Christendom and derived from the heritage of the ancient church, yet this alone will not suffice; for the real differences happen to lie just in the different manner of appropriating and "realizing" the common "fundamental potential," in the different and in part exclusive "use" made of the possessions objectively held in common! In our ecumenical wrestling we cannot evade reflecting on just these differences of appropriation, "realization," and "usus," because *here* is where we find the real causes of the divisions

in the church. So the joint recognition of the three "ecumenical symbols," for instance, of the ancient church is indeed an important and promising *prerequisite* of joint ecumenical effort; it is, however, not yet sufficient as an aim!

17. Originally, when enthusiasm ran high in the beginning of the ecumenical movement, this was the actual aim. Thus, for instance, *Archbishop Söderblom* exclaimed at the meeting in Oud Wassenaer, 1919, in preparation for the coming world conference of churches, "I pledge my support to an ecumenical council which is to present a spiritual representation of all Christendom." (F. Luepsen, *Amsterdamer Dokumente,* 1948, p. 99). Yet it was after all a rhetorical exaggeration when the World Conference for Life and Work in Stockholm, 1925, emphatically compared itself with the first "ecumenical council" of Nice, 325!

18. Here, above all, we must call attention to the report of the third World Conference for Faith and Order in Lund, 1952, (cf. W. Staehlin, ed., *Kirche, Gottesdienst, Abendmahlsgemeinschaft (Church, Worship, Altarfellowship),* Witten, 1954, p. 19 sq.), and also to the continued work on this project on the part of the different individual Faith and Order Commissions, whose results are soon to be published. Of especial importance in this connection is also the attempt to find a closer definition of the unity for which the World Council of Churches is striving as it is set forth in the official report on "The Future of Faith and Order" (Faith and Order Paper, No. 31, 1960), which was presented to the executive committee in St. Andrew, August, 1960, and which will be presented to the third plenary convention of the World Council at New Delhi in November and December, 1961. Cf. on this matter E. Kinder, "Ende der 'ekklesiologischen Neutralität' des Weltrats" *(The End of Ecclesiological Neutrality of the World Council?), Ev. Luth. Kirchenzeitung,* 1961 (Nr. 7), p. 105 sq.

19. This is meant in a twofold sense. For one thing, one's own confession in its full force is to be brought into the ecumenical effort; it is not to be mutilated or hidden (for it is just in that which is specifically confessional that we find the decisive "handle" for the central truth, and it is just this that must be brought into the discussion!); but in the second place, the confession itself in all its force is actually to be submitted to the judgment of the revelation of salvation itself according to its original canonical testimonies and must not be substituted for this revelation as being self-evidently the truth.

20. The "Basis" of the World Council of Churches is, of course, not intended as an ecumenical *creed*—for this it would doubtless be too "scanty"—it would rather give expression to the minimum requirements for promising participation in the ecumenical effort: Church bodies which earnestly confess the divinity and the redeeming work of Jesus Christ and who consider themselves in relation to this Jesus Christ, the church's head, can in a hopeful sense be members of the World Council—and in application of our present discussion may participate in an ecumenical council. (On the history and the sense of the "Basis" cf. the report of Visser 't Hooft at the meeting of the executive committee in St. Andrews, 1960, *Ökum. Rundschau,* 1960, (Heft 4), p. 208 sq., and Eberhard Fincke, "Zur Geschichte der 'Basis' des Ökumenischen Rates der Kirchen" *(On the History of the*

"Basis" *of the World Council of Churches), Evangel. Theologie,* 1960, (Heft 10), p. 465 sq.—In this connection especial notice deserves to be given to the *enlarged* form of the "Basis," which will be presented for adoption to the third plenary assembly of the World Council in New Delhi it reads: . . . *"a fellowship of churches who confess the Lord Jesus Christ according to the Holy Scriptures as God and Savior and who therefore seek to fulfill the purpose for which they are jointly called, to the glory of God the Father, the Son, and the Holy Spirit."* Here the Holy Scriptures, the serious ecumenical desire, and the confession of the Trinity are listed among the minimum requirements!

21. On this understanding of itself on the part of the World Council of Churches cf. as *documents* the *Declaration on the Nature of the World Council,* Amsterdam, 1948, (in F. Luepsen, *Amsterdamer Dokumente,* Bethel, 1948) and the "Toronto Declaration," 1950 (German text in *Ev. Luth. Kirchenzeitung,* 1951 (Nr. 8),

p. 120 sq.); *literature:* W. A. Visser 't Hooft, *Der Ökumenische Rat der Kirchen. Seine Eigenart, seine Grenzen (The World Council of Churches. Its Nature, its Limitations,* Geneva, 1947; J. Winterhager, *Der Weltrat der Kirchen. Seine Ziele und seine Problematik (The World Council of Churches. Its Aims and its Problems,* Berlin, 1949; H. Liermann, "Ökumene als rechtliche Erscheinung" *(The Universal Church as a Proper Phenomenon), Ev. Luth. Kirchenzeitung,* 1951, (Nr. 8), p. 117 sq.; E. Schlink, "Aufgabe und Gefahr des Ökumenischen Rates" *(The Task and the Hazard of the World Council), Ökum. Rundschau,* 1952, Heft 1; S. Grundmann, "Der Beitrag des evangelischen Kirchenrechts zum Selbstverständnis des Ökum. Rates der Kirchen" *(The Contribution of evangelical Church Law to the Self-Understanding of the World Council of Churches), Ev. Luth. Kirchenzeitung,* 1960 (Nr. 11), 162 sq.

22. Cf. on this, Ernst Kinder, "Protestant-Roman Catholic encounter—an ecumenical obligation," *Ecumenical Review,* July 1955.

Chapter III

Luther's Attitude Toward Church Councils

The general councils of the church can err; in fact, the Council of Constance, the sixteenth of the general councils of the church, did err when it condemned certain teachings of John Hus and Jerome of Prague. When Martin Luther was maneuvered into making this admission at the Leipzig Debate in 1519, both he and his opponents began to recognize the extent of the alienation between him and the Roman church.[1] This admission, more than either the Ninety-five Theses of two years earlier or even his excommunication of two years later, initiated the Reformation. Just a little more than a quarter of a century later, as Luther lay dying in February, 1546, another church council was in session at Trent—the nineteenth of the general councils—to discuss, among other issues, some of the doctrinal and disciplinary questions raised by Luther's Reformation.

Luther's career as a Reformer spanned the interval between Leipzig and Trent. During almost every year of that career he found himself constrained to think and speak about the problem of a church council.[2] Indeed, he had already appealed for a council on November 28, 1518.[3] He was hopeful, at least for a while, that a

37

free and ecumenical council could reopen the question of restoring the chalice to the laity.[4] In June, 1520 he composed his *Letter to the Christian Nobility,* setting forth some of the chief abuses with which such a council would have to deal and outlining the conditions under which it should be convoked.[5] Many of the themes sounded in this treatise dominated Luther's thought about a council to the end, and he recurred to them each time the prospects for a council seemed likely. Repeatedly, however, these prospects were dimmed by imperial politics or by church politics; first one party, then another, found a church council inexpedient when it was proposed. Everyone remained theoretically committed to the idea of a council, but in practice there was strong opposition to the idea both in Rome and elsewhere. During the 1530's, at the urging of Paul III, who had become pope in 1534, the council almost became a reality on two occasions—at Mantua in 1537 and at Vicenza in 1538.[6]

To prepare for these occasions, Luther and his colleagues re-examined his ideas about a council of the church in the light of the changed religious and political alignment. For each of the major forces had been altered radically since the *Letter to the Christian Nobility* of 1520. New light on the conciliar question came from another source as well, a deepened study of church history. Both the decrees of the ancient ecumenical councils and the acts of the more recent councils, especially Constance, helped to shape the ideas of Luther and his associates about what a council could and should undertake,[7] if one were ever actually to meet. The influence of this historical study is evident in many writings from the last decade of Luther's life, including some writings, such as those on the Lord's Supper, which are not specifically directed to the conciliar controversy.[8] The preoccupation of modern Luther research with "the young Luther," or at best with the mature Luther, has relegated this final decade of his career to a position of secondary significance. Yet it was during this decade that Luther was forced, regretfully and reluctantly, to formulate his personal assessment of a career that had begun with the intention of reforming the Christian church but had ended with the irrevocable division of Catholic Christendom.

Out of the theological and historical work of the Wittenberg theologians came Luther's treatise on *The Councils and the Church* of 1539.[9] It contains his most comprehensive statement about church councils past and present, summing up the themes originally sounded two decades earlier at Leipzig and in the *Letter to the Christian Nobility* but adding the variations required by the history of those fateful decades. This treatise is therefore the logical basis for a study of the topic "The Reformation and the Council"; and instead of stringing together a catena of Luther's statements of various years on this topic from various writings, this essay will proceed from a close reading of *The Councils and the Church* to an analysis of the conciliar motif in Luther's thoughts as his career was nearing its close.[10]

I. The Appeal to a Council

"We cry out and appeal for a council and beseech all of Christendom for its advice and help" (620, 9). "You say that there is no hope for such a council any longer; I suppose I agree with you" (623, 5). The juxtaposition of these two declarations in the treatise is an indication of Luther's ambivalence toward the prospect of the forthcoming council. He had been appealing for a council and to a council for twenty years, taunting his opponents with the contradiction between their protestations of loyalty to the conciliar ideal and their dilatory tactics. Now a new pontiff, Paul III, was bent on finally convoking the long expected council; and now it was Luther's turn to see his declarations about a council challenged. The strategy and propaganda of the Reformers seemed in danger of losing the advantages they had gained from papal hesitation about a council. Thus Luther had to summarize his position in a way that took account of this shift. He was convinced that there was no hope for genuine reformation in any conclave to which Rome would give its consent; yet the onus of the responsibility for this had to rest not on the Reformers but on Rome. To assure this, Luther coupled his continuing appeal for a council with a threefold attack on the motives of the ecclesiastical authorities who were summoning the assembly.

1. The very first paragraph of the treatise set forth the first attack: The pope was not sincere in his invitation to the council. He was trifling with the hopes of those who longed for a settlement of the issues dividing Christendom, as one teases a dog by waving a morsel before its snout on a knife and then striking it with the butt of the knife when it snaps at the morsel (509, 1). In substantiation of this charge Luther leveled at his opponents his oft-repeated accusation that they actually acknowledged the correctness of his teachings and knew that their own doctrine could not be substantiated from the Scriptures (511, 20). In spite of this they insisted upon having their own way. Therefore they had no right to plead ignorance, but were acting contrary to Scripture and to their own better knowledge and judgment. The willfulness of this opposition to the evident truth was proof to Luther that any council was doomed to failure even before the first session was called to order. "Thus the council is settled before it even begins: Nothing is to be reformed, but everything is to be retained in accordance with past usage. What a fine council that is!" (510, 12). Long before the Vatican Council the "irreformability of the church" was simultaneously an article of faith to Roman Catholicism and an insurmountable obstacle to Protestantism. Luther was sure that no council called by the pope could be expected to effect any fundamental changes in the life and teaching of the church.

In 1539 there were still those who held out the sincere hope that a general council of the church could effect the fundamental changes that Luther's Reformation had been unable to effect. In support of this hope they cited the precedent of the earlier general councils of the church, maintaining that "a fine reformation, in their opinion, could happen on the basis of the fathers and the councils" (519, 14). This was the conciliarist position of the fourteenth and fifteenth centuries, applied to the unprecedented schism of the sixteenth century. The reaction of Luther to this historical romanticism was as forthright as it was conclusive. His own historical studies and his experience in two decades of debate had deepened his misgivings about both conciliar and patristic authority. Neither the councils nor the church fathers had achieved true unanimity in their teaching. Therefore it was possible for either party in the controversy of the sixteenth century to select from the fathers and the councils whatever seemed to suit and substantiate its own position (542, 18). But such proof was finally no proof; for the presuppositions of the combatants, not the actual writings of the fathers or decrees of the councils, determined what was to be accorded the status of normative conciliar teaching.

2. Luther's second charge against the pope's sudden conversion to the conciliar position dealt with the question of his readiness to compromise. Although Luther may scarcely be termed a mediating theologian, he did repeatedly declare his willingness to compromise on any but the essential issues. "Thank God," he asserted, "we are not so far gone that we would permit the church to perish rather than compromise, even on weighty issues, so long as they are not against God. No, we ourselves are ready to perish and to be stripped completely . . . rather than to let calamity or danger befall the church" (516, 24). There is no reason to doubt the sincerity of this protestation. The historical studies upon which *The Councils and the Church* was based had shown Luther that conflicts of personality had been prominent in the determination of dogmatic issues at the ancient councils. He urged that in the debate over the subtler problems of the doctrine of the person of Christ, not a proud condemnation of the errorist, but "instruction with gentleness" had been called for (601, 26). Thus he knew that the recalcitrance of an orthodoxy that refused to compromise even where some compromise was permissible had to share with heresy the responsibility for schism and dissension in Christendom. For such recalcitrance permitted heretics to excuse themselves with the claim that they had been overdone, not with truth, but with violence, injustice, and a distortion of their views (594, 12). Both from his study of the history of councils and from his evaluation of the contemporary conflicts Luther knew that some concession on nonessentials was necessary if a council was to have any hope of succeeding.

Did the pope's summons to a council mean that he was prepared to make such a concession? Luther put his answer to this question frankly or, as he said, "in German." There were two fundamental concessions that the pope had to make. First, he had to abolish the tyranny of the human regulations that he had substituted for divine commandments. Second, he had to grant that even man's obedience to these divine commandments "cannot help to achieve righteousness, to atone for sin, to obtain the grace of God, but only faith in Christ, who is the King of righteousness in us through his precious blood, death, and resurrection, with which he has atoned for sin, rendered satisfaction, reconciled God, and redeemed us from death, wrath, and hell" (621, 20). From any council that did not grant these two concessions Luther expected no good. And it had to grant both of these concessions. There was to be no giving with one hand and taking away with the other (621, 9), no *Gebers Nemers*. He thought that his opponents were insincere enough to make the concession that only the grace of Christ saves, but they would immediately add the condition that works are necessary for satisfaction or righteousness. Their indifference to matters of true doctrine should have permitted them to compromise even on the issues that were most important to the Reformers; their unwillingness to grant such compromises doomed any council to failure.

3. The third argument that Luther directed against the pope's council was a criticism of its proposed composition. As matters turned out—although, of course, Luther was not yet aware of this— the delegates to the Council of Trent had one vote per capita; at Constance, by contrast, they had voted by national delegations. But Luther did foresee that the papacy would try to have priests friendly to its cause chosen as delegates, and he urged that delegates be chosen on the basis of other criteria than their loyalty to the pope: "From every country those who are thoroughly learned in the Holy Scriptures and who are seriously and sincerely devoted to the glory of God, the Christian faith, the church, the salvation of souls, and the peace of the world" (622, 11). In addition, for reasons to be expounded later in this chapter, Luther believed that some of the delegates should be chosen from the secular government, since the business of the council concerned them too. Persuaded as he was that the pope would never be willing to accept a council thus defined, Luther laid down an either-or condition: If such a council as he envisioned was impossible, there should be none at all. Impossible though this council was, Luther wanted to

be sure that he and his followers did not receive the blame for the collapse of the ideal of an ecumenical council. Therefore he continued to call for a council even when he knew that it could never be.

II. The Functions of a Council

Luther's rejection of the pope's plans for a council was grounded, therefore, not merely in a polemical position, but in a positive definition, based upon church history, of the proper functions of a council. Generalizing from his study of the first four ecumenical councils and from his own theological assumptions about the nature of the church and the meaning of religious authority, Luther sought to demarcate the rights and duties of church councils in three areas of Christian concern: Christian doctrine; Christian life, including both good works and ecclesiastical ceremonies; and secular government and law. Both his descriptions of what councils had done and his prescriptions of what any true council should do concentrated upon these three areas. In fact, he maintained that the criteria he was laying down in these areas applied to "all other councils, great or small, even though there were many thousands of them" (606, 3). For the church had "miniature councils" going on within it all the time, in its parishes and schools (616, 8–617, 24). These "miniature councils," too, dealt with the three areas. Luther's thought about each of these areas likewise manifested unresolved conflicts that belong to any exposition of the theme "Luther's Attitude Toward Church Councils."

A. Christian Doctrine

First and foremost, a council had "no authority to establish new articles of faith, even though the Holy Spirit was present in it," but only to suppress and condemn doctrinal innovations (607, 7). As later discussion will show, even the presence of the Holy Spirit in a council did not, according to Luther's definition, give such a council authority to create new doctrines. Luther went to pains to demonstrate that none of the first four ecumenical councils had arrogated to itself any such authority. Thus the Council of Nicaea had not invented a new doctrine, but had "preserved the old article of faith, that Christ is true and very God, against the innovating cleverness of Arius" (551, 12). Again, since the Council of Constantinople had itself acknowledged that its decrees were "the ancient and true faith, in which we have previously been baptized and instructed, why should we give councils the great authority of establishing new doctrines and of burning as heretics all those who do not believe them?" (581, 7). Nor did the Council of Ephesus usurp such authority; it merely "defended the ancient faith against the innovating suppositions of Nestorius" (591, 23). Finally, the last of the great ecumenical councils, the one held at Chalcedon, provided no support for the contention that councils had a right to establish new doctrines in the church (603, 15).

Here Luther drew the logical consequences of his stand at Leipzig twenty years earlier. He rejected the formal authority of church councils in matters of faith and doctrine and asserted that councils merely applied the doctrine of Scripture to the new issues that had arisen. But the left wing of the Reformation in his century and theological liberalism in our century have both pointed out the paradox that this rejection of formal conciliar authority was accompanied by a loyal submission to the material authority of the dogmas defined by the councils.[11] During most of Christian history the authority of dogmas has depended upon the authority of the church as defined in a council, and indeed upon the capacity of the secular government to enforce dogmatic orthodoxy by police power. In the eyes of Luther's Roman Catholic opponents, his repudiation of conciliar authority would inevitably lead to apostasy from the catholic faith. Luther's reply to this interpretation of his stand was a critical reappraisal both of what in principle councils could do in the church and of what in fact the great ecumenical councils had done. He argued that the dogmas of the Trinity and of the two natures in Christ, as defined by the first four ecumenical councils, did not depend for their validity upon an acceptance of the infallibility of the councils. For the fathers who formulated these dogmas did not intend to state a new doctrine but only to defend the primitive faith of the church as given in the Scriptures.

A criticism of the councils in the name of the Scriptures, therefore, was more faithful to their authentic spirit than the misplaced loyalty of an uncritical traditionalism.

As examples of this authentic spirit Luther cited the works of Athanasius and Hilary, who opposed the heretics, not with their own ideas or authority, but with the authority of the Scriptures. "At Nicaea," he insisted, "the creed was substantiated by the apostolic Scriptures. Otherwise, if it had not been for the Scriptures of the apostles and prophets, the mere words of the council by themselves would have accomplished nothing" (552, 14). What the Council of Ephesus promulgated "had been in the church since the beginning; it was not invented by the council, but preserved by the Gospel or the Holy Scriptures" (591, 26). Citing passages from both the Old Testament and the New in opposition to the Eutychian heresy, Luther summarized his interpretation of conciliar authority: "Even if I do not . . . understand [this council] correctly, I still have these passages and understand them correctly. The council itself is obliged to be guided by this Scripture, and this is more certain to me than all the councils" (604, 7). In fact, even if most of the New Testament were to disappear and only the Gospel of St. John were to remain, this one book would state the doctrines of all four ecumenical councils more amply and powerfully than they did (605, 21). Luther's rhetoric moved him to exclaim: "The poor, insignificant pastor of Hippo, St. Augustine, taught more than all the councils. . . . I will go even further: More is contained in the children's creed than in all the councils. The Lord's Prayer Our Father and the Decalogue also teach more than all the councils do" (615, 1). The genuine defenders of the councils and of their dogmas, then, were not those who claimed supreme authority for the councils, but those who, like the fathers at the councils themselves, subjected the authority of the councils to the authority of the Scriptures.

When the self-styled defenders of the councils demanded submission to their authority, they demanded the impossible. For anyone who had ever studied the councils and the fathers had learned that they were not only inconsistent, but downright contradictory (520, 12). Hence no one could obey all of their decrees at the same time. An illustration upon which Luther dwelt at considerable length was the legislation of the Council of Nicaea regarding those who left the military service for the sake of a religious profession and then returned to their old way of life; the council prescribed a long and severe period of penance in such cases. Luther cited this example to show that even those who were now clamoring for a submission to conciliar authority refused to obey an ecumenical council when its legislation did not suit them. Although the bishops and popes waged war themselves and thus violated this rule, "they incessantly shout, 'Councils, councils! Fathers, fathers!'—except, of course, that they are free to act contrary to this and to choose the things they want us to do" (534, 4). Luther did not accept this decree of Nicaea (532, 25), but he was contending that no one could be obedient to all the legislation of all the councils.

Sometimes, however, his criticism of conciliar authority went beyond this formal demonstration of inconsistency and contradiction to a material examination of the content of conciliar decrees. There were at least three such material critiques in *The Councils and the Church:* (1) the concentration of the councils upon one article of faith, at the expense of the totality of the faith (546, 14); (2) the preoccupation of the Council of Ephesus with the heretical Mariology of Nestorius rather than with the other dangerous implications of his teaching (591, 4); and (3) the endorsement of celibacy and monasticism by the very councils that condemned the heretics (609, 14).

1. As he developed the first of these critiques, Luther found himself contrasting the councils with Peter Lombard, on whose *Sentences* he had lectured many years before. The contrast came out much to the advantage of the Lombard, whose study of St. Augustine led him to summarize all the main doctrines of the Christian faith—almost all, at any rate, for he was weak on the doctrines of justification and of faith (543, 13). Ultimately, of course, neither the councils nor Augustine nor Peter Lombard, but only the Scriptures, contained the whole of Christian doctrine (546, 29).

2. It seems clear that Luther's own controversies with "the

Nestorians I myself have had" (591, 9), that is, with Zwingli and with others who denied the real presence of the body and blood of Christ in the Eucharist, had made him conscious of the far-reaching implications of Nestorian Christology. The passion of his attacks upon Zwingli's principle of distinguishing between those New Testament statements that applied to the divine nature shows how much he believed was at stake in any separation of the two natures in Christ.[12] Nothing less than the very meaning and efficacy of the saving work of Christ came under threat from such separation. Although he acknowledged that personal factors had played a role in the controversy and that the opponents of Nestorius had not understood him because they had not wanted to understand him, this did not obscure the threat to faith posed by the Nestorian doctrine. Apparently the Council of Ephesus had not grasped the real threat. Therefore "this council condemned far too little in [the teaching of] Nestorius. For it dealt only with one property [of Christ], namely, that God was born of Mary. Hence the histories record that in this council it was decided, in opposition to Nestorius, that Mary was to be called Theotokos, that is, God-bearer. Yet Nestorius denied all the properties of human nature to God in Christ, such as dying, being crucified, suffering, and whatever is inconsistent with deity" (590, 23).

3. The third of Luther's material critiques of the councils, and one to which he reverted several times in this treatise, was aimed at their failure to condemn monasticism and celibacy, which were, in Luther's judgment, logically connected with heresy. In fact, he was even ready—without historical grounds—to lay the blame for the endorsement of celibacy by the Council of Nicaea upon the presence of bishops who were inclined to Arian doctrine (539, 17). An extended excursus in his definition of what a council may legislate about good works criticized the ecumenical councils for not having condemned the dangerous novelty of the monastic life even as they were condemning the dangerous novelty of the heretical doctrines (607, 35). Thus Luther claimed that the false teachings of Arius, Nestorius, and Eutyches regarding the Trinity and the person of Christ were consistent with the false teachings of those who demanded clerical celibacy and praised the monastic estate

as a purer form of Christian obedience. The councils did not recognize this consistency; if they had, "they would have condemned the archimandrite Eutyches, not only on the grounds of faith (as they earnestly did), but also on the grounds of his monasticism (as they did not do, endorsing it instead)" (618, 19).

From these three material critiques and from his other statements about the ecumenical councils it is evident that Luther did not shrink from applying to the councils the canons of both theological and historical evaluation. As he never tired of saying, the fathers were human beings, who had never "transcended the seventh chapter of Romans" (525, 20); they were fallible as individuals, and even when gathered together in councils they could and did err. Therefore their authority was not to be put on an equal plane with that of the Scriptures, to which they themselves wanted to be subjected. Nevertheless, all of this must not be permitted to obscure Luther's thoroughgoing dogmatic orthodoxy: He pitted the authority of the Scriptures against the authority of the councils, but what he found in the Scriptures was the dogma that the councils had formulated on the basis of the Scriptures. Historically speaking, Luther could not have been the theologian he was without the help of the very councils whose infallibility he denied. Sometimes he even contended that not by assigning to the councils an infallibility they neither possessed nor claimed, but only by acknowledging their fallibility with critical gratitude could one preserve the dogmas of the councils against their enemies.

B. Christian Life and Worship

As a council was not permitted to create new articles of faith, so it had "no authority to command new good works . . . for all good works are already amply commanded in the Sacred Scriptures" (607, 18); similarly, "a council does not have the authority to prescribe new ceremonies for Christians and to require their observance as a matter of conscience or under pain of mortal sin" (613, 19). Rather, its task was to guard against the introduction of any such new rules into Christian life and worship and to condemn them when they arose. A council was to condemn not only the obviously wicked works such as murder and adultery, but also the glittering new works invented by the devil as a cover for idolatry (607, 31); these new works, of which monasticism was the outstanding instance, were "a menace to Christian faith and an offense to Christian life" (608, 2).

This did not mean, of course, that a council had no right at all to consider problems of administration and discipline for which there were no explicit commands or prohibitions in the Scriptures, or matters of liturgical usage that were neither forbidden nor prescribed there. It did mean that such administrative and liturgical regulations were not the reason for which a council should be summoned. When the bishops at Nicaea had attempted to introduce jurisdictional disputes into the proceedings, Constantine had wisely refused to be party to their "clerical squabbles" (552, 25). Liturgical details were also too trivial a matter for councils to waste their time debating. It was better left to schoolmasters, who could train the children to genuflect at the *Et homo factus est* of the Nicene Creed or to remove their hats and genuflect at the mention of the name of Jesus (619, 9). Such ceremonies were a good thing and useful in the life of the church, so long as they were not made obligatory and tyrannical. When the externals of ecclesiastical discipline or of ceremonial usage became tyrannical, it was the task of a council to speak out against them.

Nevertheless, just such externals of ecclesiastical discipline and ceremonial usage had been responsible for the first "church council," described in the fifteenth chapter of the Book of Acts. This meeting had established many precedents for subsequent councils. To determine what a council had the right to do, therefore, it was necessary to go behind the four ecumenical councils to "the very first council, that of the apostles, held in Jerusalem, about which St. Luke writes in Acts 15 and 16" (526, 18). The terms of its fourfold prohibition—"that you abstain from what has been sacrificed to idols and from blood and from what is strangled and from unchastity" (Acts 15:29)—had figured prominently in the debates of the Reformation. The prohibition was suspended in the course of later church history. This suspension was interpreted as proof for the claim that other commands and prohibitions of the New

Testament were also subject to revision or suspension by the church. It was cited to show that the church did have the right, despite the words of institution, to withhold the chalice from the laity and to administer the Lord's Supper under only one kind.[13] Fifteen years before he wrote *The Councils and the Church*, in June, 1524, Luther took up this claim in a series of sermons on Acts 15 and 16.[14] When he dealt with the interpretation of these chapters in the present treatise, therefore, he brought to it a long period of reflection and study. This much was clear to all: The apostolic council had indeed forbidden these four items, but after centuries of Christian history only the prohibition of immorality still belonged to the Christian ethic. The council in Acts 15 was therefore a crucial case in any determination of the rights and authority of church councils. Luther dealt with the case by examining various possible explanations for the suspension of these rules and then by suggesting his own, which he applied to all councils.

1. The simplest explanation for the suspension was to say that "it is impossible to carry out [the requirements of] this council, because the contrary course of action has established itself too securely" (527, 24). Luther saw that this way out of the dilemma was too facile. For one thing, if the awesome formula of Acts 15:28, "It has seemed good to the Holy Spirit and to us," meant what it said, it was illegitimate to plead that observance of the council's requirements was impossible. But it was also not true that such observance was impossible. Commenting as he did during this very time upon the patriarchal narratives in the Book of Genesis, Luther believed that man had originally been a vegetarian.[15] Hence it was possible, by avoiding meat altogether, to obey all three of the dietary prohibitions promulgated by the apostolic council. Thus the argument from "impossibility gives us no help in comforting our conscience against the Holy Spirit" (528, 11).

2. Another explanation given for the suspension of this decree was this: The church had the authority to change even the mode of administering the Eucharist, just as it had eventually amended these decrees of an apostolic council, which had been issued by the authority of the Holy Spirit. To this explanation Luther replied, first, that the church had no such prerogative to amend a divine

decree (528, 25). In addition, he pointed out a fundamental inconsistency: Although the church claimed the right to interpose its authority into the administration of a divine institution like the Lord's Supper, it demanded that its own disciplinary and liturgical decrees be obeyed and enforced as though they had been promulgated by divine right (528, 32). The institution of Christ and the decrees of the Holy Spirit could be suspended, but the institutions of the church and the decrees of the pope had to be obeyed at any cost! This was, in Luther's eyes, a basic distortion of the function of church council.

3. Yet, if the church did not have the right to amend a rule laid down with divine authorization, this did not mean that the enforcement of the prohibitions of the apostolic council had simply withered away in the course of time without any explicit action by the church at all. A jurist would point out the speciousness of such reasoning. The nonenforcement of a law at a particular place and time did not mean that the law had been repealed (529, 17). By the same argument an immoral person could argue from the prevalence of immorality that the moral law was invalid. "In fact, we children of Adam would hold a council together with the devils and conclude: 'Are you listening, God? Among us men and devils all your commandments have fallen into disuse. Therefore we should no longer observe them'" (529, 21). Despite his rejection of this argument, Luther was willing at times to reason a posteriori that the prohibitions of the apostolic council could not have been intended to be permanently binding because they had in fact lapsed. Thus he could speak of "certain incidental and external articles" that were decreed by the council, "but not with the intention that an eternal rule should remain in the church as an article of faith; for it has lapsed" (560, 4). He could maintain that "now that [*weil*] it has lapsed," it was permissible to ignore this decree (564, 15). It seems evident, however, that Luther was not contradicting his fundamental argument here, but only using this a posteriori reasoning to corroborate a repeal that he justified on other grounds.

4. In short, it was false to say that on its own authority the church had amended the apostolic council; and though it was

true to say that the decrees of the council had lapsed, this was not a satisfactory explanation. Rhetorically Luther suggested that perhaps the way out of the difficulty was to erase the word "Holy Spirit" from the record and to interpret the decree as the opinion merely of the apostles, not of the Holy Spirit (529, 30). It was obvious that this evasion would not do either: "This is ridiculous! You will have to think up something better" (529, 34). Another evasion that did not provide a workable solution was to declare that the council was speaking, not of the entire law of Moses, but only of portions of it, some of which could be imposed upon the Gentiles and others of which could not be imposed (563, 31). This would have been a new patch on an old garment and a violation of St. Peter's dictum that anyone who obeyed the law in one point would have to obey it in all points (Gal. 5:3). None of these explanations—some of them suggested facetiously by Luther and others advanced seriously by his opponents—could account for the eventual suspension or repeal of decrees that had been promulgated, not by mere bishops, but by the very apostles, not on their own, but with the supporting authority of the Holy Spirit. Did this imply that the decrees were eternally binding, or was there another interpretative device by which to show that they were not?

The interpretative device that Luther employed was to contrast the fourfold decree of the apostolic council in Acts 15:29, which was based upon the recommendation of the Apostle James in Acts 15:20, with the main address of the Apostle Peter in Acts 15:7-11, and particularly with the question of v. 10: "Why do you make trial of God by putting a yoke upon the neck of the disciples which neither our fathers nor we have been able to bear?" This contrast, which contained many echoes of Luther's more familiar contrast between James and Paul, noted that while Peter sought to excuse the Gentile converts to Christianity from the entire Mosaic law, James still wanted to require of them that they obey some of its prohibitions. Luther accused his Roman Catholic opponents, who claimed that the pope was the successor of St. Peter, of ignoring St. Peter and concentrating only upon St. James and his four points. Yet the main issue of the council was the one stated by St. Peter: that Gentile converts should know that they were saved by grace.

If there was a contradiction between this main issue and the four points of James, Luther was willing to say: "If we cannot harmonize them, we shall have to let St. James go with his article and keep St. Peter with his chief article, on account of which the council was held; for without St. Peter's article no one can be saved" (564, 4). This distinction between the "chief article" *[heubtartickel]* (564, 4), and the "peripheral matters" *[nebenhendlin]* (565, 27), the full implications of which were to become a key to the entire conciliar question, enabled Luther to dismiss the fourfold prohibition of the apostolic council as a temporary regulation. St. Peter's article had to do with faith, St. James's with love. The basis of faith was permanent; therefore St. Peter's article was intended to be binding on the church in every age. The basis of love changed from one age to another; therefore St. James's article was relevant to the problem of Gentiles who did not want to offend their Jewish fellow-Christians, but it no longer applied when the reason for this restraint was gone (567, 10). By means of this contrast and distinction Luther was able to take his opponents' arguments, based upon the apostolic council in Acts 15, and to use them in support of his contention that a council had no authority to command new good works or to prescribe new ceremonies.

C. The Role of Government

After laying down the principles that a council had no right to promulgate new doctrines or to command new good works and ceremonies, Luther continued: "A council has no right to meddle in secular law and government" (613, 31). The full implications of this principle, however, do not come into view until one sets it into the context of Luther's interpretation of the role of secular government in a council. For although he expressly forbade interference by a council in the business of government, he did not forbid interference by government in the business of a council. In fact, he maintained, both from history and from an analysis of the contemporary scene, that the convoking of a church council was the business of government. As the government was obliged to come to the rescue in the case of a fire, so it could spring to the aid of the church in an emergency by calling a council (616, 21). And he interpreted the efforts of the pope to convoke a council as proof that the pope had designs on secular authority and monarchy (523, 27).

In support of this interpretation Luther cited historical precedents. The outbreak of the Arian heresy had proved too much for the clergy of Alexandria and even for other clergy. Therefore "the pious Emperor Constantine" added his authority to theirs and convoked the Council of Nicaea (616, 13). Luther's narrative of the circumstances leading up to the Council of Nicaea described the disappointment of the emperor when the church to which he had just granted peace was torn by strife over Arianism (548, 31). Luther admired the patience and humility of Constantine and half-humorously contrasted it with his own polemical style, confessing that he could never have written as gentle a letter as Constantine did to Arius and Bishop Alexander—especially if he had been emperor! (549, 18). Hence it was thanks to the emperor, not to the pope, that the church had obtained the benefits of Nicaea. Whether Luther's opponents liked it or not, "history proves that if it had not been for the Emperor Constantine and if it had been up to Sylvester, the bishop of Rome, the first Council of Nicaea would never have been convoked" (522, 30). The same was true of all four great ecumenical councils. Bishops did call local synods on their own; but when an ecumenical council became necessary, the emperors had done the summoning (592, 21). The council after Nicaea, that of Constantinople, was summoned by Theodosius, also a "pious emperor" (576, 4). When Damasus, the bishop of Rome, had attempted to summon one without imperial authority a year later, the other bishops had refused to come (576, 10). As for the Council of Ephesus, "Latin writers would like to give the impression that the pope had a part in calling it, but the truth is that not the pope but the emperor had to summon his council" (581, 18). The same was true of the Council of Chalcedon (592, 18).

On the basis of these historical precedents Luther had maintained all along that summoning a council to meet the challenges of the sixteenth century was a responsibility also of the secular rulers. During the early years of the Reformation it had been his hope that Charles V could be prevailed upon to live up to this responsibility. He was persuaded that the pope would never consent to a council unless he was sure that he had the emperor, the kings, and the princes firmly in hand before the council was even assembled (510, 17). In the course of the years—the Diet of Augsburg seems to have been the dividing line—Luther had reluctantly come to the conclusion that the emperor could probably not be relied upon to meet this responsibility. Even in this treatise he could speak as though he meant it and say: "The emperor and the kings should take hold here. And if the pope is unwilling, they should force him, as the emperors did in the case of the four chief councils" (622, 1). But the facts of life in both the spiritual and the secular realm had made it clear by the end of the 1530's that the emperor would not take the lead in summoning the "free Christian council" for which the Reformers had been appealing. In part at least, the disappointment of his hopes about the emperor accounted for Luther's pessimism about the prospects for a council, about which we spoke in the first section of this chapter.

Yet if there could not be an ecumenical council under the auspices of the emperor, perhaps it would be possible for the emperor and the German princes to convoke a provincial synod, one confined to the German lands (623, 17). More timid souls than Luther were afraid that such a council could cause a schism, although this is difficult to understand in view of the schism that had already become obvious by this time. Luther was not put off by such fear. On the contrary, he suggested the possibility that exactly the opposite could be the result of such a provincial council. If other rulers saw the accomplishments of the provincial synod, they might be persuaded to accept its decisions even though they had not been participants in it. Perhaps a council, with its "strong voice that can be heard from afar," could accomplish what an individual theologian or preacher had been unable to accomplish. At least it was worth trying (623, 21). And if even this stratagem proved to be unrealistic and the emperor was unwilling to convoke a German council, Luther was already considering the possibility of a still narrower constituency. Perhaps the Reformation party could hold its own council, without the pope and his supporters (514, 20). Even by 1539 there were already enough problems within Protestantism itself to suggest to leaders in both the secular and the spiritual realm the idea of a purely Protestant assembly. This, too, would be a council summoned and assembled under the aegis of the government. For secular rulers, "because they are Christians, have the obligation to convoke a council" (623, 10).

III. The Primary Concern of a Council

From this detailed interpretation of the proper functions of a council and its limitations it is clear that by the time he composed *The Councils and the Church* Luther had developed a key to the interpretation of councils past and present. With its help he was able to make sense of the four great ecumenical councils, as well as of the "apostolic council" spoken of in the Book of Acts; at the same time he was able both to describe and to circumscribe his expectations of a future ecumenical council, if indeed there was to be one.

The key was this: *Every council had one primary concern, one principal doctrine, one chief issue, for the sake of which it was convoked. The decisions of the apostolic council and of the ecumenical councils on the primary concern facing them were permanently binding. Other decisions, having to do with secondary and temporary concerns, were binding only so long as the conditions that called them forth still obtained.* In opposition to the exaltation of conciliar authority by his opponents, therefore, Luther claimed to be reading the councils and fathers as they had wanted to be read, namely, as interpretations of the Sacred Scriptures, and to be concentrating upon the doctrinal questions that constituted the primary concern and the continuing importance of the councils. Using his new-found historical knowledge about the councils to good advantage (514, 26), Luther analyzed the source material before him in order to identify the primary concern of each council and hence to label as peripheral all those features of conciliar legislation which, on the strength of their being incorporated into the canon law, continued to claim authority in the church.

As we have seen, Luther founded this distinction between the primary concern of a council and its peripheral legislation upon the precedent of the apostolic council. Its primary concern was expressed by Peter's insistence that no unnecessary burden was to be laid as a yoke upon the necks of Gentile converts to Christianity. At stake in this primary concern was the Gospel itself. The other actions of the council, i.e., its fourfold prohibition, had to be seen only in the light of this primary concern. Failure to read the acts of the apostolic council in such a light could lead one to repudiate its primary concern and to canonize its temporary and external legislation. It could lead also to a distorted conception of the business of a council, the notion that a council could and should promulgate new dogmas, prescribe new good works, invent new ceremonies that were binding upon consciences, and pass new laws for the secular government. Why, even the apostles in council assembled had refused to be innovators, but had grounded their decision about the primary concern of the council in the precedents of the Old Testament (562, 34). How much less right did any subsequent council have to demand eternal obedience for its temporary legislation! The great councils of the church had been great for the very reason that each of them had paid attention to its primary concern, disposing of other issues as the peripheral problems that they were.

This, then, was Luther's basic thesis about the history of the ecumenical councils: "The decrees of the genuine councils must remain in force permanently, just as they have always been in force, especially the primary concerns for whose sake they are councils and are called such" (563, 24). The Council of Nicaea "dealt primarily with the doctrine that Christ is true God. It was convoked for the sake of this, and for the sake of this it is a council and is called such. Besides this they also dealt with certain accidental, temporal, external, and temporary matters, which are to be regarded as purely secular, not to be put on a par with the articles of faith and not to be observed as a permanent law" (559, 31). Hence fidelity to Nicaea meant the affirmation of its primary concern, not the observance of its temporary regulations about the defection of soldiers (534, 1). Similarly, the doctrine of the deity

of the Holy Spirit was the primary concern of the Council of
Constantinople, "the sole reason why it was held, on the basis of
which the intention of the council can be understood" (579, 24).
Other decisions of this second council, such as those regarding the
elevation of the bishop of Constantinople to the rank of patriarch,
were "not an article of faith, but an external and empirical work,
which even reason can and should perform" (579, 29). The Council of Ephesus condemned the Nestorian heresy; its other decrees
"have to do with temporal matters. . . . These we ignore" (583, 24).
When he came to consider the Council of Chalcedon, Luther's
sources of historical information were unclear. He confessed:
"What the reason for this council was, I myself would like to learn
from someone else" (592, 29). But his subsequent discussion of
Eutyches showed that he was still operating with his key distinction between the primary concern of a council and its secondary,
peripheral decrees.

   In short, Luther affirmed the legitimacy of church councils past
and present. But he insisted that if there were ever to be a council to deal with the issues raised by the Reformation, it had to
address itself to this primary concern. Yet Luther was convinced
that the pope wanted the council to consider everything imaginable
except this primary concern. As Part I of this chapter has shown,
he had no hope any longer that the central doctrinal concern of his
Reformation could receive a fair hearing at any council to which
a pope would consent. Therefore all he could envision was a papal
council at which the pope would insist upon a vindication of his
doctrinal position and then permit latitude and compromise on the
peripheral issues that did not really matter. Luther's historical
studies persuaded him that this was a reversal of the established
procedure of the councils of the church, as well as an evasion of
the responsibility now laid upon any church council. Although
his distinction between primary concern and secondary issues
provided later Protestants with an excuse for making their fateful
distinction between the husk and the kernel of the Christian message, it did not enable him, with very meager historical resources,
to penetrate by intuition into the issues that had confronted the
ecumenical councils and to see their continuing relevance. Even

within the council described by the New Testament he was able to distinguish between the permanent and the temporary.

Each generation of Protestants must reconsider the adequacy of this interpretation of church councils past and present. Each generation must also ask what did in fact happen when the appeal of the Reformers for a council was taken up in earnest. Certainly the Council of Trent dealt with many administrative and disciplinary problems, carrying out far-reaching reforms that permanently affected the organizational structure of Roman Catholicism. Yet it would not be accurate or fair to maintain that these reforms were at the cost of the "primary concern" that had been central to Luther and the Reformers. By its decrees on original sin, justification, and Scripture, the Council of Trent affirmed the conviction that these issues were indeed central to the Reformation controversies. The actual outcome of the Tridentine decrees may be another matter; but the evasion of the issues, of which Luther was afraid, did not in fact take place. In a formal sense if not in a material sense, therefore, Trent met Luther's requirements for a council. His attitude toward church councils obliges his descendants to look seriously, not only at the Council of Trent, but at subsequent councils as well. For the inter-relation between Luther and the councils shows how the Roman Catholicism that convoked these councils and the Lutheranism that provoked these councils are bound together in a mysterious and mutual responsibility.

Notes

1. "Disputatio Excellentium theologorum Iohannis Eckii et Martini Lutheri Augustiniani," *Luthers Werke* (Weimar edition, henceforth abbreviated as WA) 2, 288; cf. Jaroslav Pelikan, "Luther's Attitude Toward John Hus," *Concordia Theological Monthly*, XIX (1948), 747-763.

2. Theodor Kolde, *Luthers Stellung zu Konzil und Kirche bis zum Wormser Reichstag* (Gütersloh, 1876), while outdated, is still useful. See also Robert Stupperich, "Die Reformatoren und das Tridentinum," *Archiv für Reformationsgeschichte*, XLVII (1956), 20-62, especially the section on "Luthers Stellung zum Konzil im Allgemeinen," pp. 23 ff.

3. "Appellatio F. Martini Luther ad Concilium," WA 2, 36-40.

4. "Ein Sermon vom Sakrament des Leichnams Christi," WA 2, 742.

5. "An den christlichen Adel deutscher Nation," WA 6, 404-469.

6. The most recent and balanced account of these negotiations is Hubert Jedin, *Geschichte des Konzils von Trient*, I (Freiburg, 1951).

7. Cf. W. Köhler, *Luther und die Kirchengeschichte* (Erlangen, 1900) and Ernst Schäfer, *Luther als Kirchenhistoriker* (Gütersloh, 1897). This study had been facilitated by the appearance in 1538 of Peter Crabbe's edition of the acts of the councils, *Concilia omnia* (cf. WA 50, 502). Crabbe's book is in the Library of Congress.

8. Cf. Schäfer, *op. cit.*, pp. 83 ff.

9. "Von den Konziliis und Kirchen," WA 50, 509-653. Both the English translation by C. S. Smyth in

1847 and that by C. M. Jacobs in 1931 translated *Kirchen* as a plural, "churches."

10. The numerals in the text refer to the page and line of the Weimar edition with which the citation or summary begins.

11. Adolf von Harnack, *Lehrbuch der Dogmengeschichte* (Tübingen, 1932), III, 847-896.

12. "Vom Abendmahl Christi. Bekenntnis," WA 26, 319-323.

13. "Sprüche wider das Konstanzer Konzil," WA 39, 22.

14. The sermons appear, WA 15, 571-602.

15. See, for example, "Enarratio in Genesin," WA 42, 54-55.

Chapter IV

Roman Catholicism on the Eve of the Council

Two opposing, even contradictory, tendencies dominate the contemporary Roman Catholic scene. A secularist or a Roman Catholic might not see the situation in quite these terms, but such must be the judgment of the Protestant who is concerned about evaluating the present from the viewpoint of the Reformation understanding of the Christian faith. On the one hand, there is a whole complex of developments leading to an increased emphasis on what he believes are the central Christian realities. It is possible to speak of a genuine "evangelical revival" within the Roman Church, strange though this expression may seem to many. Yet there are also contrary movements, the most striking of which is the growing importance of the Virgin Mary both in popular piety and in the most recent dogma, that of the Assumption (1950). The Protestant regrets these latter tendencies just as much as he approves the former, and thus he finds it difficult to understand how both can develop together. The result is that he is tempted to ignore one or the other side of the picture and to describe contemporary Roman Catholicism either with excessive enthusiasm or, even more unfortunately, with unjustified animus and disgust. It is no doubt impossible to achieve an entirely balanced view, yet it is this for which we must strive in order to understand the role which the coming council could play in the history of the Roman church.

Before attempting a more detailed description of the evangelical renewal, it is well to remind ourselves that Roman Catholicism varies enormously from one part of the world to another. This is inevitable in a communion found on all continents, which claims five hundred million adherents, has two thousand bishops, and maintains on the foreign mission field alone a force of one hundred thousand priests, brothers, and nuns.[1] Further, the leadership as a matter of deliberate policy adapts itself to different conditions and tolerates extreme diversity on certain matters, while remaining firm on others, for it knows that only thus can it keep within the church men of widely varying races and cultures who differ radically in their political persuasions, intellectual outlooks, and style of moral and religious life. Everyone knows that Roman Catholicism in northern and southern Europe, or in North and South America, does not have the same external appearance, but the depth of the contrasts is often far greater than either Protestants or Catholics generally realize. Most non-Europeans are greatly surprised by the strength of the evangelical component in the Catholicism of transalpine Europe, especially where French or German is spoken, and in the Low countries (though it has also radiated outward to other areas). The contrary tendencies are present everywhere, but are most powerful in Spain, Italy, and Latin America. Furthermore, in some of these areas there are still abuses similar to those of the late medieval church, such as clerical corruption, pagan superstitions, and the forcible repression of other religious groups. Here the Protestant view of the Roman Church is dark indeed. In English-speaking lands conditions of still another type prevail, for while the moral level in general is high and the people are loyal to the church, yet far more than in some European circles there is a legalistic and juridical emphasis on the institution and its dogma rather than on the power of Christ's grace in Sacraments, Scripture, and preaching.

These objective differences, however, are not the only ones which produce radically divergent attitudes towards Roman Catholicism.

There is in many quarters a deep-seated conviction, fostered in part by Catholic claims of unchangeableness, that the Roman church must forever remain basically the same as it was at the time of the Reformation and during the wars of religion. As a result even more Europeans, and many more outside Europe, minimize the great changes which have taken place, and continue to regard the pope as a close relative of the Antichrist and such groups as the Jesuits as dangerous and unprincipled conspirators. Diversity of theological perspective introduces another variable. A man who agrees with the Reformers that the Bible and the early creeds have some genuine authority, or with Luther on the Sacraments, or with the Anglicans on the importance of the episcopacy will be inclined, other things being equal, to have a more favorable view of Roman Catholicism than will a radical theological liberal or an extreme congregationalist. This, to be sure, is not inevitable, for, to cite just one exception, some free-church liberals[2] have a tremendous appreciation for certain mystical movements within Catholicism which greatly trouble most Calvinists and Lutherans (as well as, it should be added, some Roman Catholics). Still another factor which influences men's judgments in these matters is their social and political views, as in the case of some Americans who argue that democratic beliefs regarding the organization of both ecclesiastical and civil society are the only proper ones for a Christian to hold.

Influential though these considerations are, the most important detriment of Protestant and Catholic reactions to each other is what I fear must be called the struggle for power between the confessions. Where this is quiescent, where the fronts have for centuries been stable, as in much of Europe, it is easier for the two parties to look at each other without undue aggressiveness or feelings of insecurity and so to appreciate each other's good points even while continuing to disagree. It is even possible for friendly, constructive relations to develop, as happened especially during the last war when both groups were threatened by a common foe. Protestants were impressed by the resistance of the Roman Church to Nazism, which in Germany, though not without hesitations, was generally firmer than their own. When priests and pastors were imprisoned together they also talked and prayed together, thereby discovering that they were far more closely united in their common faith and loyalty to Jesus Christ than they had realized. As a result of these experiences *Una Sancta* groups, concerned with *rapprochement* between the confessions, multiplied, and even now, when that movement has declined, for reasons which we shall later mention, the conversation between the theologians of the two groups grows ever more vigorous and fruitful. The focus is on fundamental doctrinal problems, on the right understanding of sin and salvation, of Christ and the church, rather than on the social and political questions which dominate interconfessional discussions in other places such as the United States. Furthermore, these doctrinal debates have generally moved beyond the hostile and sterile polemics of past centuries into a cooperative search for the fullness of the truth that is in Jesus Christ in which each side learns from the other. There is nevertheless a full consciousness that fundamental and, humanly speaking, irreconcilable differences still remain, but this is combined with a sense of genuine Christian brotherhood and a realization on the part of many that Protestants and Catholics stand united in common opposition to growing secularism, to anti-Christian movements outside the church, and to indifference and purely cultural religion within.

The situation is utterly different on most mission fields, for there the two confessions are in direct competition. Roman Catholics often resort to extreme measures to persuade prospective converts that theirs is the only true church, while Protestants are frequently convinced that the Catholics are primarily interested in power and numbers and not in genuine conversions to Christian faith. Thus real bitterness sometimes develops and the missionaries of the two groups face each other with mutual hostility and suspicion.

The worst conditions of all exist where Protestantism threatens to make inroads among traditionally Catholic peoples, such as those of Spain and South America, especially when these are of a low cultural and educational level. This sometimes leads to governmental persecution and sometimes to physically violent reactions on the part of priests and laity even when the government and the hierarchy, as in Colombia, have made at least some efforts to restrain them. Such incidents magnify the tensions in other parts of the world, for Catholics are inclined to think that they have been greatly exaggerated, while Protestants usually believe, sometimes against the evidence, that they have been engineered or favored by higher authorities in the church. Protestants are also likely to forget that similar outrages have been committed in the not too distant past against growing Catholic minorities even in places like the United States. In that country there were numerous outbreaks, especially in the decades just prior to the Civil War. Some were extremely violent, as, for example, the three-day anti-Catholic riot in Philadelphia in 1844 when thirteen were killed, fifty badly injured, two churches, a seminary, and blocks of houses destroyed, and the bishop was forced to take refuge in the home of one of the few kindly disposed Protestant ministers.[3] Such events are seared into the memories of American Catholics but are utterly unknown to most Protestants, who instead have vivid recollections of the Spanish Inquisition and the persecutions of the French Huguenots.

Although mass bigotry is no longer a problem in America, as is proved by the election of Mr. Kennedy to the presidency, both confessions are still inevitably affected by the existence of a power struggle in which Roman Catholicism continues to make gains in a traditionally Protestant land. It seems unlikely that these advances will in the future be primarily numerical, for the proportion of Roman Catholics appears to be more or less stabilized at about 33-35% of those with religious affiliations and at about somewhat less than 25% of the total population, but the influence of this minority is constantly increasing.[4] Because of their relatively recent immigrant origin, it is only in the last decades that Roman Catholics have begun to move in large numbers from the ranks of the urban workers into the middle and upper classes, and with this rise in status comes a corresponding increase in their power to shape society, especially in such sensitive areas as school policy, censorship, and medical ethics (e.g., in regard to the dispensing of birth-control information). The resulting apprehensions of non-Catholics are aggravated by the fact that American Catholic attitudes are still to a certain extent that of a belligerent, somewhat foreign, and therefore emotionally insecure minority. Perhaps in

order to compensate for this, hyper-patriotic and ultra-nationalistic
movements, such as that led by the late Senator Joseph McCarthy,
have recently developed a special appeal to many Catholics, and
this in turn further strengthens an image of Catholic totalitarianism
and reaction which is actually misleading, for the semi-proletarian
character of the Roman church in America has meant that both its
people and its leadership have in the past usually provided more
support for social reforms than have Protestant denominations.
Another result of this historical background is that American
Catholicism displays a peculiar combination of practical pro-
gressiveness and theological and liturgical rigidity. Efficiency and
flexibility were necessary in order to accomplish the tremendous
task of caring for the millions of immigrants who flooded these
shores, but this has left little time and energy for creative intellectual and spiritual concerns. One American Jesuit recently com-
mented that the seven million Catholics of Austria are "incompa-
rably more productive theologically" than the economically far
richer forty million Catholics in the United States.[5] It has also
been pointed out that not one of the bishops, archbishops, and
cardinals in the history of the American Catholic Church is the
son of a university graduate.[6] For all these reasons, the American
Protestant attitude toward Roman Catholicism is generally a peculiar compound of intellectual, cultural, and religious contempt combined with what are often unrealistic fears of its reactionary authoritarianism and power.

It should not be supposed that the reality fully corresponds to
this picture. What we have called the evangelical revival is making
rapid progress in the ranks of the priests and theologians who will
be the leaders of tomorrow and also among the growing group of
lay Catholic intellectuals. In one area many American Catholics
have been in the forefront of reform, for their devotion to American
ideals of religious freedom have made them for nearly a hundred
years an increasingly powerful force pressing for the revision of
the traditional, intolerant position that in primarily Catholic society
the church should make use of the state to repress heresy. Yet,
when all is said, it must be admitted that North American Roman
Catholicism is very different from the northern European variety,

and that both these diverge sharply from the Italian, Spanish, or Latin American forms. Which of these, many people ask, is truly Roman? What is the essential reality lying behind the diverse manifestations?

The meaning of this question often proves to be: What are the views of the hierarchy, the Vatican Curia, the pope? What sort of Catholicism do they consider ideal, and what would they like to see realized everywhere? Are not the more hopeful developments at which we have hinted simply expedient compromises, and would not the leaders like to see a restoration of what is often represented as the late medieval situation in which a juridical and legalistic religion completely rules the hearts of men by means of sacramental magic, hagiographical superstition, and the fear of disobedience?

If a man is determined to believe that this is the case, it is impossible to convince him of error even by volumes of evidence. He takes opposing facts simply as proof of the cleverness of the hierarchy in concealing its true purposes, while he seizes on every word or act which suggests restorationism—and there are many of these—as support for his thesis. Actually, there are great differences of opinion even at the top of the hierarchy as to what genuinely promotes the welfare of the church. Some dare not trust the free work of the Holy Spirit in any measure and would like to confine it rigorously within fixed patterns of thought and practice developed during the post-Reformation centuries. Others have seen that this defensiveness was disastrous, that the privileges which the church had acquired were corrupting, and that new challenges cannot be met by maintaining old forms *en bloc* but only by taking the risks of change and creativity and by greater reliance upon the power of the Gospel.

The first signs of renewal, the beginnings of a shift to this second approach, are discernible already shortly after the First Vatican Council (1869-1870) in the Pontificate of a truly great man, Leo XIII (1878-1903). He was not in any full sense a representative of the present phase of the evangelical revival but he had the courage and insight to recognize the need for "reformation" as opposed to "restoration." He forced the reactionary French majority in the church, which had come close to identifying Catholicism and royalism, to come to terms with the Republic and, going even farther in this direction, he insisted in such encyclicals as *Rerum Novarum*[7] on the justice of major parts of the socialist program, thus helping, at least in Germany and the United States, to arrest that progressive alienation of the proletariat which had resulted from the alliance of the church with the propertied classes. The intellectual backwardness and obscurantism of the past were attacked by Leo XIII's sponsorship of archeological and biblical studies and, more ambiguously, by his encouragement of the study of earlier medieval thinkers, especially Thomas Aquinas, in preference to later commentators. Perhaps most important of all was his recommendation of private Bible reading, which reversed earlier prohibitions (renewed as late as 1836) against lay use of the Bible without special permission. It is characteristic also that in dealing with the reunion of Christians in the encyclical *Praeclara* he avoided the traditional terms "schism," "heresy," "sect," and spoke of Protestants as "most beloved brethren." These may seem like small details, but they were symptomatic of a revolutionary change in atmosphere.

The progress started under Leo XIII has continued with increasing momentum down to the present day. To be sure, it has not been continuous and has at time been halted and even reversed in an effort to control forces which the Vatican considered disruptive. The first check was administered by Pius X, when in the encyclical *Pascendi* (1907) he condemned the so-called Catholic modernists, who included some of the most able and, in the opinion of non-Catholics, some of the most Christian thinkers of the time. Two of the greatest sympathizers with many aspects of modernism, Baron von Hügel and Lord Acton, were not actually forced out of the church, but the values for which they stood were stifled, and only now are some of them beginning to emerge from a cloud of suspicion.

Further action against excessive freedom in doctrine or practice has been taken in the last two decades especially by the limiting of ecumenical discussion with non-Roman Catholics (the *Monitum* of June 5, 1948, which was moderated by the Instruction *Ecclesia*

Catholica of Dec. 20, 1949),[8] by the warning against various theological and philosophical developments in Humani Generis (1950), and by the disbanding of the French worker priests which started under Pius XII and was completed by the present pope, John XXIII, in 1959.[9] The Reformation Protestant regrets these measures, not because he entirely approves of what they condemned—modernism had its dubious aspects and the loss to Communism of some of the generally admirable worker priests clearly had to be stopped —but because these papal actions often rejected the good together with the bad, violated evangelical freedom, and seem to have been concerned more with maintaining ecclesiastical power than with the Gospel. Nevertheless it is clearly wrong to argue, as is sometimes done, that such incidents prove that Rome has in no way changed. Rather they are eddies in a current of renewal which has been flowing now for over eighty years.

External aspects of the church have been affected by reforms, such as those started by Pius X (1903-1914), which have eliminated certain abuses from the Vatican Curia, improved its administrative responsibility and efficiency, and simplified the luxurious and archaic etiquette which surrounds the pope. When John XXIII— to mention just one small detail—walks rather than is carried in triumphal state into St. Peter's, he reminds the Catholic faithful of what a Christian pastor should be rather than of the worldly princelings which past popes have so often been. The internationalization of the church has also progressed enormously through the consecration of native bishops in China, India, and Africa, and through changes in the College of Cardinals, in which now for the first time since the Reformation Italians are in the minority. As a result of these and similar improvements, the Roman church is reported on the basis of an extensive independent investigation to be administratively more efficient than are most first-rate business corporations.[10] It must be remembered, of course, that progress of this sort is purely instrumental and can be used either for good or ill. When it is employed, as often seems to be the case, in order to increase what even many Catholics consider the excessive centralization of power in Rome, it is to be regretted. There is now, however, much discussion about measures which can be taken to increase the authority and independence of the bishops, perhaps even by supplementing and thereby modifying the impression left by the Vatican decrees on the infallibility of the pope.

More unequivocally good is the extensive withdrawal of the Roman church from that direct involvement with the state which has been one of the greatest sources of its corruption. There is a growing conviction, echoes of which are heard even in Spain, that it is not only inexpedient but unchristian for the church to utilize temporal power in order forcibly to maintain its position in society. This position is represented by the great majority of post-war Roman Catholic writers on this subject and was even reflected in Pius XII's speech on toleration in 1953, which contained what has been widely interpreted as an indirect rebuke to the rigid traditionalism of Cardinal Ottaviani (who is still, however, one of the leading figures in the Curia).[11]

Improvements in canon law were also made in the codification of 1917, and these open up the possibility of greater and much needed changes in this mass of legalistic, casuistic regulations which govern so large a part of a Roman Catholic's life. It is too easily forgotten that many of the most typical features of the Roman church, such as clerical celibacy and the withholding of the cup from the laity in Communion, belong in the area of things which can in principle be altered and that, as a matter of fact, these two practices do not exist in those Oriental churches that are in communion with Rome. In recent years there has been speculation about the possibility of making all sorts of canonical concessions to any Protestant groups which may be interested in union with Rome, and in Europe the ban on married priests has actually been lifted in several instances in order to make possible the ordination of Protestant ministers who were converted to Catholicism.

Much more significant in the long run, however, is the increasing role which the laity is playing in the Roman church. The most impressively visible example of this—the many kinds of work carried on by Catholic Action—however, has generally been tightly controlled by the clergy, though this is decreasing. Lay orders are being formed, more and more lay men and women are studying theology, and such thinkers as Gilson and Maritain (to mention only those who currently have the greatest international reputation) have exerted a greater influence even on theologians than have all but a handful of clerics. The previously neglected doctrine of universal priesthood (which, according to Roman Catholics, all believers share, though in subordination to the special priesthood) has become one of the favorite themes of contemporary theology and was also emphasized in the papal encyclicals *Mystici corporis* (1943) and *Mediator dei* (1947). This has even led to the suggestion that it might be possible to establish a lay College of Cardinals which would restore to the people some of the influence in the direction of the church which they had in the early centuries.[12]

Supporting and inspiring this movement is the great progress which has been made in the study and use of the Bible. On the scholarly side the encyclical *Divino afflante Spiritu* (1943) is of special significance, for it together with various decisions of the Papal Biblical Commission silently rescinded many of the repressive measures taken at the time of the modernist controversy, and it also acknowledged that the Hebrew and Greek originals have greater authority than does the Latin Vulgate, which for four hundred years had been supreme. Roman Catholics are now as free to reach unbiased decisions on textual problems as are Protestants, and the differences in recent translations prepared by the two groups are so minor that in 1960 arrangements were made in America to start on the preparation of an interconfessional English edition of the Bible. There has also suddenly developed a surprising degree of agreement with Protestant scholars on critical, historical, and exegetical questions. Catholics are willing to admit that they have learned much from non-Catholics about the Scriptures, and Protestants in turn acknowledge that Catholics are now beginning to produce quantities of first-rate biblical work. This has important theological consequences, as is illustrated by the many Roman Catholic scholars who, while still criticizing Luther's understanding of faith at certain points, nevertheless admit that he is much closer to the Apostle Paul on this matter than were Catholic theologians and catechisms of the past few centuries. Thus biblical studies constitute the one area in which cooperation between the confessions is already extensive and constantly becoming more so.

This biblical revival has not been confined to the scholarly level but has also penetrated deeply in some places into the lives of the people. Many new translations have been widely circulated, so that in marked contrast to the situation even a generation ago, it is now usual rather than unusual for Catholic homes in many lands to have a Bible. It is already half a century since daily scripture reading was first recommended to all Catholics by a pope, and while such admonitions have only gradually taken effect, this practice is now followed by millions of Catholics, especially in areas where the bishops are concerned to encourage it. Bible courses have been instituted and extensive guides to the study of the Bible have been prepared and widely circulated among the laity in Europe, as well as during the last couple of years in the United States. These follow the doctrinal standards of the church, but the distortions of the biblical message are substantially less than in the past, so that the Protestant cannot but rejoice that the religious life especially of devout Catholics is being increasingly nourished by Scripture.

In the judgment of Roman Catholics, however, the modern liturgical movement is of surpassing importance for the growth of Christian life among the people. It provides, they believe, the proper soil for the development of both lay participation and a biblical orientation. In the Roman Catholic setting, contrary to what is often true in Protestant circles, there is no opposition between liturgical and scriptural interests, and they are generally combined in the same persons. Despite later accretions, the liturgy is still primarily biblical, and furthermore, the reforms are directed towards regaining the liturgical emphases of the early centuries which are even more unmistakably scriptural. All efforts are concentrated on restoring congregational worship to its original primacy, and in this there is a similarity to one of the major concerns of the Protestant Reformation (even though it should be added that preaching the Word, while not entirely neglected, is not as important for the modern Catholic liturgical movement as it was for the Reformers). What is important is that the entire congregation learn to participate intelligently in the central worship service of the church. In this way an effort is made to overcome both the extreme objectivism of the older views, according to which the priest alone acts and the congregation is entirely passive, and also the accompanying subjectivism and individualism, especially popular during the nineteenth century, which recommended that the devout believer busy himself with his own prayers and meditations during the mass. Now all are urged to "pray the mass" instead of "praying in the mass."[13]

Pius X was the first of the popes to press the cause of liturgical reform, as he did especially in the encyclical *Musicae sacrae disciplinae,* which urged congregational participation in the mass. His initiatives have been continued by later popes, culminating in 1950 in the greatest liturgical change in many centuries, the reshaping of the services for Holy Week. The Vatican has also done much to encourage more frequent communion and the use by the people of translated missals enabling them to follow the mass in their own language. The last of these innovations has become well-nigh universal in northern Europe and in North America, though in the latter area it is still recent. In 1928 only fifty thousand vernacular missals were in circulation, while by 1956 a single one of the nineteen available editions had sold thirteen million copies in the United States.[14] One of the long-range objectives of the liturgical movement is the replacement of Latin by the mother tongue, first in the sacramental rites (Baptism, marriage, burial, etc.) and ultimately in the entire liturgy, except for the sacramental words proper. The first steps in this direction have been taken in much of transalpine Europe, but North America and, even more, South America, lag behind, largely because the people and bishops have generally not been interested in requesting the necessary permission. There are therefore few dialogue masses and nothing comparable to the vernacular hymn singing so common in Germany, where the songs are often the same as those used in Protestant churches. The objective in a great many churches seems to be the operation of an efficient production line in which the thousands of parishioners are rushed through a forty-minute routine, including both confession and mass, which requires little more than their physical presence.

Even in North America, however, the style of church sanctuaries

74   *The Papal Council and the Gospel*

has been influenced by liturgical reforms favoring simplicity—often greater simplicity than is found in Protestant churches. The altar, which was formerly removed from the congregation and often hidden behind a choir screen, is now advanced towards the people and sometimes becomes an altar-table behind which the priest celebrates mass while facing the congregation. A cross or crucifix is central, while other statues and pictures are either banished entirely or exiled to the periphery. Everything is done to overcome the traditional view that the mass is a priestly act done for the benefit of spectators, and to replace it with an experience of common worship in which the priest and the congregation together participate in a personal manner in the one and only sacrifice of Christ on the cross which is here made present for the salvation of the world.

Those familiar with Reformation controversies recognize that the liturgical movement meets many of the most serious of the original Protestant objections to Roman Catholic sacramentalism. It centers worship on God's saving acts in Jesus Christ and, as is evident in many European parishes, pushes into the background the historically more popular forms of Catholic devotion, such as pilgrimages, indulgences, novenas, and the veneration of saints and relics. The magical attitude towards the Sacraments is replaced by a sense of personal involvement and commitment. Such doctrinal affirmations as that of transubstantiation are persistently maintained, but the practical religious meaning of these is largely transformed when the mass is viewed, not as a ritual in which the priest "makes God" (to cite a phrase which was current before the Reformation), but as the way in which Christ gives himself in his full divine-human reality in order that men "may know him and the power of his resurrection, and may share his sufferings, becoming like him in his death" (Phil. 3:10 RSV). It is in terms such as these that the theologians associated with the liturgical revival explain the Sacraments. Their favorite themes are the incorporation of the Christian into Christ and into the church as his mystical body—which in the past was often considered a dangerous notion. For them the Sacraments are not rituals which God has empowered certain men to perform in order impersonally to produce all sorts of good effects, from the cure of sick cattle to the release of souls from purgatory, but they are rather the means whereby Christ makes himself present in his church and incorporates men into himself.

It would be an exaggeration to suggest that the full dimensions of these views have penetrated deeply into the parishes of even the most liturgically (and evangelically) advanced areas of Europe. In English-speaking lands, not to mention Latin countries, born knowledge and sympathy are largely absent, and the relatively slight reforms of worship which occur have been met by incomprehension, indifference, and even resistance. The American priest who used the title of Shakespeare's play "Much Ado About Nothing" to describe the liturgical movement is by no means an exception.[15] And yet the progress made in parts of Europe and in smaller circles in other regions should not be underestimated. It is as a result of this that a German Roman Catholic theologian asserts that the piety of the most active Catholics is now Christocentric and theocentric, grounded in the Bible and the liturgy. He continues:

Despite all the defects which we have mentioned, one should not fail to note a great religious upsurge in the Catholic Church of this century. Further, it will be necessary in these matters to have patience and not require from uneducated Catholics the same as from educated, from a southern temperament, the same as from a northern, from areas which have no living contact with Protestantism and its concerns, the same as from the confessionally mixed and therefore in many respects more awakened regions. Definite beginnings are to be found everywhere, and for the future the Catholic elite is more important than the often sluggish Catholic masses. We discover time and again . . . that the spirituality of the religiously leading Catholics and Protestants has come to be very similar—and spirituality is more important than a multitude of divisive externalities. Time and again Catholics and Protestants who have come to know each other well discover with astonishment how alike they have become despite their abiding differences. This is a likeness which is ultimately grounded on faith in the same Father through the same Jesus Christ, in praying the same Lord's Prayer and the same Psalms, in meditating on and studying the same Holy Writ, in life out of the same Baptism, the same spirit, and the same—still too little recognized—great common Christian tradition.[16]

Roman Catholics who are as close to Protestants as this quotation suggests have inevitably come to view the Reformation with far greater sympathy than would have been imagined possible half a century ago. Leading Roman Catholic historians of that time still argued that Luther was fundamentally a fornicator. Great scholars such as Denifle and Grisar were more subtle, but they still pictured him either morally corrupt or psychopathic. An almost complete reversal of this view is represented by the contemporary Roman Catholic Johannes Hessen, who regards Luther as a prophet raised up by God to reform Christendom, forced out of the church primarily because of the sinful stubbornness of the authorities and only secondarily because of his own attitudes.[17] This is somewhat extreme, and more representative of Roman Catholic opinion is Lortz's description of the Reformer as a man of truly Christian faith who attacked genuine evils within the late medieval church, but who was betrayed by his excessive subjectivism into a break with Rome.[18] This is now the standard view in German theological circles, and it is being increasingly accepted in other parts of the world. Progress is slow, however, especially in polemical popular literature, and even "For many a Catholic student of theology, *pecca fortiter sed fortius crede* ("sin boldly but believe more boldly") is the formula which genuinely, adequately, and loyally expresses the complete thought of Luther."[19]

Associated with this re-evaluation of the Reformation is a new emphasis on the need for constant reform within the Roman Catholic Church itself.[20] It is admitted that the church badly needed to be purified in the 16th century, but it is then argued that this has been largely accomplished and that additional and never-ending progress is possible. All Roman Catholics firmly maintain the traditional teaching that the divine institution and constitution of the church are spotless and irreformable, but it has now been suggested by one author that human and divine elements are so intertwined that it is misleading simply to say, as is customary, that "there are sinners in the church but the church itself is sinless." One must also speak of "a sinning church." After all, two of the collects repeated each year in every Roman Catholic congregation speak of God as "purifying his church," thus implying that "the sin in the church affects, burdens, wounds, and distorts the church itself" and must be constantly struggled against in all the areas of its life.[21]

These attitudes have made possible a new—and, it must be granted, more effective—Roman Catholic apologetics which repudiates those ill-tempered and often historically dishonest polemicists who try to derive all the evils of the modern West from Protestant and secularist departures from Rome. Instead of this, it is granted that Catholics, including many of the leaders, have contributed much to these evils and that, on the other hand, a great deal of good has developed outside of Catholicism. Thus, for example, Father Bouyer says of the Reformation that all its positive concerns were good and valid.

This Roman Catholic author approves Luther's emphasis on justification by faith, Calvin's stress on the glory of God, and even, to a certain extent, the Reformation insistence on primacy of Scripture and the priesthood of all believers. The trouble with the Reformation, he says, was that to each of its positive and genuinely Christian emphases it attached a corresponding and unnecessary negation. Justification by faith resulted in a neglect (perhaps not by Luther but by his followers) of the doctrine of sanctification. The rightful concentration on the glory and power of God was combined with the depreciation of human worth; the *sola scriptura* was associated with an attack on reason, and the priesthood of all believers was interpreted in an individualistic way which destroyed any proper notion of the church. Now, Bouyer continues, these principles should be held together, rather than be made into opposites. When they are made into contradictory, rather than complementary, assertions, then what has happened in Protestantism becomes inevitable. Men swing from one extreme to another. After neglecting sanctification at the expense of justification, they come to do the opposite, neglect faith and the grace of God, and make salvation a matter of Puritanic moralism or else of "social-gospel" activism. Indeed, in a good deal of modern Protestantism there has been a more radical works-righteousness, a more complete indifference to God's grace, than was ever true of the theology—whatever may have been true of the practice—

of the Middle Ages. The same pendulum movement can be seen
in other aspects of Protestantism. After elevating God at the expense of man, man has been exalted so as to throw God in the
shadow and an anti-rational biblicism has often been replaced by
an anti-biblical rationalism. The lesson to be drawn from all these
observations, so Bouyer maintains, is that the only way to preserve
the positive and proper truths of the Reformation is to hold them
within the balanced structure of justification and sanctification, of
the glory of God and the dignity of man, of reason and faith,
Bible and tradition, individual and church, which is represented
by Roman Catholicism. So this Roman Catholic author concludes
that in the future, even if not in the past, the positive aspects of the
Reformation have a better chance of prospering inside the Roman
church than outside. The future of the Reformation lies within
Romanism, and the best way to be a good son of Luther or Calvin
is to join the Roman Church.[22]

Any Protestant whose primary concern is that the Gospel of
Christ be preached, whether by Catholic or by Protestant, will
rejoice at the unprecedentedly evangelical accents of these new
apologists. He will be thankful for the progress which has been
made and will pray that it may continue. Yet he will also find
himself wondering about the relation of these Catholics, to whom
he feels so close in spirit, to all the unreformed and unchristian
elements in the Roman church. How can they reconcile themselves
to the official toleration and even encouragement of popular superstitions, to the unscriptural and irreformable dogmas, to the idolatrous absolutization of the human element involved in ecclesiastical
authoritarianism and papal infallibility? He will try to ask these
questions without self-righteousness, fully conscious that within
Protestantism are to be found indifference, unbelief, and a capitu-
lation to a de-christianized culture which are, in their way, fully as
bad as Catholic corruptions, but also fully convinced that as a
Protestant he has a freedom which he dare not surrender—even
though he exercises it far too little—to withstand in obedience to
God all evils in his own and other churches without being forced
into the excuses and compromises which he sees as inevitable in
Roman Catholicism.

There are two contemporary Roman Catholic developments which especially trouble the Protestant observer. First, in defining the dogma of the Assumption of the Virgin Mary in 1950, the Roman church clearly and explicitly claimed the authority to promulgate a dogma which, even by its own official admission, is without direct biblical warrant. This has inevitably aroused fears that, despite the biblical revival, future dogmatic developments may be increasingly independent of Scripture.

Second, Protestants fear that the Mariological movement will continue to grow, thus leading to even further departures from the original foundations of the church. Marian shrines and apparitions, such as those at Lourdes and Fatima, arouse enormous popular enthusiasm, and this occurs with at least the acquiescence of the hierarchy, while Marian congresses and Marian literature—982 new titles are listed in a bibliography for 1948-1950[23]—have full approbation. It is with bewilderment that a Protestant reads of recent popes dedicating all mankind to Mary, appealing to her for mercy, grace, and help in time of misfortune, speaking of her as receiving the same lot as Christ in order to atone for the sins of men, and even affirming that she offered up the Son in her own way so that there is a sense in which it is proper to speak of her as having redeemed the human race together with Christ.[24]

The explanations for such statements given by biblically oriented Catholics must be listened to attentively no matter how tortured they sometimes seem. They say that nothing is attributed to Mary which cannot also be said of the church and, in a lesser measure, of every Christian. This means, first of all, that she has nothing of her own independently of Christ, for all that she has received has been given her because of him. Paul says that Christ is "to be glorified in his saints, and to be marveled at in all who believed" (2 Thess. 1:10 RSV). Surely, so the argument goes, this is preeminently true of Mary, to whom alone is given the right in the New Testament to say, "Henceforth all generations will call me blessed" (Luke 1:48 RSV). Just as other Christians can become spiritual parents in the Lord, so Mary is supremely the spiritual mother of all. Just as one asks fellow believers for their prayers, so one begs Mary especially to intercede with her Son. So also

when she is called the "Queen of Heaven," one should remember
that the Bible speaks of all the saints ruling together with God in
the Kingdom. The Catholic apologists argue that to a degree which
surpasses what is true of any other creature, the whole being of
Mary, the very reason for her existence, is directed towards bringing Christ to men and men to Christ, so that all those who are
saved, even if they are Protestants who do not give special honor
to Mary, are "born into Christ through Mary." Lastly, it is maintained that Mary's cooperation with Christ in the atonement and in
redemption does not differ in kind, though it is vastly greater in
degree, from the co-redemptive activity of all Christians of which
Paul speaks: "In my flesh I complete what remains of Christ's
afflictions for the sake of his body, that is, the church" (Col. 1:24
RSV).[25]

This is not the place to deal in detail with the Protestant objections to these attempts to give a scriptural foundation to the
veneration of Mary (as well as of other saints.) Our only purpose
is to indicate in an extremely general way the character of what
might be called evangelical Roman Catholic Mariology, and thus
to make more comprehensible how many men and women whose
piety is in large measure Christocentric are nevertheless astonished
at the suggestion that the role of Mary in the Roman Church
dangerously compromises the centrality of Christ. They are not
conscious of any tension in themselves between their love of Jesus
and their love of his mother and thus often—and in the case of
theologians, irresponsibly—overlook the Mariolatry present in their
church.

When one looks beneath the surface, however, one discovers
signs of what appears to be a conflict between the Marian developments and evangelical renewal. We have already mentioned that
in the areas penetrated by the liturgical revival secondary devo-
tions, including those to Mary, decline in importance. The differences in these matters are sometimes explained as the result of a
contrast between a "northern" (French and German) and a
"southern" (Spanish and Italian) temperament, but clearly more
than this is at work, as becomes evident when one compares liturgically awakened and unawakened circles within a single country

such as the United States. Further, there is a striking contrast between the Marian theology produced by those aware of evangelical concerns and the "Marian maximalism" which is uninterested in interpreting the Virgin's place in biblical categories and instead proceeds by metaphysical speculations and logical deductions from the concept of the divine maternity to make Mary in effect, though of course not explicitly, into a semi-divine being mediating between Christ and men. When even theologians do this, it confirms Protestants in their suspicions that popular devotion to the Virgin is indeed often idolatrous.

The silence on these dangers, especially on the part of the Magisterium, is disheartening, but there are in Europe a few influential theologians who have protested against the way in which the full manhood of our Lord is ignored by those who think that Mary is more sensitive and sympathetic to our sin and suffering than he is.[26] One theologian, after mentioning theological and popular phenomena which are to be challenged "as without doubt predisposing factors for an obsolutizing of the Mariological," then goes on to say:

Now the Catholic is completely clear that such tendencies will never bring an outbreak of cancer, that means they will never lead to the degeneration of Catholic doctrine into a Marian heresy. The theologians affected by these tendencies would not wish to diminish by one iota the sovereignty of Christ in redemption, and still less would they want to set their teaching against the teaching of the church. All that is involved is a certain tension and disharmony between their Christology, which is faithful to tradition, and their new Mariology. Frankly, such a tension is not beneficial and is good for nothing. . . . Factors predisposing to cancer should be eliminated from Marian doctrine even though they cannot lead to the heresy which some fear.[27]

The attitude reflected in this quotation is typical of many Roman Catholics. They wish to purify the Church of what they agree are corruptions, but from the Protestant point of view, they are strangely tolerant of abuses. This is true not only in Mariology but also in reference to such often superstitious or doubtful practices as the veneration of relics and gaining of indulgences, which they wish to correct but not eliminate. One of the leading German-language

Roman Catholic theologians asks whether the doctrine of indulgences is coming to be a truth "which existentially (though not theoretically) is non-existent among Christians." Yet he is not happy over this neglect of what is, after all, one of the unalterable doctrines of his church, and so he wishes to restore the practice of indulgences in a new and better form, which makes clear that the church has no legal rights in reference to the temporal punishments whereby God chastens even the forgiven sinner, but that it only intercedes on behalf of those who repent so that "the free and gracious will of God shall grant the remission of temporal punishments in view of Christ's sacrifice and the sanctity of the saints which is dependent on it."[28] Another writer, who is widely considered the leading contemporary Roman Catholic dogmatician, says that an indulgence, rightly understood, is a constant exhortation "not to neglect repentance and to replace defective external works by ever deeper readiness to repent and by union with the glorified brothers and sisters who reign with Christ."[29]

The same effort of reform is directed towards the use of relics and of pilgrimages. For example, the literature which was placed in the hands of the multitudes who thronged to Trier in 1959 in order to see what purports to be the seamless robe of Christ insisted at length on the absence of historical verification of the authenticity of this relic and the permissibility of supposing that it may not have been the robe of Christ. It also emphasized that the primary purpose of the pilgrimage was to pray for the reunion of Christians so that they might all be knit together seamlessly even as was the holy garment.[30] Such an "enlightened" use of ancient practices is unthinkable in many parts of the world, but it should not be forgotten that there are also millions who participate in this "reformed" use of relics and pilgrimages.

Yet those interested in reform also show great indulgence to unreformed and crassly superstitious practices. They often justify their attitude by a line of reasoning, first developed by Cardinal Newman, according to which Jesus also was tolerant of superstition. He did not, for instance, rebuke the woman with the issue of blood who secretly touched his garments in the superstitious belief that they had magical healing power which could be stolen. Christ saw the faith behind the superstition and simply said, "Take heart, daughter, your faith has made you well" (Matt. 9:22 RSV). What our Lord chiefly condemns, Newman argues, is "the adoration paid to rich men, the thirst after gain, ambition, and the pride of life, idolatries worse in his judgment than the idolatory of ignorance, but not commonly startling or shocking to educated minds."[31]

It is only fair to add that such attitudes do not always involve an unlimited toleration for popular abuses. Bishop Straubinger, for many years active in Argentina, wrote with anguish of the displacement of Jesus Christ through the cult of Mary in South America: "Here Mary is everything, absolutely everything. God has yielded all power to her, and Christ still exists for very many only in the Host. These conditions were able to arise and grow in the time when the Word of God in the Holy Scripture was (or is) practically inaccessible to the people."[32] In reference to a similar situation, this time in Chile, we even find acknowledgment of the good work done by sect groups such as the Pentecostals who

with a very poor insight into the Gospel, succeed in obtaining from their numerous converts *a deep feeling of their redemption by Christ, a real detachment from material goods, great zeal, great generosity,* [which] shows us *what we ourselves could obtain from them* by teaching them to know and appreciate the real message of Christ.[33]

We have so far said little of the specifically theological situation in contemporary Roman Catholicism. In a way it would be repetitious to do so, for each of the tensions we have mentioned is reflected also in the technical discussions between theologians. This is often extraordinarily difficult for either Protestants or Catholics to realize, for the traditional passivity of the Catholic laity, and the reluctance to air controversies on the part of theologians, has resulted in treating all the theological interpretations presented by catechisms, priests, or professors as if they were official dogma. On the popular level, little effort is made to distinguish between that which must be accepted and those explanations of dogma which sometimes, from the viewpoint of other Catholics, are extremely questionable. As a result, the impression has arisen that it is easy to ascertain on almost every point what correct Roman Catholic doctrine is: Simply consult any catechism or theological textbook and you will find what all Catholics believe stated in a form which clearly agrees with all the catechisms and textbooks throughout the world in past and future centuries!

Such notions are utterly misleading. On closer inspection, the much acclaimed theological unity of Roman Catholicism sometimes seems to the outside observer to be an external shell consisting of agreement on the authority of the church to prescribe the acceptance of dogmatic formulae which by themselves are relatively empty. The content, the religious meaning, given to these formulae is sometimes astonishingly diverse, as we have already mentioned in connection with Mariology and indulgences, and as could be illustrated from most other areas of theology, including justification by faith and the infallibility of the pope. One of the great and liberating changes of the last few decades is that the possibility of such variations has been admitted more explicitly even by the Magisterium. As Pope John XXIII said in the encyclical *Ad Petri Cathedram* in 1959:

> There are quite a number of points which the Catholic Church leaves to the discussion of theologians, both in so far as these points are not absolutely certain and, also, as the famous English writer, John Henry Cardinal Newman, noted, in so far as controversies of this kind do not tear asunder the unity of the Church, but rather greatly help (by striking new light out of the friction of the various opinions) to a deeper and better understanding of the dogmas, and level and strengthen the path to the attainment of that unity.[34]

Among the factors contributing to this greater theological freedom and creativity are views of the development of dogma similar to those first proposed by Cardinal Newman.[35] These are now generally accepted by evangelically inclined writers, as well as by their opponents, though there is still some resistance in traditionalist circles. According to the newer view, each additional dogma proclaimed by the church is to be understood, not as an extrabiblical truth transmitted by oral tradition, but as the unfolding, the making explicit, of a previously only implicit aspect of the full and final revelation given by Christ to the apostles, and by the apostles to the church. This has the bad consequence, from the

Protestant point of view, of justifying doctrines not found in the Bible on the unverifiable grounds that they are there in germ and have only later been unfolded in the consciousness of the church; but it also implies, as becomes clear in the works of such theologians as Schmaus,[36] that all dogmatic formulations, while unchangeably true, are nevertheless partial and inadequate statements pointing towards the full and unitary revelation that is in Jesus Christ. It is therefore possible to supplement and thereby improve them indefinitely, and this may be necessary in order to free doctrines of the past from misuse or misunderstanding. They must be understood *in the context of, and in subordination to, what the Bible says about Jesus Christ,* and this means that many traditionally important teachings, while not denied, may nevertheless be reinterpreted in a more biblical direction.

Another stimulus to this more flexible view of theology in its relation to dogma is the vast increase in historical study and consciousness. French writers, especially the Dominican Yves Congar, characterize the entire contemporary renewal of Roman Catholic thought by the word *resourcement*—back to the sources: back to great medieval theologians like Aquinas in preference to later commentators; back to the Greek and Latin Fathers from whom the medievals drew so much; back especially to the Bible, which is the greatest source of all. Knowledge of all these sources has increased enormously, and this has given the theologian far more material with which to work. It is his dogmatically imposed task to utilize the entire tradition of the church, for all of it is in one degree or another authoritative. He must take seriously such men as St. Bernard and St. Augustine, on whom the Reformers also were heavily dependent, and with the progress in objective historiography, Catholics and Protestants agree more closely in their understanding of these great Christians of the past. Because of this increased emphasis on history, we often find Roman Catholic theologians twisting and turning the meanings apparently intended by the authors of dogmatic statements in order to reconcile them with other parts of the tradition and with the Bible. They must do this, for it is their conviction that, despite variations in the words and concepts used, the faith of the church has not changed.[37]

From the Protestant point of view, there is something unsatis-factory about this procedure, for it may be utilized not only in order to reinterpret doctrines in a biblical direction, but also for the contrary purpose of distorting scriptural teaching in order to make it harmonize with later views. Fortunately there is reason to believe that at present these techniques are being increasingly used to give a genuine, though excessively limited, priority to the Bible.

It would be a mistake, however, to suggest that the tensions which run through all areas of the Roman Church's life at the present time are summed up by the opposition between the "bibli-cal" and the "unbiblical" in any narrow sense of these terms. A more comprehensive description can be given in terms of the con-trast between two antagonistic attitudes towards the proper rela-tion of ecclesiastical authority and personal freedom and responsi-bility. The more traditional one is rigid and fearful, interested in preserving or restoring the past; while the other, though also con-cerned with maintaining ecclesiastical discipline, is more open and adventurous and strives to obey God and meet the needs of the modern world by greater use of personal initiative. They are per-haps rarely found in their pure forms, but that is the way we must describe them.

The newer approach[38] has been gaining strength at least since Leo XIII. It recognizes that obedience cannot be simply a matter of submission to institutionalized authorities, for this drives those of independent vitality and force out of the church and threatens to reduce those who remain to mindless automatons incapable of responding effectively to new situations and unable to attract to Catholicism any except fearful souls desirous of a slavish security. Instead, obedience must spring from a mature love and sense of independent responsibility so that all men, including the laity, will have the courage to seek for new and effective ways of thinking, preaching, and practising the Christian life. This necessarily in-volves the risk of ecclesiastical censure, for a man can never be sure that the authorities will approve what he does on his own initiative in response to what he takes to be God's guidance. It is argued, however, that it is the duty of the mature Catholic, of the truly obedient Catholic, to take this risk, willing at the same time to submit to bishops or popes if they pronounce against him, willing to bear the often painful and unjust suspicions of his fellow churchmen, yet always seeking within what he understands to be the limits marked out by the church to actualize the fullness of the Christian reality which he has encountered in his own personal life. To the non-Catholic this often seems to be a matter of trying to follow God except when the church says "no," but the Roman Catholic of this persuasion believes that God speaks both through ecclesiastical spokesmen and directly to his own heart. More and more, though far from universally, we find greater emphasis on God's personal address to men, while the Word of God as it comes through the teaching office of the church is viewed in large part as a necessary corrective to the sinful human tendency to confuse the imaginations and desires of one's own heart with divine truth.

One of the results of this freer outlook is a much broader view of what is permitted by the church. The restorationist mentality tends to think that only that is safe which is specifically commanded by higher authority, whereas in this other approach, everything is at least possible which is not specifically and clearly prohibited. It thus becomes the duty of theologians to re-examine views, such as those of the Reformers and of modern philosophers, which are heretical, in order to see whether they do not contain Christian truths which have not before been taught with sufficient clarity by the church. It is also his duty to review traditional teachings and practices in order to discover whether or not they contain misleading applications, or even contradictions, of that Christian consensus, starting with Scripture, which the Roman Church claims to follow. The administrative and practical directives of the hierarchy are given the same scrutiny. If they seem to contradict what mature and prayerful reflection leads one to believe is the right or best policy, one must, if the issue is important, seek to have the directive changed, or in extreme cases actually disobey even if this leads to serious penalties. Such courses of action are arduous, but they are not opposed to Roman doctrine, which admits the fallibility of all ordinary decisions and pronouncements of the bishops and the popes up to and including excommunication (which, while it would always have, to the Roman Catholic, the extremely grave consequence of prohibiting access to the normal Means of Grace, can be, the church admits, unjust and invalid in the sight of God.)[39]

Those imbued with this outlook are convinced that it is more orthodox than is an attitude of passive submission, for it resembles that combination of a strong sense of personal responsibility with ecclesiastical loyalty which characterized living Christian faith in its first millennium, and which supported large numbers of those whom the church has canonized in their frequent and difficult struggle against obstructive superiors. In all of these cases there was a firm conviction that though the offices of bishop and pope are instituted by God, the men who filled them were often not inspired by the Holy Spirit—indeed, were sometimes damned—and must therefore (always within limits) be resisted. In this way the divine assistance believed to be given the rulers of the church is understood primarily as a safeguard against error on those rare occasions when dogma is defined rather than as a guarantee of positive inspiration in the ordinary conduct of business. The representatives of the opposing attitude, while accepting the same doctrinal formulations, tend to think it presumptuous and dangerous for groups or individuals to suppose that they might be right over against higher authorities. This is probably still characteristic of most Catholics in most places. While theoretically admitting the possibility of exceptions, in practice they seem to believe that God speaks only through official channels. If any reforming is to be done, the pope will do it, and yet when the pope does act, as in 19th century France, these passive believers frequently greet his initiative with howls of protest and begin to wonder what is happening to their dear old church.

Future developments within Roman Catholicism depend in large part on which of these two attitudes prevails. The difficulties of the freer approach are evident, for it is not at all easy to maintain creative individual responsibility within the limits of an authoritarian church. Those who succeed, often at the cost of great personal suffering, are the mainstays of the church, for they goad it into action and reform. But many who try to walk this road find that they must break with Rome, sometimes out of obedience to God, sometimes because they find the tension insupportable. The pressures to which they are then subjected by their former co-religionists are often severe, for it is maintained both by the decrees of the Vatican Council and by Canon Law that those who leave the church do so without "just cause."[40] Legalistic and juridical means of preserving unity are so deeply rooted in the Roman church that it would undoubtedly in the future, as in the past, react to any sizable defections by suppressing freedoms which it now allows. It is therefore always possible that the new evangelical developments might sometime be condemned, just as were the old ones.

There seems, however, to be very little likelihood of this occurring in the foreseeable future, for the reforming forces are clearly providing vitality which the Roman church can ill afford to lose. In contrast to most of the movements which have been suppressed in the past, the leaders of the contemporary renewal are intensely loyal to the church and insist upon its authority. It is largely through their efforts that Roman Catholicism is maintaining, or even regaining, its influence and prestige in large parts of the secularized modern world. In those areas in which it can no longer depend on the power of the state, or on sheer traditionalism, to preserve its strength, it is discovering that it must allow greater freedom in order to survive.

Moderate optimism is also supported by the fact that the modern way of looking at history now seems too deeply rooted to be eradicated. Theologians and scholars everywhere recognize as a matter of course that the words and conceptual categories in which doctrines are expressed change their meaning in the course of time, and that in order to preserve the same truth in a new age—and even more, in order to make it vital—new modes of thought and action must be found. But the moment one stops repeating the same formulae and the same practices, the moment one tries to be faithful to the spirit, and not simply the forms, of the creative periods of the past, room for genuine development and renewal is opened.

We have in this discussion looked at Roman Catholicism from the viewpoint of specifically Protestant concerns, so it will be well for us in conclusion to recall the transformation in the public image of the Roman church which has taken place since the turn of the

century. In those days it was almost universally regarded as a kind
of atavistic survival from the Middle Ages, a fortress of fossilized
superstition and obscurantism. Protestants had a tremendous cultural superiority complex over Roman Catholics, and these latter
were intellectually on the defensive. They felt themselves to be
aliens in a hostile modern world. In both amount and competence
their scholarship was far from impressive, and the learned publica-
tions which they put out were a mere rivulet beside the mighty
flood of Protestant writings. A tremendous change has taken place
in the last sixty years. Protestant intellectual work has diminished,
while the Roman has greatly increased. In Europe it now surpasses
the Protestant in quantity and, in some fields, in quality. What is
more, its prestige is now much higher than it was in non-church
intellectual and academic circles. This is particularly true because
Roman Catholics of theological competence are doing much work
in non-theological areas, in science and philosophy, in literature,
sociology, and psychology, while Protestants often seem to be
becoming more detached from the cultural interests of the day.
The same growth of influence is evident in the political sphere.
In Italy, France, and Germany a half century ago the state was
in each case bitterly opposed to the Roman church, depriving it
of its old privileges and even oppressing it. Now the Vatican is
once again on friendly terms with the Italian government and
exercises great influence in its homeland, despite its failure to stop
the growth of Communism. In France and Germany the hierarchy
has learned from bitter experience to avoid as much as possible
open involvement in politics, but the political leadership of these
countries since the war has in large part been devoutly Roman
Catholic. The United States has elected its first Catholic president.
All this would have been inconceivable in 1900.

   To be sure, this impression of progress is in part misleading, for
both Protestants and Roman Catholics are confronted with ad-
vancing anti-Christian forces, not only in Communist areas and in
mission lands, but also in so-called Christian countries where the
apparent friends of the church often do it the greatest damage by
trying to pervert it into a mere prop for western civilization. Yet
there are also fresh voices, many of them in Catholicism, calling on

the churches, whether Roman, Orthodox, or Protestant, to repent, preach Christ, serve justice, and love the neighbor without calculating worldly advantages but in simple obedience to the Lord God who will establish his kingdom in his own time and his own way. It is in the response to this call that the health of the church is to be found, not in any earthly success or failure.

Notes

1. M. Williams, *The Catholic Church in Action* (revised edition), New York, 1958, pp. 202, 207, 208.

2. The Quaker author Rufus Jones and the Congregationalist William Hocking are examples.

3. The best documented account of these incidents is by a Protestant, R. A. Billington, *The Protestant Crusade, 1800-1860*, New York, 1938.

4. *An American Dialogue*, by Robert McAfee Brown and Gustave Weigel, S. J., New York, 1960, p. 38.

5. W. J. Ong, *American Catholic Crossroads*, New York, 1959, p. 109.

6. *The Catholic Church,* U.S.A. Edited by L. J. Putz, Chicago, 1956, p. xvi.

7. The more important passages of this and of most other papal documents cited below are found in H. Denzinger, *The Sources of Catholic Dogma* (English translation by R. J. Deferrari of 30th edition of *Enchiridion Symbolorum*) St. Louis: Herder, 1957.

8. *Osservatore Romano,* June 6, 1948; *Acta apostolicae sedis,* 42, 142 ff. Cf. English translations *American Ecclesiastical Review,* 119, p. 215; 122, pp. 321 ff.

9. *Commonweal,* 71, pp. 102 ff.

10. American Institute of Management. "The Roman Catholic Church," *Management Audit,* Vol. 5, No. 15, February, 1956.

11. D. F. Carrillo de Albornoz, *Roman Catholicism and Religious Liberty.* Geneva: World Council of Churches, 1959. p. 6, n. 1 and *passim.*

12. Hans Küng, *Konzil und Wiedervereinigung,* Freiburg, 1960, p. 136.

13. The liturgical revival began in the nineteenth century in such French monastic communities as Solesmes and Maredou and, somewhat later, in Germany at Maria Leach and Beuron. It has been led by a galaxy of notable scholars and theologians such as Odo Casel, Romano Guardini, Pasher, and Jungmann. In Europe, the best known periodicals of the movement are *Ecclesia Orans* and *La Maison Dieu,* while in the United States the excellent review *Worship* must be mentioned. It is published by the Benedictines of St. John's Abbey in Minnesota, who are the leaders of the liturgical movement in North America. Perhaps the best comprehensive account in any language of this entire development is written by the American Lutheran E. B. Koenker, *The Liturgical Renaissance in the Roman Catholic Church,* Chicago, 1954, who gives more detailed references to the authors and literature mentioned in our discussion.

14. L. J. Putz (editor), *op. cit.,* pp. 306-307.

15. See H. A. Reinhold, *The American Parish and the Roman Liturgy,* New York, 1958, p. 20.

16. Hans Küng, *op. cit.*, pp. 139-140.

17. *Luther im Katholischer Sicht*, Bonn, 1947.

18. Joseph Lortz, *Die Reformation in Deutschland*, 2nd ed. Freiburg: Herder, 1949. *Die Reformation als religioses Anliegen heute*, Trioer, 1948.

19. Gustave Weigel, S. J., *A Catholic Primer on the Ecumenical Movement*. Westminster: Newman, 1957, p. 70.

20. Yves Congar, *Vraie et fausse reforme dans l'Eglise*, Paris, 1950.

21. Küng. *op. cit.*, pp. 46-49.

22. Louis Bouyer, *Du Protestantisme a l'Eglise*, Paris, 1954. (English tr., *The Spirit and Forms of Protestantism*, London, 1956).

23. G. Besutti, "Bibliografia mariana," *Marianum*, 1950.

24. See K. E. Skydsgaard, *One in Christ*, Philadelphia: Muhlenberg Press, 1957, pp. 200, 204-205. R. Graber, *Die Marianischen Weltrundschreiben der Papste in den letzten hundert Jahren*, Wurzburg, 1951, pp. 156 and 83.

25. Examples of this approach are mentioned in footnotes 26 and 27.

26. E. G. Yves Congar, *Le Christ, Marie et l'Eglise*, Paris, 1952, 80-93. (English tr. *Christ, Our Lady and the Church*, London, 1957, 68-82.)

27. Alois Muller, Maria als Bild der Gnade und Heiligkeit," *Begegnung der Christen* (edited by M. Roesle and O. Cullman), Frankfurt am Main, 1960, pp. 594, 595.

28. Karl Rahner, *Schriften zur Theologie*, Einsiedelm, 1956, Vol. 11: pp. 186 f. and p. 194.

29. Michel Schmaus, *Katholische Dogmatik*, Munchen, 1952-1958, Vol. III/2, p. 401.

30. *Christus sei euer Kleid: Festzeitung Heilig-Rock-Wallfahrt, Trier, Vom 19. Juli bis, 20. Sept. 1959.*

31. John Henry Newman, *The Via Media of the Anglican Church*, 3rd edition, London, 1877, Vol. I, p. lxviii.

32. Quoted by Otto Karrer, *Das Reich Gottes Heute*, Munchen, 1956, p. 334.

33. Fr. F. Legrand in *Christ in the World*, Vol. 3, no. 1, 1958, pp. 111-112. Italics in the original. Quoted by Bernard Leeming, S. J., *The Churches and the Church*, Westminster: Newman Press, 1960, p. 235.

34. English tr. in *The American Ecclesiastical Review*, Vol. 141, p. 204. The reference is to Newman's *Difficulties of Anglicans*, London, 1885, Vol. I, pp. 296 ff.

35. *An Essay on the Development of Christian Doctrine.* This has been many times reprinted in many languages.

36. See *supra*, n. 23.

37. H. Küng, *Rechtfertigung: Die Lehre Karl Barths und eine Katholische Besinning*, Paderborn, 1957, 105-127. G. Lindbeck, "The Evangelical Possibilities of Roman Catholic Theology," *Lutheran World*, VII (1960), pp. 142-152.

38. See Karl Rahner, *Free Speech in the Church*, New York, 1959; Friedrich Heer, "The Rebirth of Catholic Obedience," *Cross Currents*, Vol. 6 (1956), pp. 119-130.

39. *Codex juris canonici*, can. 2195, par. 1.

40. See Joseph Klein, *Skandalon: um das Wesen des Katholizismus*, Tübingen, 1958, esp. pp. 1-88, for a discussion of this. Denzinger, *op. cit.*, 1794 and Can. 2314, par. 1, pp. 2 and 3 cf.

Chapter V

The Coming Council
Its Purpose and Problems*

I. The Announcement of the Council

When Cardinal Giuseppe Roncalli was elected to be the successor of Pius XII on October 28, 1958, many people believed that the new pope, being seventy-eight years old, had been chosen—as was said half apologetically—as a "transitional pope," that is, as a pope who would lead the church only until a younger and more eminent man could be chosen.[1] Nothing could have proved to be more wrong. The new pope immediately showed himself to be a very energetic and dynamic overshepherd, not only in his capacity as bishop of Rome, but also as the supreme director of the whole Roman Catholic Church. Within a short time many became aware of the fact that a new era of the church had begun.

The greatest surprise was afforded by John XXIII to the Catholic Church and the whole of Christendom when on January 25, 1959, the last day of the Octave of prayer for the unity of the church, he announced an ecumenical council without any previous intimation having been given concerning it. Even the closest co-

*For helping me to prepare the material for this chapter I am indebted to my assistant, the Reverend Gerhard Pedersen.

93

workers of the pope were exceedingly surprised, and some of them certainly were also frightened. Indeed, even to the pope it came as a surprise. He confesses that the idea of the council was not the result of long deliberations. It came "like the sudden flowering of an unexpected spring,"[2] a divine impulse during prayer,[3] an inspiration "the immediateness of which we felt in the humility of our heart as a sudden, unexpected touch."[4] The announcement was made in the Church of San Paolo fuori le Mure, where the pope had gone to celebrate the feast of the Conversion of the Apostle Paul and the close of the week of prayer for the unity of the church. During the preparation for this service "he felt intensively the inspiration to call together the Catholic family."[5] After the service an improvised secret consistory of the seventeen cardinals who were present was held in the Benedictine monastery attached to the church and here John XXIII communicated his plan in a Latin address. In a brief text which was given to the press[6] it is stated: "As the supreme pastor of the church the pope has pointed to the dangers that most severely threaten the religious life of the faithful, namely, the false doctrines appearing in various places and the boundless attraction of material goods which has grown more powerful than ever today by reason of technical progress." "In order to meet the present needs of Christian people, the supreme pastor, being inspired by the ancient customs of the church, has announced three events of utmost importance, namely, a diocesan synod of the city of Rome,[7] the observance of an ecumenical council for the universal church, and the modernization of canonical law,[8] which is to precede the impending publication of the code of Oriental canon law.

"With respect to the celebration of the ecumenical council, according to the pope's intention it is to serve not only the edification of the Christian people, but is also at the same time to be an invitation to the separated communities to search for the unity for which so many souls in all the ends of the world are yearning."[9]

The most important of these three events is undoubtedly the coming ecumenical council. In the Roman Catholic view there is no greater event in the life of the church than a council, in which the *whole* church assembles and in which all local churches are present in the persons of their bishops, in order to deliberate together and adopt resolutions. Only very seldom and under quite definite, threatening, and urgent conditions is such a step taken. Between the Council of Trent and the First Vatican Council there was an interval of three hundred years, and almost a hundred years have passed since the latter was held. What caused the pope to convoke an ecumenical council?

As has already been mentioned, the calling of it occasioned extreme surprise; no one thought of the possibility of a council. After the First Vatican Council, which was prematurely broken off by reason of the occupation of the Pontifical State by the Italians, it was for several years expected that it would be resumed. And when nothing happened the idea arose that since the declaration of the infallibility of the pope in 1870 the time of councils was definitely past.[10] Thus Paul Hinschius, the canonist, could say in 1883: "The general council has become unnecessary and superfluous for the Catholic Church. Since the Vaticanum it no longer has any independent legal significance alongside the papacy."[11] The Roman prelate who remarked to the Bishop of Metz during the First Vatican Council, "I am pleased that the bishops have gone to Rome to see that the pope is everything and the bishops nothing,"[12] appeared to have been right!

All the greater surprise, therefore, that John XXIII has now convoked a general council. There would seem to be no definite emergency at the moment, no heresy that threatens the faith, no manifest abuses in the church. On the contrary, seldom in its history has the Catholic Church experienced such flowering and obvious success, and not for a long time has it had either so much influence or enjoyed so much esteem as now. Naturally the question arises: Could not the things that must be done be handled by the pope and the curia without resorting to such an extraordinary measure as the organization of an ecumenical council?

Be that as it may, the pope himself has stated that the seriousness of the time and the development of the world which impinges upon man in all areas of our existence, its complete difference from earlier times, require the concerted thinking and spiritual concentration of the whole church. The church's situation has changed.

Whereas the last council was still exclusively a European-Latin council, in which the Asiatic and African Catholics played hardly any part, the Catholic Church has in the meantime regularly received into itself elements from all parts of the world. Hence it is presented with a host of difficult problems which cannot be solved by the Roman curia alone or from a purely European point of view. The *whole* church in all its variety and diversity must come together to take counsel together concerning the situation and the future and to take new, authoritative measures. Perhaps the pope's certainty that a council must be held was far greater than the consideration of what was actually to take place at the council. In any case, this much seems to be clear at the outset: that the renewal of the Roman Catholic Church and the unity of Christians will play an important role in it. We shall have to deal with these two main thoughts in what follows.

At first the precise meaning of the words "an ecumenical council" called forth a certain confusion, not only in Catholic, but also in non-Catholic circles particularly. The explanation of this circumstance must be sought in the fact that in recent times the word "ecumenical" has in non-Catholic usage been connected exclusively with the so-called "ecumenical movement" and the World Council of Churches. It was used in this sense even by Catholic theologians (cf. Père Congar, *Chrétiens desunis, Principes d'un* OECUMENISME *catholique,* 1937) and the highest Catholic doctrinal authority (cf. the instruction *"De moutione* OECUMENICA" of December 20, 1949.)[13] It was, therefore, not strange that non-Catholics should have been subject to the error of thinking that the ecumenicity of the council consisted in the fact that all church bodies, Catholic as well as non-Catholic, were to assemble in order to find their way back to each other after centuries of separation. Thus the pope's statement that it would be the task of the council to be an *"invitamentum seiunctis fratribus"*[14] was understood as an invitation to participate in the council. The pope often speaks without a manuscript and his addresses sometimes contain astonishing phrases, which are omitted in the official version. On January 30, 1959, a few days after the announcement of the council, he said at a retreat of Roman priests with reference to the Eastern Church: "We do not wish to institute a historical trial. We do not want to try to show who was right and who was wrong. The responsibility is divided. We wish only to say: Let us come together, let us put an end to the divisions."[15] Statements like this quite naturally gave rise to the temporary supposition that the pope actually contemplated a union council, similar to the councils of Lyons (1274) and Florence (1437), and that this time it was to include not only the ancient Orthodox Church but also some of the Protestant church bodies. It was suggested from various quarters that in the course of the ensuing months John XXIII was obliged to modify his original, almost intuitive feeling.[16]

It was not long, however, until this lack of clarity disappeared as it was clearly established that the word "ecumenical" used in connection with a Roman Catholic council has a very definite meaning established by centuries of usage: "An ecumenical or general council means a solemn assembly of the bishops of the Catholic world convened by the authority of the pope which deliberates and decides concerning the affairs of the whole of Christendom under the presidency of the pope."[17] According to the Roman Catholic view, an ecumenical council is therefore not a parliament made up of representatives of various parties in which one hopes to achieve unity through discussion and possibly compromise; nor is it an international congress in which one seeks through cooperation to reach favorable results in some particular areas. Nor can an ecumenical council be compared with a constitutional assembly which adopts or revises the constitution of a country, for the "constitution" of the church already exists, that is, it is given by Christ himself and can never be modified. The pope and the bishops of a council are not representatives appointed by the Christian people, but rather the plenipotentiaries of God. They are there not only to deliberate, but primarily to make decisions and proclaim the truth with divine authority.

According to the established canon law *(Codex Juris Canonici,* can. 222-229), the regular members of an ecumenical council are:

1. the cardinals (even if they are not bishops);

2. the patriarchs, resident bishops and archbishops, the abbots, and other dignitaries with their own areas of jurisdiction;

3. the abbots primate and the heads of monastic congregations, along with the superiors general of orders of priests independent of the local bishop.

Of these only the resident bishops, who are the legitimate successors of the apostles, are members of a council by virtue of *divine* right. They are present as authoritative witnesses of the faith *(testes fidei)* and judges of truth and falsehood *(judices fidei).* The council is first and foremost the concern of the bishops *(concilium esse episcoporum).* The cardinals and monastic dignitaries participate on the basis of special *privileges* or ancient rights, and the titular bishops and the general heads of orders of priests which are not dependent upon the local bishop may be invited as *extraordinary* members.[18]

II. Brief History of the Preparations

This council is proceeding in four periods of time:[18a]

(1) The more remote preparation, which will serve as a preliminary inventory; the so-called *commissio antepraeparatoria* is working on this. (2) The actual preparatory work, the carrying out of which has been delegated to a number of commissions on special questions and the available theological and canonico-legal advisers. (3) The official observance of the general church assembly at which the fathers of the council will frame the final and authoritative resolutions and "which undoubtedly will be a very moving and magnificent spectacle." (4) "The proclamation of the acts of the council," that is, the publication of the conclusions, statements, and decrees for the promotion of faith and life, the perfection of the spirit and action, and the glorification of the Gospel of Christ.

1. The More Remote Preparations

On Pentecost Sunday, May 17, 1959, the pope announced the appointment of the so-called *commissio antepraeparatoria.* Its prefect was the papal secretary of state, Cardinal Domenico Tardini. All the members were from Roman congregations and were almost exclusively Italians. To this commission were assigned the following tasks: "To establish contact with the Catholic episcopate of the whole world in order to secure advice and suggestions; to gather formal proposals from the office of the Roman curia; to work out the main lines of the topics which are to be reviewed at the council, including the securing of the opinions of faculties of theology and canon law in Catholic universities; to propose the composition of the various organs (commissions, secretariats, etc.) which are to undertake the further preparation of the tasks which the council has set itself to do."[19]

These tasks were tackled in the following way: On June 18 a circular letter was sent to the approximately twenty-seven hundred bishops, prelates, and religious members who are to participate in the coming council. In this letter they were urged to state with the utmost candor and clarity the problems which in their opinion should be dealt with at the council. In the same manner the central offices of the general church administration in Rome were asked to make proposals. As the replies began to come in they were photo-copied and the material was catalogued according to subjects and countries, in order that the characteristic features of the individual countries and their special desires and suggestions would be brought to the fore. The responses of the faculties of theology and canon law in the Catholic universities were dealt with in the same way. They contained not only suggestions for topics but also elaborated discussions of important theological questions which it is assumed that the council will concern itself with.[20] After the gathering of this considerable mass of material has been completed it will be presented to the pope himself, since he alone can decide which topics the council is to deal with.

The work of the commission for preliminary preparations was concluded about June 1, 1960.[21] Hardly any previous council was prepared for by such thorough canvassing of the bishops, the Roman curia, and the Catholic universities.[22] A highly placed prelate expressed the opinion that there was enough material to keep ten councils busy! Cardinal Tardini expressed himself similarly: The replies of the bishops dealt *"de omnibus et quibusdam aliis"* ("with everything and even more")![23] On the basis of the materials sent in an index of almost two thousand topics as suggestions for the work of the council was prepared. These topics were divided among the preparatory commissions and with that the council entered the phase of actual preparation in which it now is.

All the replies, those of the bishops, the Roman curia, and the universities and faculties, have appeared in a number of volumes as the first series *(Series Prima, Antepraeparatoria)* of the total material of the council: *Acta et Documenta Concilio Oecumenico Vaticano II Apparando.*

Volume I of this introductory series contains the *Acta Summi Pontificis Ioannis XXIII,* the addresses and writings of the pope concerning the council from January 24, 1959, to June 5, 1960. The addresses are reprinted almost exclusively in accord with the reports in the *Osservatore Romano.*

Volume II of the series, which consists of eight large volumes, contains the proposals and requests of the bishops and prelates: *Consilia et vota episcoporum et praelatorum.* A systematic synopsis of these has been prepared in two volumes (1,537 pages). Here all the doctrinal and disciplinary questions of the Roman church are summed up in 8,972 statements.

Volume III in one volume (427 pages) contains the replies of the Roman offices or congregations: *Proposita et monita Ss. Congregationum Curiae Romanae.*

Volume IV consists of the studies of the Catholic universities and faculties, *Studia et vota universitatum et facultatem ecclesiasticarum et catholicarum,* in three volumes. The first two (a total of 1,054 pages) contain the studies of twelve universities and faculties in Rome, the third those of thirty-seven universities and faculties outside of Rome.

Together this first series consists of fifteen large volumes of 9,520 pages in quarto, of which the last was presented to the pope on March 29, 1961. Thus this impressive work was accomplished within less than two years *(Oss. Rom.,* March 29, 1961).

Volume I is available to the public, but the remaining portions are available only to the members of the commissions and advisers. They will be made available to the public, however, at some time, either before, during, or after the council (Cf. *Oss. Rom.,* Oct. 15, 1960, pp. 3-4).

2. The Actual Preparations

On Pentecost Sunday, June 5, 1960, one year after the establishment of the commission for the more remote preparations, John
XXIII published the *Motu Proprio "Superno Dei nutu,"* which
ordered the appointment of preparatory commissions for the coming council.[24]

The commissions have the following designations:

1. Theological Commission.
2. Commission on Bishops and the Governing of Dioceses.
3. Commission on Regulations for the Clergy and the Christian People.
4. Commission on Religions.
5. Commission on Regulations about the Sacraments.
6. Commission on the Sacred Liturgy.
7. Commission on Studies and Seminaries.
8. Commission on the Eastern Churches.
9. Commission on Missions.
10. Commission on the Lay-Apostolate, to have to do with Catholic
action, religious or social.[25]

In addition there are three secretariats, one that concerns itself
with modern means of communication (such as newspapers and
magazines, radio and television broadcasts, films, etc.), one for the
unity of Christians, which will be discussed more fully later, and
one for the administration of the council.

Finally a Central Commission set above all the others and under
the presidency of the pope was established, its function being "to
follow the labors of the individual commissions, to coordinate them
if necessary, and to report their results to us after due examination,
in order that we may determine the subjects of discussion for the
ecumenical council."[26]

It is apparent from the writings of the pope that he has followed
the work of preparation personally. "We have made it our business
to give careful consideration to the advice and suggestions of the
sacred prelates, the admonitions and proposals of the Roman curia,
and finally the proposals and investigations of the universities."[27]

First the prospective themes of the council must be carefully
studied in the commissions. Their members are cardinals, bishops,
and members of the secular and monastic clergy, "who are outstanding for their virtue and learning. We want them to be chosen

from all parts of the world so that they may be a shining example of the universal and catholic nature and mission of the church."[28]

In addition to these members there is available to the commissions a number of consultors who, though they do not have the right to vote, are often persons with unusual insight and extensive knowledge.

It is important to the pope that this work is not an affair of the Roman curia. In his Pentecost message of 1960, which can be regarded as an authentic commentary on the *Motu Proprio*, the pope says that the structure and organization of a council dare not be identified with the function of the various offices and congregations of the Roman curia. "Here there is a clear difference: the regular government of the church is one thing, the council is something else."[29] Thus the conjecture which has occasionally been made that the Roman congregations have replaced the earlier councils is disposed of. The congregations are the central offices of the papal government. The councils, however, are the whole church, that is, all local churches of the whole world represented by their bishops.[30]

Another important reference made by the pope which is connected with this applies to the universality of the council. It cannot be either a Roman or an exclusively European-North American affair; it is a world concern. Therefore no large region of the world has been left without representation. The mission countries have been carefully taken into account. It is likely that the reactions of the missionary bishops to the pope's questions concerning the coming council will be the most interesting and the most radical. They live in areas where the Catholic Church must live and work quite differently from the way it does in the old world. "It is a fundamental principle which has meanwhile entered the consciousness of every believer of the holy Roman Church that the Catholic is as such a citizen of the whole world and must also actually conduct himself correspondingly."[31]

In the following months the members and the advisers of the commissions were appointed.[32] On November 14 they were received in audience by the pope, at which time he gave them the following fatherly admonition: "The preparatory study naturally requires a great deal of time, steadfast patience in labor, and the exertion of love. . . . Everything at the council should be surrounded by great restraint and soberness on the part of every participant."[33]

These preparatory commissions have been working under high pressure since November, 1960. The individual questions are first dealt with in the subcommissions, then presented to the commission as a whole for revision, and finally submitted to the *Central Commission*. According to the above-mentioned list of persons, this commission, which is headed by the pope, has as regular members fifty-three cardinals, thirty-three archbishops and bishops, four generals of orders, and twenty-seven episcopal and monastic clerical consultants. Here it is decided whether the *schemata*, i.e., the material proposed for the final documents, can be submitted to the fathers of the council in their original form, whether they must be re-examined by the proper commission, or whether they should possibly be dropped altogether.

What has been said here is naturally only a sketchy description of the preparatory work for the council. As we have already mentioned, everything is done under the seal of silence and in secrecy.

We conclude this section with a number of facts about the council itself. It has already been established that it will be called "The Second Vatican Council."[34] The name selected demonstrates that it is not a resumption of the First Vatican Council. At the same time, however, it contains the suggestion of a connection with the council of 1870, whose work, after all, was not concluded. The dogma of the infallibility of the pope was decreed, but a doctrine of the church—though it had been prepared—was not conclusively defined.

With respect to the time at which the council shall be held there has been a long period of suspense. It now appears that it will occur either at the close of the autumn of 1962 or the beginning of the year 1963, probably the former. It is the express wish of the pope that the paper preparations be so thorough that it will not be necessary to spend much time at the council itself, since the pope does not wish that the bishops should be absent from their dioceses any longer than is absolutely necessary.[35]

The language of the council will be Latin.[36] This has great advantages, but will also create many difficulties, especially for the eastern, Uniate bishops. From American quarters has come the proposal that simultaneous translations be employed as is done at other international meetings, but this suggestion has been rejected. Cardinal Tardini gave as the reason for this the fact that the Latin language "is singularly suited to express dogmatic concepts and the norms of discipline precisely, clearly, and succinctly."[37] It is, however, the express wish of the pope that the bishops who cannot express themselves in Latin should have the opportunity to do so in another language.

On the supposition that all present ecclesiastical offices are filled it may be expected, according to an article by P. Kerkhof,[38] that 2,816 fathers of the council will come to Rome; 313 will come from Italy and 415 from Europe—apart from Russia and the Baltic countries. This means that there will be a decisive preponderance of Italians, since the Catholic population of Italy constitutes only nineteen percent of European Catholics whereas the bishops who represent them constitute forty-three per cent of all the European bishops.

Of the other continents 31 representatives will come from Oceania, 196 from the United States of America, 356 from Asia, 400 from Central and South America, and 186 from Africa.

These figures, which naturally are only approximate, can be reduced to the following percentages. (The figures in the first column indicate the percentage of population in relation to world Catholicism and the figures in the second column the percentage of fathers of the council in relation to the total number of participants in the council.)

Europe	47 %	38.0 %
America	43 %	31.5 %
Asia and Oceania	7 %	20.5 %
Africa	3 %	10.0 %

For the purpose of comparison we may add that the European participants of the First Vatican Council constituted sixty per cent of the whole number of participants in the council.

III. The Pope's Purpose for the Council

Since the announcement of the council the pope has not ceased to speak about the coming council, not only to the bishops and theologians, but also frequently to various groups of lay people when he has received them in audience. These public statements have usually been confined to generalities, however, and little that is concrete can be drawn from them. As has already been mentioned, the pope's thoughts concentrate upon two foci: the council as an intra-Catholic concern for the renewal and strengthening of the Roman church and the council as a step toward the unity of all Christians in the Roman Catholic Church. We shall elucidate these two thoughts further at this point.

On June 29, 1959, the pope issued his first Encyclical *Ad Petri Cathedram* with a heading that is characteristic of John XXIII: "On Truth, Unity, and Peace, and their advance in a Spirit of Charity."[1]

Doctrinally the content is altogether traditional and not at all extraordinary. If one expected the opposite, one would have been disappointed. The tone of the document, however, is peculiar. It would appear that the pope was intentionally avoiding difficult questions. "There are no flashes of lightning, no rolling of thunder, one does not stand before Mount Sinai and tremble. Hence no striking, sharply pointed dogmatic sentences can hastily be excerpted and handed over to the world press, no names of persons affected can be whispered from mouth to mouth. Rather one must allow oneself to be carried along by the quietly flowing stream of positive statements and allow the warm love of the good pastor to have its effect."[2]

In this encyclical we find three points that sum up the purpose of the council as follows: "to bring about the growth of the Catholic faith, the restoration of sound morals among the Christian flock, and the appropriate adaptation of church discipline to the needs and conditions of our times."[3] The council will, therefore, deal with the faith, with the Christian life, and with church discipline.

When the Christian faith is spoken of, this has both an objective and a subjective significance. It refers to the content of faith (the *fides* QUAE *creditur*) as well as the act of faith (the *fides* QUA *creditur*). Naturally, in connection with a council the objective significance plays an exceedingly large role. A clear witness to the faith is to be made, perhaps in the form of a new, liturgically structured symbol as a positive expression of the Catholic faith in our time. In the eminent sense every council is a *dogmatic* council. This is inherent in the structure of the council itself, for the history of the councils is nothing else but the history of Catholic dogma in which the *depositum fidei* (the faith deposited) has been developed. According to the Roman Catholic view, every council has contributed in some way to this development. That which had come alive through the great theologians, through the liturgy, and through the collective faith and thinking of the Christian flock was purified, defined, and furnished with authority at the councils by the teaching church.[4]

There are many of the faithful—laymen, bishops, and priests—who desire the definition of a new dogma of Mary: Mary as the mediator of all grace or Mary as coredemptrix. Insofar as one may permit oneself to prophesy anything at all about the coming council, it may be said that one may expect in vain a concrete definition of dogma.

It is certain that there are many prelates who would like to see the condemnation of certain free tendencies in Catholic exegesis and in dogmatic thinking. It is equally certain that there are not a few who wish that the many "errors of the times," naturalism, materialism, secularism, and existentialism, shall be denounced. One does not get the impression, however, that the chief concern of the pope is concentrated on this point. The pope may express concern, give pastoral admonition, or even give severe rebuke; but isolated, negative condemnations will surely be missing. His interest is directed rather toward positive corroborations and constructive statements. One may probably assume that Cardinal Tardini was expressing the thoughts of the pope when he said at a press conference: "This council is not directed against anyone. Those who have written or said that a condemnation of a person or a thing is planned are mistaken. The council is rather intended much more to attract those who are outside the church than to condemn them."[5]

Nevertheless, what has been said here does not rule out the fact that this council will be a dogmatic council, or *lex credendi* (the law of faith), *lex orandi* (the law of prayer), and *lex agendi* (the law of action), inseparably bound together. One of the most important functions of a council is to determine the correct interpretation of a doctrinal statement which is in controversy in theology, to reject dangerous ideas, and in certain cases also to condemn errors.

An indication of this is the fact that the Theological Commission is the first and the only one the scope of whose functions has been specified in detail: "It has the task of considering and examining the questions which relate to the Holy Scriptures, the Holy Tradition, Faith, and Morals."[6] The Theological Commission was divided into five subcommissions, but no further particulars concerning the actual work can be given at the present time. That a clarifying and authoritative position with regard to the ecclesiological questions will be in the foreground is beyond all doubt. It cannot be denied that since the definition of the infallibility of the pope in 1870 the doctrine of the church according to the Roman Catholic view has in a certain way been out of balance. Everything appeared to concentrate in the person and the office of the pope. After 1870 Rome increasingly became the spiritual and organizational center of the church. One was obliged to ask: Are the bishops in the last analysis anything more or other than delegates or representatives of the pope in their dioceses? Do they receive their authority directly from the apostles or only through the mediation of the pope? Does not the authority of a general council become illusory if the decrees of the council have no ultimately binding power unless they are confirmed by the Roman pope and promulgated by his command (*CJC, can.* 227), indeed, if only the pope of Rome can convene a council (*CJC, can.* 222, sec. 1)? This absolutization of the papacy was expressed in the strictest possible way in the following statement of the solemn definition of infallibility: "Such definitions of the Roman Pontiff are irreformable *of themselves (ex sese)*, and not from the consent of the church."[7]

All these questions touch upon a problem which is being very avidly discussed in the Roman church itself. One of the great wishes cherished for this council is the reassessment of the episcopal office,[8] and it is openly said that this is the intention of the pope. What is being thought of here is not a reformation of the legal status of the bishops, but rather a comprehensive clarification of their ecclesiological importance and function. According to Roman Catholic doctrine the commission of the bishops was given through Christ himself in that he founded the church upon Peter *and* the apostles. Hence the bishops have their authority *directly* from Christ. Therefore the pope cannot exercise his functions without the bishops, but only together with them. Conversely, it is also true that the bishops are lawful bishops *only* in fellowship with and subordination to the pope in his capacity as the successor of Peter.[9] The church is not one-sided by "monarchical" but also "collegial." The coming council, it has been said, is not to define anything *new*, but rather to bear witness to the genuine Catholic truth against all misunderstandings which have crept in through one-sided emphases and "indurations." The office of the pope was precisely defined in the First Vatican Council; it will be the task of the Second Vatican Council to clarify the status of the bishops.

The balance of Roman Catholic ecclesiology which "was seriously jeopardized by a hasty and shortsighted acceptance of the 'Vatican dogma'" must be restored.[10] Extremely interesting in this connection are the words of Cardinal Newman shortly after the First Vatican Council which are often cited by Catholic authors: "But we must have a little faith. Abstract propositions avail little— theology surrounds them with a variety of limitations, explanations, etc. No truth stands by itself—each is kept in order and harmonized by other truths. The dogmas relative to the Holy Trinity and the incarnation were not struck off all at once—but piecemeal—one council did one thing, another a second—and so the whole dogma was built up. And the first portion of it looked extreme—and controversies arose upon it—and these controversies led to the second, and third councils, and they did not *reverse* the first, but *explained* and *completed* what was first done. So will it be now. Future popes will explain and in one sense limit their own power. This would be unlikely, if they merely acted as men, but God will overrule them. Pius has been overruled—I believe he wished a much more stringent dogma than he has got. Let us have faith and patience."[11]

A part of the ecclesiological task of the Theological Commission is also the question of the laity in the church. Hardly any other topic is such an urgent order of the day, theologically, practically, and concretely, as is this question in the Roman Catholic Church. Both clergy and people belong to the body of Christ, and both are equally necessary. As baptized persons the laity have their place in the structure and the living function of the church exactly as do the clergy, even though on a different level. Every baptized person has responsibility for the church in the world, though this does not affect the hierarchical order of the church. This is a new concern for which the Roman curia previously has had no organization. Among the preparations for the council the pope has empowered a special commission to deal with the practical implications of this question.

The wording of the description of the Theological Commission indicates that the question of Scripture and tradition will be dealt with. We know that the exegetical situation in the Roman Catholic Church is tense and that differing tendencies exist beside side by side, not without difficulties.[12] In recent years there has been a tremendously intensive preoccupation with the basic idea of tradition without achieving agreement: Are there two sources of revelation, Scripture *and* tradition, or is there only one, the Holy Scriptures, which is then interpreted by tradition?[13] Will the coming council express itself authoritatively on these difficult questions?

Topics which are being dealt with simultaneously in the various commissions are given thorough theological treatment in the Theological Commission. The results of this work will be awaited with great and anxious eagerness, not least within the Roman Catholic Church itself.

Along with the Theological Commission the nine other commissions are at work. A host of questions and problems in all areas of the life of the Roman Catholic Church are being tackled. Official statements with regard to these studies are not available. By way of suggestion a few of the most important subjects may be mentioned here. The question of the episcopal office is being dealt with theologically in the Theological Commission, but it also has its practical, organizational side, and the Commission on Bishops and the Governing of Dioceses is handling this. After 1870 there followed a period of rigid centralization; this council will surely be followed by a period of decentralization. This will require measures that involve reformulations of the canon law. "The principle of subsidiarity" will again be recognized in the church.[14] Two controversial questions, which will have to be solved by the Committee on the Sacraments and the Committee on the Liturgy, are that of the introduction of the vernacular, not only in the sacramental of the Mass, and that of the reintroduction of Communion in two kinds, if not in all cases, at least on special occasions. Here the reintroduction of the diaconate as a special office, possibly including permission for deacons to marry, will likely be discussed also. This would mean taking a step, though a short one, toward the solution of the difficult question of celibacy.[15]

The Commission on Seminaries and Studies will direct its attention to the proposals for an urgent reform of the training of Catholic priests which have become audible in recent years. The situation of priests behind the Iron Curtain and the position of the Catholic Church with regard to Marxism and atheism must also be clarified.[16]

Every evangelical Christian who is at all familiar with the missionary tasks of the church will understand that the Commission on Missions will have to contend with tremendously difficult problems. The great world religions have awakened and for decades have been in a process of revival in conscious opposition to Christianity, "the religion of the white colonial masters."[17] Will the mission of the church be able at all to keep pace with the fantastic growth of population in Asia, Africa, and Latin America? Will it be equal to the missionary efforts of other world religions? According to a Roman Catholic source, Islam has gained forty million new adherents within the last thirty years, whereas the Catholic Church has gained only about fifteen million.[18] But this by no means exhausts these problems. What happens when a church which is stamped by a particular culture and its tradition is transplanted to an Asiatic or African milieu? Consequently, special care will have to be devoted to the education of the priests and heads of these young churches. A further aspect of the mission fields, and one that is of utmost importance ecumenically, is the relationship of the churches to one another, a problem attended with many difficulties, as every missionary knows. Here the precarious question of religious freedom plays a large role.[19] Evangelical Christendom cherishes the hope that this matter too will receive positive discussion in the work of the commissions.

Essential as the doctrinal side of a council must be, the pope has nevertheless strongly emphasized that his purpose in calling the council was primarily *pastoral,* that is, the council is to contribute to the inner renewal of the life of the church.

This was evident already in the first announcement of the council: The world is in many respects in a sad state, "above all through the misuse and the breakdown of freedom of man, who is wholly absorbed in the pursuit of the so-called goods of this earth. He closes himself to heaven, which is open, and to faith in Christ, the Son of God, the Redeemer of the world, and the Founder of the church. The chase for the goods of this world comes from the influence of him whom the Gospel calls the prince of this world."[20]

"All this . . . diverts men from striving after the higher goods, weakens the energies of the spirit, leads to the relaxation of discipline and the good old order, to the severe detriment of that which constitutes power of resistance of the church and her sons against errors." All this leads "to spiritual and moral decay and the downfall of nations."[21]

In his address to the members and consultors of all the preparatory commissions in St. Peter's Cathedral on November 14, 1960, the pope said that in the past the ecumenical councils had for the most part given answers to urgent questions of pure doctrine with reference to false doctrine and errors. And this, he said, was also true of the Council of Trent and the First Vatican Council. This council is different. "In the modern period the face of the world has changed profoundly, and it is hard for it to stand its ground against the attractions and the perils of a constant and almost exclusive pursuit of material goods . . . the question is not so much one of some particular point or other of doctrine or of discipline that has to be brought back to the pure fonts of revelation and of tradition, as it is of restoring the substance of humane and Christian thinking and living (for which the church has served as custodian and teacher through the centuries) to full force and to its proper splendor."[22]

It is a question, therefore, of the substance of the Christian life, of the whole man, and of the revaluation of the Christian faith and life. The church is facing a new era. It must reflect upon the task that this presents. It must find renewal and strengthening in order to be able to fulfill the mission which has been committed to the church by its Lord. The council should be devoted to a pastoral adaptation of the apostolate of priests and laity to the changed conditions of the time.

This point of view recurs again and again in the pope's addresses. "The council will be a revivification of power and energy for the apostolate, in order to show once more how the Gospel is able to permeate the world with its beauty, its power, and its uplift."[23] "The council will be an event of utmost importance whereby the spiritual life of the church will be increased, the confession of the Catholic faith will be given new growth, and the morals of Christians will flourish with the help of divine grace."[24] It will be a "wonderful spectacle of truth, unity, and charity, which will be clear to all who observe it attentively."[25] The glory of the church, "the city upon the mount,"[26] will become apparent even in the mission fields. The council will be the beginning of a new universal missionary epoch.[27] It has been convened above all "because the church in the radiant diversity of its various rites, in its multifarious activities, and in its unbreakable unity has resolved to gain new power for its divine mission."[28]

The council will be a new Pentecost. It is not accidental that the three festivals of Pentecost, 1959, 1960, and 1961, constitute the turning points in the preparations for the council and that on all three occasions the pope related the coming council to Pentecost. Even before his election to the papacy, shortly before the conclave, the then patriarch of Venice wrote in a letter to the bishop of Bergamo that "the soul takes courage in the hope that a new Pentecost will give new strength to the church through its new head and through the reorganization of the ecclesiastical organism for the triumph of the truth, the good, and peace."[29]

The coming council will bring together all the bishops of the whole world who live in concord with Rome as to a new Pentecost. "This meeting, based on profound and large-scale preparations, will bring, with God's help, increased sanctification of the clergy and edification of the Christian flock. It will be an encouraging spectacle for all people whose thoughts are lifted to faith and peace."[30] In the prayer to the Holy Spirit composed by the pope[31] and in his admonition to prayer to Mary in the month of May[32] he also spoke of the council as a new Pentecost.

"God wills this council, and we are all convinced that the council will glorify the Lord."[33] The highest thing that an ecumenical council can aspire to and to which it can contribute is "the triumph of Jesus Christ."[34]

The first condition for the happy success of the council is the fervent prayer of all the faithful. Again and again the pope has exhorted to prayer, which "is more important than all human efforts and the most careful diligence."[35] It is recommended that the faithful in praying the rosary pray especially for divine aid for the council.[36] The bishops are enjoined to observe services of prayer for the Holy Spirit in connection with the feast of Pentecost, 1961 everywhere in their dioceses, that he may enlighten and in a special way fill with his grace all those who are engaged in the preparation of the council. All must take refuge in the intercession of Mary, the mother of grace and the heavenly patroness of the council. The pope himself on Pentecost Sunday, 1961 has consecrated several bishops in St. Peter's Cathedral whom he has called to proclaim the Gospel in distant lands.[37]

The pope is convinced that a good result of the council will be to prepare the way for real peace among the nations. Though the council is not a "peace congress" and neither desires nor is able to occupy itself with the great international problems, a direct way will lead from this council, at which the right principles of life will be clearly expressed, to the peaceful cohabitation of men and nations.[38]

We now turn to the pope's second main thought: the council as a step on the way to the unity of Christians. It is not too much to say that with John XXIII a note is struck which has in fact not been heard from Rome for centuries. "For the first time since the Reformation the government of the Roman Catholic Church has departed from a more passive attitude of waiting, tentativeness, aloofness, and calling others back to the church. Through the personal initiative of its supreme pastor it has now moved toward a vigorously active readiness to meet others."[39] The unity of Christians lies upon his heart in a way that it did not in the case of scarcely any previous pope. In his written and oral statements the pope hardly ever neglects an opportunity to mention the "others" with love and respect. The pope prefers to use the term *"fratelli separati,"* the separated brethren. This term is said to have been used for the first time in the inaugural encyclical of Pius XII, and it is known that it was the then Nuncio Roncalli who begged the pope to use this term.[40]

More and more it has become evident that the council is to be viewed as an "intra-Catholic concern." The enthusiasm with which certain parts of non-Roman Catholic Christendom received the announcement of the council has been very much dampened. It is true that the pope expresses his joy over the great amount of appreciation shown by non-Catholics, but at the same time he says emphatically that the council "is to occupy itself *above all and exclusively* (author's italics) with that which concerns our mother, the Catholic Church, and its inner organization."[41] The council is *not* primarily directed toward the unity of Christians, but rather has to do "exclusively" *(esclusivamente)* with the Roman Catholic Church. This was a great disappointment to many. But the words "above all" *(zunachst)* indicate that the pope has another idea about the council, although this idea plays only an *indirect* role: the unity of Christians.

A clear picture of this aspect of the council is provided by the inaugural encyclical, *Ad Petri Cathedram.* We quote several important excerpts from the third part of this encyclical "On the Unity of the Church":[42]

"It is a matter of record that our Divine Redeemer founded a society which was of such a nature that it alone would exist until the end of the world. This He promised in the words 'Behold, I am with you all days even to the consummation of the world' and for this he prayed ever so ardently to His heavenly Father. This prayer of Jesus, 'That all may be one, even as thou, Father, in me and I in thee; that they also may be one in us' was without a doubt accepted and heeded because of its deep reverence. By this, we are given the most gratifying hope and assurance that, at some time, all the sheep that are not of this fold will earnestly desire to return to it. Thus, in accordance with the sentiment expressed by our Divine Redeemer, 'there shall be one fold and one shepherd.' (John 10:16)

"The promise of this hope has already stirred us deeply to the action of announcing our intention of convening an Ecumenical Council to which Bishops from every corner of the globe will come to consider the serious problems confronting religion. Its special concerns will be the growth of the Catholic Church, the renewal of the spirit of the Gospel in the hearts of people everywhere and the adjustment of Christian discipline to the exigencies of modern day living. This will surely be a particularly remarkable display of truth, unity and love, a display which those who are cut off from this Apostolic See will observe. We sincerely hope that they will receive it as a gentle invitation to seek and acquire that unity which Jesus Christ prayed for so ardently to His heavenly Father.

"In regard to this, we are aware, and this is a consolation to us, that the faith and teachings of the Catholic Church have struck a responsive chord in the souls of many among several communities separated from the Chair of Peter. Then, too, considerable respect toward this Apostolic See has arisen and has grown daily as the desire for truth has meant the downfall of prejudice. In addition, we have noticed that almost all those who are called Christians,[43] even though they are separated from us, have again and again held congresses for finding a bond of unity among themselves and have established Councils for this purpose. What further proof do we need that they are experiencing a desire of coming to at least a basic unity?" (There follows an exposition of the concept of unity in the church, unity of doctrine, unity of government, and unity of liturgy.)

"We direct a plea to all you who are separated from this Apostolic See. May this wondrous manifestation of unity by which the Catholic Church shines forth for all to see, and may her prayers from the heart by which she begs this unity from God for all of you, move you in a deep and salutary way. . . .

"Please note that when we call you tenderly to the unity of the true Church, we are not inviting you to a strange home, but to your very own, the common home of our Father. In our longing, permit us to exhort all of you 'in the heart of Jesus Christ' (Phil. 1:8) to call to mind your fathers 'who spoke to you the word of God. Consider how they ended their lives and imitate their faith' (Heb. 13:7). The illustrious cohort of saints which every one of your nations has sent before you into heaven, and in particular, those who in their writings have handed down true and lucid explanations of the teachings of Jesus Christ, seem to invite you by the example of their lives toward that unity with this Apostolic See to which every Christian community was, for so many years, so strongly connected.

"Again we address all of you who are separated from us as brothers on the strength of these words of St. Augustine: 'Whether they wish it or not, they are our brothers. They will only cease to be our brothers if they cease to say "Our Father." ' . . .

"In union with Catholics the world over, we repeat these pleas with earnest prayers. This we do, not only because we are motivated by ardent love toward all peoples, but because we are stirred by the humility of spirit in the Gospels. We are fully aware of the lowliness of our person whom God, not on any merit of ours but in His secret counsel, has deemed worthy to raise to the throne of the Supreme Pontificate. Wherefore, to all our sons and brothers who are separated from this Chair of Peter, we repeat these words: 'I am . . . Joseph your brother' (Gen 45:4). Come! 'Make room for us' (2 Cor. 7:2). We desire nothing more, we pray nothing more from God save your salvation and eternal happiness.

This quotation clearly shows that the pope sees only one possibility for the unity of Christians and that is the visible unity of the non-Roman Catholic Christians with the Apostolic See, the incumbent of which is the bishop of Rome as the successor of Peter. The pope's statements are unequivocal and in this respect do not deviate from traditional Catholic teaching. If one had expected something else, one would have been decidedly disappointed. But how could one expect anything else from the pope?

Evangelical Christians must never forget that according to the Roman Catholic faith the clause in the Apostles' Creed that reads, "I believe in the holy, catholic church," is subject to only one unalterable interpretation: The church was founded upon Peter and his successors by Jesus Christ himself; wherever Peter and his successors are there is the one church of Jesus Christ.

The pope allows no doubt to arise concerning what he means by unity. Unity means first unity of *doctrine*, as that doctrine has been proclaimed until now on the foundation of the Bible and the written and oral tradition in the Roman Catholic Church. Further, unity means unity of *government*, which according to Jesus' institution is episcopal and papal, and finally, unity is unity in *cultus*, since the church has faithfully preserved the seven sacraments "which it received from Jesus Christ as a holy inheritance" and among which the eucharistic sacrifice plays a special role. To this unity the "separated brethren" are invited. There are things that are less crucial, in which liberty may therefore be allowed. But here there is no doubt as to what is crucial and necessary.

The pope quite unqualifiedly employs the terms "return" and "reunion." These terms recur constantly. This may appear strange, since many people in the Roman Catholic Church have given up these expressions—even though for different reasons.[44] The words *"reunio"* or *"reditus,"* they say, are in fact subject to misunderstanding if they are not more precisely defined.[45] The word "return" can give the impression that what is meant is a return to the Roman Catholic Church of the sixteenth century, as if the reformatory work of a Luther or Calvin had had no importance at all. According to the opinion of many Roman Catholic theologians, however, this is not the case. The Catholic Church is *not* the same as it was four hundred years ago, but rather presents a much changed face today. The non-Catholic Christians should not feel that they are the only ones who should take a forward step while the Roman church can remain passive. An attitude something like this: The Catholic Church cannot change itself. The Protestants can. Let us hope that they do so!

It is very important that the non-Roman Catholic Christians should not be expected to believe that everything in the Roman church is irreformable, and that in this church there can be no distinctions between what is essential and what is nonessential, between time-bound traditionalism and genuine Catholic truth. Here points of view are touched upon which must be more clearly worked out in the future and which contain far-reaching theological implications.

Another reason, it is said, why the terms mentioned should be avoided is this: The words "reunion" and "return" are inappropriate and subject to misunderstanding because this is not a matter of moving backward but rather of *going forward* in faith, in which everything truly Christian in one's own church is preserved. The movement is a movement forward to greater "fullness." The Roman Catholic Church has within itself the fullness of truth, even though a historical situation can bring it about that even important sides of the faith are pushed aside. The "separated brethren" do not turn "back" but rather go from a limited to a fuller knowledge of faith, from an incomplete faith to "full faith." Indeed, it is added that the separated brethren, if they come back to the paternal home, will not come as poor and needy suppliants, but will even bring gifts to their Catholic brethren, new points of view, which are a part of the genuinely Catholic stock of faith, but which for various reasons have been neglected.[46] This rather modern "fulfilment theory" is contested by evangelical theologians, but also by not few Roman Catholic theologians. What is meant by "fulness"? What is meant by "complete faith"? One must here guard against speaking quantitatively or quasi-biologically. The faith of an Apostle Paul, who knew nothing about the "complete faith" of the present-day Roman Catholic believer, was the expression of a "fullness." Also the faith of Luther, who disputed the "full faith" of his opponents, was the expression of a "fullness," though of a different kind from the "Roman Catholic fullness." And what does "going forward" mean? Actually, is there in this view anything more than a subtle circumlocution of the term "return"?

In present-day ecumenical theology, including that of the Roman Catholic Church, there lives, though quite scattered, an idea that provides a pioneering argument for the elimination of the term "return" in the customary sense and that is that Christian unity is a *mystery*. None of the churches, not even the Roman Catholic Church, can statically set itself up "as the possessor of unity."[47] The ideas we have about unity are often all too shortsighted and narrow-minded, limited by particularistic complexes. We pray for the unity of the church, but we do not dare to leave it to God as to how *he* desires to effect this unity. There is a theology of prayer that does not first discuss or set up theses and antitheses that collide like impersonal principles, but rather first vows in prayer to Christ the Lord. *Unitas* means oneness in the one church of Jesus Christ, it means a new Pentecost in which the Holy Spirit gathers together in concord the separated Christians of all the world into the one flock of God. This does not mean the return of one party to the other, but rather *both* going forward. Why then not speak of "return" in such a way that it would mean for both a return to Jesus Christ? Why not accept this very term again in its radical sense? This would be to set out on a road that would be for both a road of repentance and humiliation, of deeper knowledge of the truth and purified faith. The day of such *unitas* would not be a day of triumph for any of us, for then, not we, but God would have won the victory. Only so would the true fullness have been reached.[48] The saying of Jesus, "He who finds his life will lose it, and he who loses his life for my sake will find it" (Matt. 10:39), has its deep and disquieting meaning also in the life of the churches with one another.

We go back to the pope's thoughts. As has been said, he apparently employs the old terms in the same old way. And yet it may be questioned whether he uses them altogether in the "traditional" way. The way in which John XXIII uses the words, as well as his whole way of speaking and acting, shows that one must read very carefully and give heed to many small features. When the pope

speaks of return he does not mean simply absorption in the Roman
Catholic Church. Return does not signify unification *(Gleich-
schaltung)* with a "Latin" or Western church. The truly *catholic*
church is far greater. It is quite simply a matter of the right understanding of the *catholicity* of the church. Are we mistaken in the
surmise that the pope is at one with those who see a danger in the
exclusive domination of a "Roman-Latin" church? The pope desires
no absolutism and no exclusive ascendancy of the Western "Roman"
church. "Genuine catholicity is not dependent upon the Roman
ritual or the use of the Latin language."[49] This must be said in
reply to those who believe that the Catholic Church and the West
are one and the same. The church must, so to speak, "de-European-
ize" itself, that is, it must take seriously the thought that Christendom is not bound up with a particular system of society or a particular culture. The catholicity of the church embraces a large
number of different cultures, spiritualities, rites, and theological
peculiarities. According to the pope's view, genuine catholicity quite
simply rules out "Roman uniformity." It means variety and freedom
and—at the same time—visible union with and subordination to the
apostolic see. The two definitions do not rule each other out; they
are rather complementary definitions of catholicity. The Roman
Catholic Church represents today, wherever it has really become
a world church, a great "ecumenical" question, with all the difficulties connected with it, on the solution of which the minds of men
are divided. In this burning, intra-Catholic concern John XXIII
appears to stand on the ecumenical side, though he lives in the
midst of Rome, indeed, in the midst of the Vatican and in the curia!

In his capacity as the bishop of Rome and patriarch of Western
Christendom the pope is on a par with the other patriarchs. The
uniqueness of his position lies in the fact that, according to the
Roman Catholic view, as the successor of Peter and by virtue of
divine right he is the supreme pastor of *all* Catholic churches on
earth. But this does not hinder him from allowing differences or
even welcoming them, as his relationship to the Orthodox Uniate
churches and his great love for the Orthodox Church as a whole
shows. That extraordinary event in the history of the Roman
church, in which a Roman pope for the first time personally con-

secrated an Orthodox Uniate bishop according to the Greek rite in the Sistine Chapel on April 16, 1961, may be regarded as a symptom.[50] Also the fact that more and more Africans and Asiatics are being appointed as cardinals and bishops is significant in this connection. These bishops and cardinals represent communities which have their own stamp, which dare not be "Latinized" but which will have to shape the Catholic life in *their* way.

The relationship to evangelical Christians who derive from the Reformation is naturally much more difficult. To what extent the pope even knows, for example, the peculiar character of evangelical Lutheran Christianity is difficult to say. He does not say a word about the way in which such a reunion could take place. Perhaps at this moment it is impossible for the pope to indicate an exact way. He can hardly be thinking of numerous individual conversions. He is content to express an invitation in the name of the whole Roman Catholic Church as urgently as possible and to do everything that in his opinion might make possible the acceptance of this invitation.

When John XXIII expresses his thoughts concerning the unity of Christians and the coming council we are struck by two peculiar points of view. First, he looks upon this event as in itself something so grand that it will have the effect of a gentle invitation to return. Repeatedly he speaks of the council as a *"mirabile spectaculum veritatis, unitatis, et charitatis."*[51] The council as an historical event and with its painstaking preparations, on which men from all parts of the world are working together, will present a witness of divine truth, unity, and charity and cannot be without effect upon the separated brethren, if they are *bona fide.*[52] The council will manifest a church that has no intention of exerting compulsion or convincing by means of many words and syllogisms, but rather will in itself have the effect of a "demonstration of the Spirit and power." To this end all human energies must be united with the grace of God and its power.

The second point of view is closely related. The separated brethren are not *simply* invited into the Roman Catholic Church *as it is now.* Something must first happen in the Catholic Church. Not any change in doctrine, but rather a renewal in head and

members. The church must first attend to its own purification and
harmony. There are things that must be done "first" and others
"afterward." The council is first an intra-Catholic concern, a council of renewal. Through this it will also serve the unity of Christians.
Afterward the "separated brethren" can be invited.

In an address to the heads of the Italian Catholic Action the
pope said: "With God's grace, therefore, we shall celebrate this
council. We shall prepare for it by endeavoring to see to it that
what is most necessary on the part of Catholics be healed and
strengthened as our Lord has taught us. When we have carried out
this laborious task and thus eradicated what could hinder speedy
progress in the human area, we shall show forth the church in all
its splendor, *sine macula et ruga* (without spot or wrinkle) and say
to all others who are separated from us, the Orthodox and the
Protestants, etc.: 'Behold, brethren, this is the church of Christ.
We have endeavored to remain faithful to her, to pray to the Lord
for grace that she may always remain as he desired her to be.
Come, come, this is the way to meeting, the way that leads to
homecoming. Come, and occupy or reoccupy your place, which for
many of you was the place of your forefathers.'" What is intended
is the restoration of the whole Christian family.[53] We shall come
back to this remarkable text. Here it is sufficient to point out that
for the pope "the reunion of separated Christians is bound up with
the internal Catholic renewal, to which the coming council should
make an essential contribution."[54]

When the pope invites the "separated brethren" to reunite with
the apostolic see, this invitation is not on his part a claim to power
over souls. According to the pope's clear statement, which has just
been quoted, there is only one motivation: the salvation of men for
whose sake Jesus came into the world. We must believe what the
pope says. The coming council is not *ultimately* concerned with
goals of an ecclesiastical, political, or "religious" kind, but with
God's saving act for men. This gives force to his words, for here
the whole concern of the council is seen from the eschatological
point of view: with one stroke it is lifted out of the penultimate
perspective and set before God, *coram Dei.*

But this at the same time confronts us with the deepest problem of this council, which will be dealt with in the last two chapters.

In conclusion I should like to say a few words about the establishment of the Secretariat for the Fostering of the Unity of Christians, *Secretariatus ad unitatem Christianorum fovendam.* On both sides the desire arose among many—both Catholics and Protestants—to have an organ within the Roman Catholic Church which would concern itself quite specially with "the others" and provide information, contacts, and conversations.[55] Even shortly before the time when the papal *Motu proprio* was issued, however, it was not at all clear whether the pope would consider this wish and give an affirmative answer to it despite many direct requests. Certainly not everybody in the Vatican was for it, and there was not a little surprise when the *Motu proprio* made the following statement: "As a clearer expression of Our love and good will toward those who bear the name of Christian but are separated from the Apostolic See, and to enable them to follow the Council's activities and thus find it easier to discover the path that will lead them to the unity that 'Jesus Christ sought from the Heavenly Father with fervent prayers,' a special committee or secretariat, headed by a cardinal to be chosen by Us and set up in the same way as the commissions mentioned above, is hereby established."[56]

The head of this secretariat is the former professor at the papal Bible Institute and co-author of the Biblical Encyclical, *Divino Afflante Spiritu,* Cardinal Augustin Bea. The secretary is also not a stranger, Monsignore Johannes Willebrands, a Dutchman who had been assigned by the episcopate of his country to assume responsibility of ecumenical work in the church of the Netherlands and at the same time had been deeply engaged with ecumenical questions in his capacity as secretary of the circle of leading theologians called the *Conference catholique pour les questions oecuméniques.*

Among the members and consultors of the secretariat are many of the men who have previously worked upon theological and interconfessional problems with great candor and expert knowledge and often at personal risk.

The fact that this secretariat did not receive the designation of a commission is attributable on the one hand to the fact that it was certainly not established only for the coming council, but is to be permanent, and on the other hand that it is thereby given more freedom to gain experience in unaccustomed areas and to act accordingly.[57] According to the wording of the announcement, this new workshop has a twofold function: to make it possible for non-Roman Catholic Christians to follow the work of the coming council and to help the churches separated from Rome to reunite with the Roman Catholic Church.

The first task makes it clear that the council is not a matter that concerns only Roman Catholic Christians. It also has a side that is turned toward "the others." The Catholic Church, says Father Congar, does not exist for itself without interesting itself in the others. What is thought and said at the coming council must also be thought and said with consideration of non-Roman Catholic Christians. The whole operation, before the council as well as at the council itself, must be carried out "under the eyes of the others."[58] The fact that an information bureau has been set up on the highest level is in itself of great significance. Its purpose, however, goes beyond that of furnishing information. As Father Congar emphasizes, its purpose is also theological. The secretariat must act as an intermediary between the non-Roman Catholic Christians and the council. The Protestant concern is to be presented at the council and thus to come up against a "Vatican insularity" which takes hardly any account of the spiritual events in the evangelical world.[59] This is a high and difficult task. It gives to this workshop a very special mission within the various commissions which means that it must not merely allow others to set tasks for it but rather seek out its own range of functions independently. This requires a thorough and sympathetic knowledge of the theology and the central concern of the other churches. Though the work is now proceeding in secret, it is nevertheless evident that the secretariat is taking this side of its task seriously and has selected for thorough study topics which are a part of the essential and unrelinquishable faith of the Reformation. We expect in the future a lively theological activity which cannot be without its influence upon our side also.

This side of the work of the secretariat raises the question of

participation of non-Roman Catholic theologians in the preparations for the council and at the council itself. Naturally, direct
participation lies quite beyond the bounds of possibility. Yet from
the beginning it has been clearly said that Rome has been con-
templating the participation of observers from other churches.
This became apparent as early as the press conference held by
Cardinal Tardini on October 13, 1959.[60] Father Congar even proposes that theologians of the various churches should be present
during the council in Rome in order that Roman Catholic theologians might enter into conversation with them on various important
topics. It would be an event if the Roman Catholic Church could
at this council for the first time in history enter "into a structure
of dialogue" *(dans une structure de dialogue)*.[61] At the moment
there are deliberations in the secretariat as to how participation
in the council by theologians of other churches is concretely possible, assuming that the other churches are willing to send such
theologians.

The other task is naturally closely related to this latter aspect:
to help the churches separated from Rome to achieve the true unity
of Christians.

In the formulation in which the establishment of the secretariat
was announced the terms *"reunio"* and *"reditus"* are not to be
found; the word that is used is *"unitas."* The fact that this word was
used was by no means a matter of course; this word was fought
for. In the decision to use *unitas* instead of *reditus* or *reunio* lies a
definite intention, which reflects the situation in the Roman Catholic Church today: The question of the unity of Christians is not
so simple as many Roman Catholic theologians have thought. We
have already discussed the problems involved.

The new secretariat will not think that its task is an easy one.
Its members and its consultors know better than most Roman
Catholic bishops and theologians how narrow and difficult this
road is. We can only wish for them that they may have the wisdom
and the courage to go deeply, to keep themselves open to new
insights, and to beware of pragmatic and illusory solutions.

The question which this new workshop presents to us is this:

Are we evangelical Christians on our part open to new insights, and are we willing to listen to the witness of the Roman Catholic Church today?

IV. Response in the Roman Catholic Church

It is being repeatedly emphasized in the Roman Catholic Church that the coming council is not the business of the pope and the bishops *only* but also definitely the concern of the *whole* church: the priests, theologians, and also the laity. It would, of course, be an exaggeration to say that the council is actually felt to be the concern of the whole church: the great masses appear to be fairly untouched by it. When a Belgian newspaper posed the question, Are the laity interested in the council? the answer turned out to be rather negative.[1] People are hardly concerned about the council, they know too little about it, and they consider that it is an affair of the bishops. And since one has nothing to say in this matter one really considers oneself a passive and useless spectator. "*Roma locuta.*" . . . So what is the use of worrying? And yet with the announcement of the council a new situation has come into being in the Roman Catholic Church, a situation of unrest and ferment, of spontaneous criticism and relief, of impatient expectation and confident hope. "The council will be the fulfilment of a great hope or a great disappointment. The fulfilment of a small hope would be—considering the seriousness of the world situation and the plight of Christendom—a great disappointment."[2]

In the preceding section we attempted to set forth the purpose the pope had in mind in calling the council. Here on the basis of the many comments that have been made in Roman Catholic Christendom since the announcement of the council we give a brief sketch of some reactions within the Roman Church.[3]

One basic thought is predominant everywhere and that is that the church is facing a new epoch and that it is high time that it recognizes this situation and proceeds to act. "Is the council coming too late?" a number of Catholic students asked.[4] And someone has mockingly called the coming council "the council of the last chance"! The time has grown short. In the greetings that Archbishop Jaeger of Paderborn sent to his diocesans at New Year, 1960, he analyzed this new situation as follows: "There is coming into being a new world culture, a new world view, and it has already made broad inroads upon those who are swayed and stamped by the spirit of a secularized technological civilization." "Not only humanity but also the church stands at a turning point in its history. The so-called 'Constantinian age' is coming to a close." This term indicates an epoch in which the state took the church under its protection and its high point was in the Middle Ages. "Perhaps the time is not far off when Christianity will no longer be the common foundation of human thought, values, and conduct as it has been since the times of Constantine the Great." "In the face of the tremendous revolution of the last fifty years, neither a naive optimism nor a paralyzing pessimism is in order, but only the indestructible Christian hope. It lives by that faith and that love which are never inactive."[5] So far the archbishop.

To summarize this new situation: The world has come "of age" and can no longer be dominated and dealt with like a child. The whole of Christendom must understand perforce that there are one or more independent worlds outside itself with other norms and ideals, other religions and views of life. The colossal technological development which inescapably stamps the mentality of men, the increasing spread of atheism, the dynamic power and expansion of the great world religions, the explosive awakening of the non-European peoples and their struggle for freedom and equality, and not least the threatening indifferentism, indeed, the apostasy, of great masses in older Christendom, all this is a tremendous challenge to the Christendom of today.

In this completely new situation the council was announced in order to show the world that the *whole* Roman Catholic Church is summoned to reflect upon its mission and mobilize itself to carry out this mission. There is among Roman Catholics a consciousness of the fact that the changed conditions demand of the Catholic Church that on the one hand it remain faithful to the message of the Lord and on the other keep itself open to an inner transformation, an "accommodation" to the new situation. The Catholic Church has more than once in its history lived through crises of adjustment which have required the mobilization of all its vital energies. Despite the hierarchical structure of the church, which also determines the structure of a council, a council also requires the cooperation of the laity. Here we touch upon a point which has entered the center of discussion with regard to the coming council. How will the laity influence the coming council? It is said that the laity will be present at the council through its bishops. After all, the bishops are not only teachers of the faith, but also witnesses, and this they are only in intimate connection with the whole community of the faithful. "He will listen in his diocese to hear what the faithful expect of the council, how they look upon things. Therefore the laity, especially those who through knowledge and genuinely Catholic spirit are capable of doing so, can and should help to create public opinion in the church. . . . Thus before and during the council, as well as in his entire pastoral work, the bishop will carry on a never-ending dialogue with the people of God committed to his care. . . ."[6] It is a question, however, whether the contribution of the laity to the council can be made only in this *indirect* way. Otto Roegele, the well-known German journalist, thinks not.[7] He says, "Just because the most important task of the council according to Pope John XXIII is [to consist in] the 'adaptation of the church to the requirements of the present,' one will be in large measure dependent upon the laity not only in the period of preparation but also during the council itself." Why does not the layman have his place in the commissions and consultations, in the committees for the "preparation and elaboration of certain texts which are to serve the fathers of the council as working materials and bases for discussion?" Roegele finds it discouraging and contrary to the call for a "mature laity" that up to this time not a *single* layman has found a place among the commissions.

Extraordinarily interesting are the questionnaires which have been circulated in various countries and the results which have been published. Through them one gains a clear impression of the diversity of minor and major wishes and hopes which are connected with the council by the laity. The opinions cover a lot of ground: age limits and the garb of priests, the censorship of books and celibacy, liturgical reforms, serious political, theological, and pastoral topics, and the burning problem of reunion, all these are questions in which the laity are interested.

In Spain there has been an ecumenical information service for more than a year. An introductory statement says among other things: "The division of Christians is a tragedy for which all of us are in one way or another responsible."[8] And from the question box of a Spanish weekly I quote the following statements as examples: "I expect a close relationship between clergy and people." "I plead for the complete use of the vernacular, as in the East." "Preaching which is more evangelical, more biblical, less vulgar and less inflated! The preacher should make Christ manifest, but not his own ideas or those of an antiquated sermon manual."

"Why cannot modern contemporary thinking be adopted to a large degree in order to set forth and intellectually deepen the eternal teaching of the gospel?" Revision of the *index librorum,* "a factor of confusion and the cause of severe problems of conscience."

"A simpler, more spiritual, more modern canon law, which will be suited to what the man of today expects in the law of the church." "Many problems of clericalism could have been avoided if the laity had been conscious of their own value within the church." "Today the endeavors to secure concordats must have the honest aim of completely separating the ecclesiastical and civil spheres of jurisdiction in order not to give any occasion for confusion whatsoever." "I wish, insofar as this is possible without violation of the dogmas, a revision of all those norms and arrangements which render more difficult the restoration of Christian unity." "Oh, that after the council the nations may more than ever before see in the church the place where believers are to be found! Oh, that they might seek in it more the treasure of the 'Word of eternal life' than influence in earthly things! Oh, that the faith of the church and not its power would attract the attention of those outside!"[9]

In the Belgian periodical *Evangéliser*[10] we find a series of very interesting and candid replies. To the question: Are there any dogmas which in your opinion should be defined? one answer was: "That as few as possible be defined. That *'anathema sit'* (may he be accursed!) be avoided. I hope that the council will set aside peripheral definitions that could provoke the Protestants even more." "I leave this to the theologians." Another wrote, "It is time to complete the teaching of the First Vatican Council concerning the primacy of the pope with a statement which will define the rights and responsibilities of the bishops and the laymen in the church." Many desire an extensive decentralization.

"Every kind of tutelage and colonialism, especially in the realm of religion, must be relegated to the past." Almost all wished a clearer definition of the place of laymen in the church. Many are in favor of a simplification of church life. The external apparatus of the church is much too complicated and completely out of date. "Pomp, genuflections, ostentatious titles in the superlative, all this readily produces flattery on the one hand and complacency on the other." Unanimously the council is called upon to carry out consistently the liturgical innovations already begun. "Not liturgy for liturgy's sake, but rather in order through the liturgy to show forth the mystery of redemption." A universal wish is also the use of the vernacular in the liturgy.

Many surprising answers were printed in the well-known Belgian paper *La Revue Nouvelle*.[11] Cardinal Pizzardo's condemnation of the worker-priests has bitterly disappointed many. One reason given for the negative solution of this problem was "the danger of the environment," and the question is asked whether a *bourgeois* environment is not a danger for the priest. "Does not the 'bourgeois priest' *(le prêtre bourgeois)* find himself in a materialistic environment, harmful to his spiritual life and his chastity?" Should one not be consistent and demand the withdrawal of the "bourgeois priests"? "Many of the faithful have a deep yearning for a humble and poor church, much simpler, less hierarchical, less an administrative machine." Occasionally one finds reactions against the exaggerations and confusions of the cult of Mary: "The more the Virgin is put in her rightful place the more will she be honored." A member of the legislative assembly remarks: "I ask myself whether the clergy, especially the higher clergy, are sufficiently aware that the unbelievers, including the political opponents, are also a part of their church. It seems to me that many ecclesiastical statements would be framed quite differently if they were edited with some regard for the nonbelievers. It appears to me on the contrary that often someone takes pleasure in shocking these people and that, because they are not sufficiently understood, they are unjustly treated." A few express their qualms concerning the church's compromises with political systems of a Fascist or reactionary stamp, as is the case in Spain or Portugal. "The compromises are in any case just as pernicious if they are entered into on the other side."

These samplings may suffice to give an impression of the ideas about the council which are being discussed in the Roman Catholic Church at large. They indicate plainly the spontaneous criticism and the hope for a renewing reform. And once all the various replies of the bishops, and not least those from the mission areas, are available, the many diverse currents which are stirring in the Catholic Church in anticipation of the council will emerge even more clearly. All this indicates the tremendous responsibility of those who have to do with the coming council, whether they are now engaged in the preparations or whether they have the deciding voice later. "The question is: Will this council move on the level of the proclamatory, apologetic, and secondary matters, or will it create, through a broad-minded renewal of the Catholic Church, *fundamental preconditions* for union? This would be the fulfilment of a great hope—including the hope of the pope."[12] These are the words of a well-known Roman Catholic theologian.

Notes

Sections I-II

1. *Orientierung* 24, 1960, p. 149.
2. *Herder Korrespondenz (H.-K.)* XIII, 1959, 273. *Acta et Documenta Concilio Oecumenico Vaticano II Apparando*, Rome, 1960 (*A. et D.*), p. 45. On this work see p. ——.
3. *A. et D.*, p. 69.
4. *A. et D.*, p. 19.
5. *A. et D.*, p. 85. See also the Motu Proprio of June 5, 1960, "*Superno Dei nutu*" ("on the basis of divine inspiration"), *A. et D.*, p. 93, *H.-K.*, XIV, 1960, p. 513.
6. *H.-K.*, XIII, 1959, p. 273.
7. This synod was held in Rome January 25-31, 1960. Present were all the priests of the diocese of Rome, according to statements by the press between eight hundred and twelve hundred. Questions concerning religious conditions in modern Rome were dealt with: the life and work of the

Roman clergy, the liturgy, the Christian education of the young, the lay apostolate, social questions, etc. (H.-K., XIV, 1960, p. 277). The result of preliminary work by several commissions was seven hundred and fifty-five articles which were presented to the synod. Since only three real working days were available, the "treatment" of the articles consisted almost exclusively in the priests simply listening to the reading of them. On June 29, 1960, the publication of the actions of this synod was celebrated with a festival service in the cathedral of St. Peter (Cf. Osservatore Romano, June 30-July 1, 1960). On November 1, 1960, they became effective as law for the diocese of Rome.

The significance of the synod must be sought primarily in the fact that it was the first of its kind in the diocese of Rome since the Council of Trent, though Canon 356 of the Canon Law prescribes that a synod shall be held in every diocese at least once every ten years. The hope is cherished by Roman Catholics that this synod will be followed by others and that gradually it will be possible to carry out in the diocese of Rome at least a few of the many urgent reforms which have been neglected for many years.

Only in a secondary sense did the synod have significance as a kind of prelude to the great event of the ecumenical council. (Cf. A. et D., pp. 52 and 64.)

Literature:

Prima Romana Synodus, Roma, Typis Polyglottis Vaticanis, 1960, XVI 622 pp.

Address by His Holiness, Pope John XXIII at the First Synod of Rome, Rome, Typografia Poliglotta Vaticana, 1960. H.-K., XIV, 1960, pp. 274-278.

8. The canon law, which in its present form is rooted in the medieval collections of ecclesiastical law and the decisions of the Council of Trent,

was assembled under Pope Benedict XV and published (on May 27, 1917) as the Codex iuris canonici, containing 2,414 canons. Many of the provisions of this collection of laws bear the stamp of past ages, and an adaptation to the conditions of our time has long been considered. Since a council is above canon law, it is natural that this task should be assigned to it in order that there might be at least certain guiding principles for a thorough revision: "In general the revised canon law should be more of a skeleton law than the present one, which would permit a certain freedom of action according to the circumstances of the time and the national situation" (Orientierung 24, 1960, p. 153).

The modernization of the canon law which the pope has announced will consist primarily in drawing the canonical consequences from the decisions of the council. Therefore the new edition of the specifically Oriental canon law (in force in the Uniate churches), which had already been begun under Pius XII, was discontinued, so that no further installments will appear until the council has concluded its work.

From Roman Catholic sources come reports of concrete modifications in the legislation concerning marriage (especially with respect to conditions in the mission fields), in ecclesiastical penal law, and in the provisions concerning the censorship of books. (Orientierung 24, 1960, p. 153; cf. Felix Lector: "Der Index der verbotenen Bücher," Orientierung 23, 1959, pp. 124-129, and Hans Küng, Konzil und Wiedervereinigung, p. 225.)

9. The Latin text was published later; see Acta Apostolicae Sedis (AAS), LI, 1959, pp. 65-69.

10. Dom Olivier Rousseau in Le Concile et les Conciles, p. xv.

11. Das Kirchenrecht der Katholiken

und Protestanten in Deutschland, 1883, (reprint, Graz, 1959), III, p. 630.

12. R. Aubert, *Le Pontificat de Pie IX*, Paris, 1952, p. 329.

13. *H.-K.*, IV, 1950, pp. 318-320. Cf. *The Ecumenical Review*, II, 1950, pp. 296 f. and W. A. Visser t' Hooft, *Der Sinn des Wortes "Ökumenisch,"* Stuttgart, 1954, p. 31.

14. *A. et D.*, p. 15.

15. *H.-K.*, XIII, 1959, p. 274.

16. See e.g. *Chronique religieuse* in *Irenikon*, XXXIII, 1960, p. 198.

17. Lorenz Jäger, *Das ökumenische Konzil, die Kirche und die Christenheit*, p. 87.

18. Cf. Hinschius, *Kirchenrecht*, III, pp. 603ff.; H. Jedin, *Kleine Konziliengeschichte*, *(Ecumenical Councils in the Catholic Church, An Historical Survey*, 1960), p. 9; L. Jäger, *Das ökumenische Konzil, die Kirche und die Christenheit*, p. 98; and *Orientierung* 24, 1960, p. 150.

18 a. Cf. the address of the pope at Pentecost vespers in St. Peter's Cathedral on June 5, 1960, *A. et D.*, p. 101, *H.-K.*, XIV, 1960 pp. 494-496.

19. *A. et D.*, pp. 22-23, *H.-K.*, XIII, 1959, p. 464.

20. *A. et D.*, p. 161.

21. Cardinal Tardini supplied information concerning the progress of the work at a press conference on October 30, 1959. See *A. et D.*, pp. 153ff., *H.-K.*, XIV, 1960, pp. 103-106.

22. *A. et D.*, pp. 89-92.

23. *A. et D.*, p. 162.

24. *AAS.*, LII, 1960, pp. 433-437; *A. et D.*, pp. 93-96; *H.-K.*, XIV, 1960, 513-514.

25. On Nov. 18, 1960, a *Commissio Ceremonialis* was appointed in addition.

26. *H.-K.*, XIV, 1960, p. 514.

27. *Ibid.*, p. 514.

28. *Ibid.*

29. *H.-K.*, XIV, 1960, pp. 494-495; cf. *A. et D.*, p. 92.

30. Nevertheless the heads of the commissions are all curia-cardinals, who are prefects or secretaries of curia offices corresponding to the commissions. *Herder Korrespondenz* calls attention to this fact which is surprising, considering the pope's statement, and to the exact correspondence between the range of functions of the individual commissions and the corresponding curia offices. Only the Commission on the Lay Apostolate is new. In view of such homogeneity, one might fear a certain overemphasis of the Roman curia and its functions. People who see in the council the beginning of a new era in the church see in this "curial" structure a not to be underestimated danger of a "Romanizing" of the council, which was precisely what the pope's words, "the council is something else," were intended to prevent. *Herder Korrespondenz* quotes a statement by Father Yves Cougar in the French newspaper *Témoignage chrétien* (June 17, 1960): "From my contact with non-Catholics, nonbelievers, and Catholics, who really stand with both feet in the world, I ask myself whether sufficient account is always given in Rome to the serious motives of dissatisfaction or criticism which are expressed with reference to Rome" (*H.-K.*, XIV, 1960, p. 497). Cf. the plain words of O. Roegele in *"Was erwarten wir vom Konzil?"* 1961, pp. 106ff., and the very outspoken article by the Jesuit P. Rouquette, *"La Préparation du Concile"* in *Messager du Coeur de Jésus*, Feb. 1961, pp. 49ff., in which a reform of the curia is proposed as one of the themes of the council.

31. *H.-K.*, XIV, 1960, p. 495.

32. A list of the members and advisers of all the commissions and secretariats, complete up to Christmas,

1960, has been published by the Central Commission: *Pontificie Commissioni Preparatorie del Concilio Ecumenico Vaticano II*, Rome, 1960. New appointments are constantly being made which are announced in *Osservatore Romano*. The study of this small book is not uninteresting. According to *La Civiltá Cattolica*, 112, 1961, pp. 300ff., the following statistics emerge up to January 24, 1961:

698 persons are participating directly and actively in the work of the preparatory commissions. Of these 49 are cardinals (17 curia-cardinals and 32 resident bishops), 6 patriarchs, 102 archbishops, 114 bishops, 176 secular clergymen, 26 monks, and 7 laymen (1 in the Studies Commission and 6 in the administrative secretariat).

Of these 699 persons, 48 belong to the Oriental Rite (among the 29 bishops) and these "Orientals" come from 22 different folk groups.

If one inquires further as to the origin of these persons, the figures are as follows:

Europe 528
Asia 43

Africa 14
North America 70
Central and South America . 48
Oceania 9

Of the European members 82 come from France, 60 from Germany, 14 from England, 12 from Ireland, 174 from Italy, 22 from Holland, 45 from Spain, and 9 from Russia.

Many of the foreign members already reside in Rome since they are employed in the Vatican; this applies to 274; 58 live in Italy outside of Rome, 201 in the other European countries, 47 in Asia, 26 in Africa, 60 in America, and 11 in Australia.

33. *H.-K.*, XV, 1961, p. 168.
34. *A. et D.*, p. 60.
35. *H.-K.*, XIV, 1959, p. 106.
36. Cf. the article by Cardinal Antonio Bacci in *Osservatore Romano*, July 3, 1960, p. 3.
37. Cf. Cardinal Tardini's press conference of October 30, 1959, *A. et D.*, p. 157.
38. Article in the Flemish newspaper *Streven*, April 13, 1960, pp. 601-604, quoted from *La Civiltá Cattolica*, 111/3, 1960, pp. 411ff.

Section III

1. "De veritate, unitate et pace caritatis afflatu provehendis." *AAS*, LI, 1959, pp. 498ff., A. et D., pp. 33-39, *H.-K.*, XIII, 1959, pp. 538-548.
2. *Orientierung* 23, 1959, p. 149.
3. *Ibid.*, p. 151, A. et D., p. 24.
4. On the significance of the councils in the life of the Roman Catholic Church see L. Jäger, *Das ökumenische Konzil, die Kirche und die Christenheit*, 1960, and "*Le Concile et les conciles. Contribution a l'histoire de la vie conciliaire de l'Eglise*," Chevetogne, 1960.
5. *H.-K.*, XV 1960, p. 83.

6. *H.-K.*, XIV, 1960, p. 514. The Theological Commission corresponds to the Holy Office, which is headed by the pope and has absolute supreme authority in all questions of faith and morals. The secretary of the Holy Office is the very conservative Cardinal Alfredo Ottaviani, who was appointed the head of the Theological Commission. The secretary of the latter is the Dutch Jesuit, Peter Sebastian Tromp, who has worked in the Holy Office for years and in 1943 played an active part in the promulgation of the famous encyclical of

Pius XII, concerning the church, "*Mystici Corporis Christi.*" A number of the most eminent Roman Catholic theologians are collaborators in this commission. Among them two names stand out especially: the two Frenchmen, *Yves Congar* of the Dominican order and the Jesuit, *Henri de Lubac.* The pope saw to it personally that these two outstanding theologians, who were under controversy and at one time placed under the restrictions of the Holy Office because of their theology, were appointed, not, it is true, as voting members, but as advisers of the commission. All the more regrettable is the fact that the name of one of the most distinguished and independently thinking theologians of Germany, Professor *Karl Rahner* S.J. is missing among the regular members of the Theological Commission. At a relatively later time Karl Rahner was appointed a consultor to the commission on regulations about the sacraments. (*Osservatore Romano*, March 23, 1961.)

7. Denzinger - Rahner, *Enchiridion Symbolorum*, Nr. 1839. Neuner/Roos, *Der Glaube der Kirche in den Urkunden der Lehrverkündigung*, Nr. 388.

8. Hans Küng, *Konzil und Wiedervereinigung*, 1960, p. 197.

9. Cf. the declaration of principle by the German episcopate after the First Vatican Council (1875), quoted by Hans Küng, *Konzil und Wiedervereinigung*, pp. 237ff., and the express words of Leo XIII in his evangelical *Satis cognitum* (1896): "Just as the authority of Peter is always necessarily present in the bishop of Rome, so the bishops in their capacity as successors of the apostles are also the heirs of the lawful authority of the apostles, so that the office of bishops (*ordo episcoporum*) is necessarily a part of the essential structure of the church."

These words were not incorporated in Denzinger/Rahner, *Enchiridion Symbolorum.* They are quoted here from J. Hamer, *Le Concile, engagement de toute l'Eglise,* (*Lumiere et Vie,* 45, 1959, p. 51).

10. George Florovsky, "*Le future Concile de l'Eglise Romaine,*" in *Le Messager Orthodoxe,* 6, 1959, p. 4. See also M. Schmulders, "*Theologische Überlegungen zu einem künftigen Unionskonzil*" in *Orientierung,* 23, 1959, pp. 165-171.

11. John Henry Newman in letter to Miss Holmes (Wilfrid Ward, *The Life of John Henry Cardinal Newman,* London, 1912, Vol. II, p. 379).

12. Symptomatic, though unusual in form and content, is the article in *Divinitas,* 3, 1960, pp. 387-456, by Mons. A. Romeo, "*L'inciclica 'Divino afflante Spiritu' e le 'Opiniones Novae.*' " Cf. the reply to this in *Verbum Domini,* 39, 1961, pp. 3-17, "*Pontificium Institutum Biblicum et recens libellus R.mi D.ni A.* Romeo," Le Blond, "*L'Eglise et L'histoire,*" *Etudes,* 1961, pp. 85-88 and *H.-K.,* XV, 1961, pp. 344-346: "*Eine Kontroverse im Rom.*"

13. See Peter Lengsfeld, *Überlieferung. Tradition und Schrift in der katholischen und evangelischen Theologie der Gegenwart,* 1960.

14. See Hans Küng, *Konzil und Wiedervereinigung,* pp. 209ff. Cf. O. Roegele, *Was erwarten wir vom Konzil?* p. 75f:—"The Roman centralism and the world of tomorrow," in which the author turns strongly against the centralizing tendencies in the Roman Catholic Church today. The great question is whether the centralism of the Vatican is compatible with the New Testament concept of the church.

15. Some Roman Catholic theologians go still farther and propose that in certain cases the celibacy of priests be set aside. See for example B. R. Spiazzi O. P. in *Monitor Ecclesiasti-*

cus, 1959, pp. 389ff. Cf. Documenta-
tion Catholique, 42, 1960, pp. 402ff.
During the Roman synod John XXIII
emphatically opposed this, saying that
celibacy was one of the great glories
of the church which could never again
be given up (H.-K., XIV, 1960, p.
275). See further P. Winniger and J.
Hornef, "Le renouveau du diaconat.
Situation presente de la controverse,"
Nouvelle Revue Théologique, 93,
1961, pp. 337-366.
    16. Interesting in this connection is
the fact that recently an institute for
the investigation of atheism has been
established at the papal university "De
Propaganda Fidei."
    17. Klostermaier in Orientierung,
23, 1959, p. 104. The pope himself
has spoken concerning the manifold
problems of present-day missions in
the encyclical "Princeps Pastorum"
of November, 1959. H.-K., XIV, 1960,
pp. 170-180.
    18. Evangéliser, 14, 1960, p. 606.
    19. Cf. De Albornoz, Roman Cath-
olicism and Religious Liberty, 1959.
    20. A. et D., pp. 4-5, H.-K., XIII,
1959, p. 388.
    21. Ibid.
    22. H.-K., XIV, 1961, p. 167.
    23. To Asiatic and African Stu-
dents, April 6, 1959, A. et D., p. 16.
    24. To the Cardinals in Secret Con-
sistory, Dec. 14, 1959, A. et D., p. 62.
    25. In his first encyclical "Ad Petri
Cathedram," A. et D., p. 34.
    26. A. et D., p. 15.
    27. To the leaders of the papal
work for Propagation of the Faith.
A. et D., p. 86.
    28. To the Commission for More
Remote Preparation, June 30, 1959,
A. et D., p. 41.
    29. A. et D., p. 87.
    30. In the address of the pope in
St. Peter's Cathedral on Pentecost,
1959. A. et D., p. 25, H.-K., XIII,
1959, p. 464.

    31. AAS, LI, 1959, p. 832, A. et D.,
p. 48.
    32. A. et D., p. 21.
    33. A. et D., pp. 85-86.
    34. A. et D., p. 104.
    35. A. et D., p. 37, H.-K., XIII,
1959, p. 544. Cf. A. et D., pp. 20-21.
    36. In the Marian encyclical "Grata
recordatio," Sept. 26, 1959, A. et D.,
p. 49.
    37. In the Littera Apostolica "Cele-
brandi Concilii Oecumenici" addressed
to all bishops, April 11, 1961. Osservatore Romano, April 19, 1961.
    38. See, for example, H.-K., XIV,
1960, p. 496, XV, 1961, p. 169 and
A. et D., p. 81.
    39. Hans Küng, Konzil und Wieder-
vereinigung, p. 12.
    40. Orientierung, 24, 1960, p. 206.
See also Hochland, 1959, p. 501.
    41. H.-K., XV, 1961, p. 168. Cf.
Osservatore Romano, Nov. 14/15,
1960, p. 2.
    42. In the first encyclical letter of
John XXIII, Ad Petri Cathedrum,
pp. 20-28. Paulist Press, N.Y.
    43. The Latin text reads: "qui
christiano nomine decorantur," i.e.,
those who are adorned with the Christian name (or the name of Christians).
According to the whole intention of
the pope it is impossible to find anything derogatory in this, such as that
the Protestants adorn themselves with
a name to which they are in reality
not entitled!
    44. Also The Chair of Unity Oc-
tave, the head office of the Apostolate
for Reunion, which is directed by the
Franciscan Friars of the Atonement,
who insist upon a "return," has under-
taken an alteration of the intentions
of the week of prayer. For example,
instead of the words, "For the return
of all sheep to the one fold of Saint
Peter" the words now read, "For the
union of all Christians in the one true
faith of the church." Instead of the
words, "That the Lutherans and all

other Protestants of the continent of Europe may return to holy church" the words, "For the reconciliation of European Protestants with the holy see." "This is not merely a change of wording," says *Herder Korrespondenz,* "but a change of attitude, to which Pope John XXIII has always attached great value" *(H.-K.,* XV, 1960, p. 107. Cf. *Unitas,* XII, 1960, pp. 213-214). Nevertheless, they oppose the prayer intention which, as is well known, was introduced in 1934 by the Franciscan priest Paul Couturier. That form read: "Pray for the unity which Christ wills for his church by the means that he wills. Pray for the sanctification of all Christians and the confessional groups." This form is severely criticized in the book by the Rev. David Gannon, S.A., *Father Paul of Graymoor,* N.Y., 8th ed., 1954. Employing an analysis of the encyclical *Humani Generis* (1950) and other papal documents, this book argues controversially against "this destruction and watering down of the Catholic truth of faith." It is only an attempt to set forth the question of the unity of the church for those who are not Roman Catholics in a more pleasing and milder form.

For an understanding of the prayer for unity in Paul Couturier's sense see the two articles by Maurice Villain, *"Gebetsgemeinschaft"* and *"Das Geheimnis der christlichen Einheit"* (*Orientierung,* 25, 1961, pp. 16-17 and 28-31) and his book *Introduction a l'oecuménisme,* 1959, pp. 168 f.

In the first volume of the documents of the council there is reprinted a very laudatory letter which the pope sent to the Superior General of the Franciscan Friars of the Atonement on October 28, 1959 (*A. et D.,* p. 54).

45. See the fine exposition of these ideas by Johannes Willebrands in the periodical *Rocca,* published by *Citadella Christiana,* Assisi, Feb. 1, 1961, p. 22.

46. See, for example, Karl Adam, *Una Sancta in katholischer Sicht,* 1948, pp. 110 ff.

47. M. Villain in *Orientierung,* 25, 1961, p. 29.

48. A good example of an ecumenical theology in this sense is represented on the Roman Catholic side by M. J. Le Guillou, *Mission et unité. Les exigences de la communion.* I-II, Paris, 1960. Cf. *H.-K.,* XV, 1961, pp. 276-280.

49. K. Klostermaier, *"Auf dem Wege zur Weltkirche,"* Orientierung, 23, 1959, p. 104.

50. *Osservatore Romano,* April 17/18, 1961. Cf. the article *"Un rito e un centenario," Osservatore Romano,* April 19, 1961, p. 1. In a private audience the pope said to the Maronite Patriarch Meouchi: "We desire that the oriental churches should zealously preserve their rite, their language, their traditions, and their privileges" (*H.-K.,* XIV, 1959, p. 60).

51. See, for example, *A. et D.,* pp. 15, 34, and 65.

52. Here an important idea of the First Vatican Council is taken seriously: "Even through itself the church is a great and constant incentive to veracity and an irrefutable testimony to her divine mission, by virtue of her wonderful propagation, her outstanding holiness and inexhaustible fruitfulness in all good, in her catholic unity and invincible steadfastness." Neuner/Roos, *Der Glaube der Kirche,* Nr. 356, Denzinger/Rahner, *Euchiridion,* Nr. 1794.

53. *A. et D.,* p. 46, *H.-K.,* XIV, 1959, p. 9. See also XIII, 1959, p. 515.

54. Hans Küng, *Konzil und Wiedervereinigung,* p. 16.

55. See, for example, Yves Cougar,

138   The Papal Council and the Gospel

"Le Concile, l'Eglise at 'les Autres'"
in "Le Concile Oecuménique" (Lumi-
ére et Vie, 45, 1959, p. 84), German
translation in Trierer theologische
Zeitschrift, 1960, pp. 129-147. Cf.
Peter Meinhold, "Was erwarten evangelische Christen vom angekündigten
Ökumenischen Konzil?" Una Sancta,
15, 1960, pp. 39-40.
    56. A. et D., p. 5, H.-K., XIV,
1960, p. 514.
    57. On this secretariat see C. J.
Dumont, "Le secretariat pour l'unité,
in Istina, XIII, 1960, pp. 65-70. Cf.
"Entwicklungen in der römisch-katholischen Kirche. Aus dem Bericht des
Exekutivausschusses des Ökumenischen Rates vom August 1960," Ökumenische Rundschau, 9, 1960, pp.
204 ff.

    58. Lumiere et Vie, 45, 1959, p. 89.
    59. A. Ebneter, "Die Protestanten
und das Konzil," Orientierung, 24,
1960, p. 233.
    60. H.-K., XIV, 1959, p. 104.
    61. In Lumiere et Vie, 45, 1959,
pp. 90-92. See Orientierung, 23, 1959,
p. 182, and O. Roegele, Was erwarten
wir vom Konzil? pp. 29 ff., in which
the author goes very far and makes
the proposal that a contact committee
be established "which would discuss
all appropriate questions, before they
reach the plenum, with the Lutheran,
Reformed, and Orthodox theologians
in order to ascertain their reaction to
the content and the proposed formulation of the council decrees" (p. 31).

Section IV

    1. Evangéliser, 15, 1960, pp. 3 ff.
    2. Hans Küng, Konzil und Wieder-
vereinigung, p. 183.
    3. An excellent introduction to the
problems facing the council is given in
Wort und Wahrheit (15, 1960, Heft
4-7): Impulses and Hopes for the
Second Vatican Council. 1. The
Church on the Road to One World
(pp. 245-262). 2. Faith and Life in
the Age of Technology (pp. 325-346).
3. Renewal in Proclamation and Canon
Law (pp. 405-422).
    4. Hans Küng, Konzil und Wieder-
vereinigung, p. 193.
    5. Katholisches Amtsblatt für die
Erzdiözese Paderborn, 1, 1960, pp.

4 ff. Quoted in Orientierung, 24, 1960,
pp. 13 ff.
    6. Cardinal Julius Döpfner, Berlin.
Quoted in O. Roegele, Was erwarten
wir vom Konzil? p. 20. Cf. L. Jaeger,
Das ökumenische Konzil, die Kirche
und die Christenheit, pp. 94-104, and
J. Hamer, "Le Concile oecuménique,
engagement de toute l'Eglise" in Lumiere et Vie, 45, 1959, pp. 57 ff.
    7. Was erwarten wir vom Conzil?
pp. 24 ff.
    8. H.-K., XV, 1960, p. 58.
    9. H.-K., XV, 1961, pp. 153 ff.
    10. 15, 1960, pp. 3-20.
    11. 15, 1959, pp. 532, 547.
    12. Hans Küng, Konzil und Wieder-
vereinigung, p. 183.

Chapter VI

The Council and
Evangelical Christians

Having briefly attempted in the preceding to see the coming council in its Roman Catholic context, we are now faced with this difficult question: Does this council concern *us?* Us, the "others," who are not Roman Catholics? This question the "others" must ask and seek to answer, each in his own way and according to his premises. This applies especially to the churches which originally belonged to the Roman Catholic Church, the Orthodox Church, the Anglican Church, the Reformed Church, and the Lutheran Church. What position does the evangelical Lutheran minority take with respect to the coming Roman Catholic council? This question will be dealt with in the last two chapters of this book.

First, is there any point at all in posing this question? Have we not grown so far apart that it will be asked seriously only by a very few? For the great majority of evangelical Lutheran Christians the council is an alien affair that lies completely outside their Christian sphere of interests and hardly finds a place in their thoughts. And for the overwhelming majority of Catholics and certainly also the fathers of the council the evangelical Lutheran Church is an equally alien area, something so peripheral and

139

Christianly irrelevant that they can hardly attach any importance
to the answer to such a question. We must not labor under any
delusions about this fact.

But even more serious: Has not the relation between these two
churches been so thoroughly destroyed that our question has
become futile from the outset? We cannot forget that Martin
Luther was officially excommunicated, nor that this same man
saw in the pope the Antichrist. Why was the break so radical at
that time? Naturally many reasons can be given, but one thing we
dare never forget: the break was so profound because in the Reformation, quite apart from how one may judge it in other respects,
such ultimate decisions were arrived at as perhaps never before
in the history of the church. This break was no superficial wound;
it went to the ultimate depths. Other churches may walk together
on an easier, less thorny path; the Roman Catholic Church and
the evangelical Lutheran Church, because of the original core of
the Reformation, are not spared a toilsome road.

When we forget this in our ecumenical age we render the whole
thing so harmless that henceforth everything we propose to do can
no longer be taken seriously. Must we not honestly admit that our
relation to the Roman Catholic Church and its coming council can
be only a negative one? Does the council ultimately concern us?
Is this anything more than an "intra-Catholic affair" at which we
can be only critical spectators? Naturally, a great deal can happen
between these two groups of Christians in the personal realm, but
there is no chance whatsoever between the *churches.* The rift can
no longer be bridged, and in view of the many confusions and
many false hopes it is salutary, though painful, to admit that we
are facing a clear Either-Or: Either evangelical Christian or
Roman Catholic Christian. In making this statement we also best
serve our Catholic fellow Christians. Thereupon we must do all in
our power to live with one another in the "civil" domain as well
and honestly as at all possible, we must show genuine tolerance of
each other, and work together in areas where this can be done
without misunderstandings.

This solution seems to be consistent, and yet it is wrong: Roman
Catholic and evangelical Lutheran appear to be mutually exclu-

sive. For both this is a shocking fact, the full weight of which must be realized by both sides and should give us no rest night and day. *Yet* we cannot stop with this solution. Life contradicts it. Life fights against the "logic of mutual exclusion." This paradoxical situation must not only be borne in faith but also at the same time be broken through in faith. Both parties have never been quits with each other and certainly are not today: Christians of both churches meet, and theologians have entered into conversation which is not a futile collision of long-established principles or mutually exclusive theses and antitheses, but rather a dialogue that means a living encounter of human beings in the realm of truth. Interconfessional speech, like every other kind of human speech, is always tainted, but our time has shown that a dialogue between the confessions is possible, a dialogue in which language does not always separate but rather opens up new common insights, and thus leads those who are separated closer to each other. Here no sense of superiority or of knowing better can help, but only the common responsibility for the Gospel of Jesus Christ and his church. To think ecumenically means to include and take the others into account. Thus there is required of both parties a spiritual attitude in which one does not see in the other primarily the apostate from whom one must separate oneself in fear of aversion, or, considering ourselves the "*beati possedentes*," the one to whom we address ourselves as missionaries, but rather as someone who is of importance to us, one who has been given to us by God as our nearest neighbor, as a gift and a responsibility. In him too the Holy Spirit is at work, producing his fruits, not only for him alone but also for us.

The existence of this "other one" confronts us with a theological problem which we dare not evade. The problem is, how can we take this "other one" into our theological thinking? If the "other" exists because God has so willed, then he turns out to be not merely an opposing church or a church which has not yet been realized, but a brother on whom we depend in our existence as a church and with whom we must share the common responsibility despite all our differences.

It is not good that the man should be alone, not even as a theologian and—*sit venia verbo!*—not even as a church. It is not good for the Lutheran Church to remain alone. Then it all too easily becomes a "particularist church" *(Sonderkirche)*, which Luther himself feared. A "particularist church" is a *contradictio in adiecto*. There can be no such thing as a church "for itself," a monological church. If the Lutheran Church does not constantly listen to the question presented to it by the Roman Catholic Church, but rather looks upon the confessional problem as solved and therefore disposed of, then this is a sign of an inner stagnation in which that for which the Reformer fought has been forgotten. Then our church would content itself with a separate existence in which access to the living history from which it flows and to which it belongs had become very small, indeed, perhaps entirely closed. It dare never desire to be alone—for the sake of its own life. It must always be willing to let the others tell it something, in order that in this way it may repeatedly be pointed back to its origin. This is precisely the way in which it fights against the forces that threaten it. Every church has its *tentatio,* and certainly the Lutheran Church does too. In togetherness with the others it is aided by the Spirit of truth himself in order that it may not perish because of its "particularity."

The fact that the Roman Catholic Church cannot exist alone has been demonstrated by its own history. This is why in the last analysis the Reformation was a great blessing to it. It too cannot and dare not content itself with its separate existence, no matter how universal its structure. It is very difficult for every church to assent to this truth, but doubtless most difficult of all for the Roman Catholic Church. This is inherent in the very nature of its understanding of itself. It must be bluntly said, however, that if the Roman Catholic Church—however hiddenly this may occur—is not open to the positive question addressed to it by the Reformation which goes straight to the center of the Bible and to the insight into the salvation of God through Jesus Christ given there, then this is a sign that it has departed far from the determinative center. Then it too has become a particularistic tradition. It too cannot get along without the others. If it believes it can do this it is deceiving itself. Not only for the evangelical Lutheran Church but also for the Roman Catholic Church togetherness with others is a gracious ordinance of God which we dare not think of as something external and imposed or simply accept superficially, but rather must accede to gratefully. We do not like to give our assent to this truth of mutual, necessary aid—*confusione hominum—providentia Dei*—but we must and we may do so.

If these judgments are true, then what happens among the others cannot be a matter of indifference. Love also drives us to this realization. Love and truth belong together because in the deepest, hidden sense they are *one*. Love breaks through all barriers and goes to the utmost limits, but it is never without the truth. On the other hand, truth likewise can *never* be without love. Otherwise it atrophies in killing harshness and coldness. If Jesus had been only the truth, he would have been the death of all sinners. He is the truth, because he is love. It is a dreadful sign of the Fall that we are capable of separating truth from love and that we actually do so—even in relation to our Christian brothers. Cautious, calculating reason says: First comes truth, and often this means: first we must agree on what *I* consider to be the truth, *then* comes love. But this is a distortion, not only of love but also of truth.

Love knows no boundaries. Love goes on working even where in my deepest conviction the other is not in the truth. Love seeks out the other and can never act as a passive spectator. It cannot dismiss him either with cool condemnation or with reserved, ultimately negative speech. For I am not dealing with a stranger but with my brother, from whom I am separated but who is nevertheless my brother just as truly as I stand with him before the cross of Jesus.

In view of what has just been said, it is clear that we are not permitted to view the coming council merely as an "intra-Catholic" concern with which *we* have nothing to do. In one way or another we are involved! In the last chapter of this book the great tensions in the area of doctrine will be dealt with. Here we shall deal in somewhat more detail with several concrete points of this council which we have already touched upon in preceding chapters.

One peculiarity of this council is the reason given for its convocation. Here already we are involved, and in a very direct way. The Roman Catholic Church has seen that it is facing a new era.

Many of its faithful have realized that today it is not the church that addresses questions to the world, but rather that it must answer the very serious questions of the world. To the world it appears that the face of the church has grown warped and old. "Three-fourths corpse," said a nonbeliever who traveled about Europe several years ago!

It is necessary to see this one thing: The reason given for the council is an unavoidable question addressed to us and, *so* understood, an invitation to us and the other churches! In this connection what may alienate and trouble us so far as the inner structure and the external course of such a council is concerned is quite immaterial. If the council really came into being because of the needs and the overwhelming problems of our time, then we have an obligation to it. For we are confronted with the same need and the same problems. Our church too has received the commission to proclaim the Gospel and perform the works of love in the midst of this world. Evangelical Christians are struggling with the same difficulties—down to many details—even though they may arrive at quite different solutions. It would be a bad thing if the evangelical Lutheran Church, simply on account of pure zeal to look upon the others critically, were no longer to see the challenge of the world. In common wrestling with the same problems we do each other a salutary service, even though we cannot accept or must contradict the others' solutions.

When this common situation is understood and taken seriously the result for evangelical Christians is the demand that they give expression to their criticism. This criticism is not motivated merely by the desire to say No, but springs from an insight into the Gospel which obligates us.

The coming council desires a *renewal* of the church. Renewal is related to *reformatio*, and reformatio means, as Hans Küng rightly says, "to give back an earlier, better form, to reorganize and give new form to something deformed," "to form according to its real nature."[1] In Protestant theology the phrase *"Ecclesia semper reformanda"* has become almost too fluent, but the thought that lies behind it is right and necessary. In his published addresses Pope John speaks very much of renewal. What does he mean by it? Renewal means above all new strength for the divine mission of the church, the revival of piety and the works of the Catholic Church, and an energetic "adaptation" to the new world. The church desires "with energy and strength to establish upon the tracks of her ancient tradition her own life and her cohesion over against the manifold relationships of the present world and thus bring forth usable norms for life and action. In this way the church will appear in her full splendor before all the world."[2] In a statement already quoted the pope says that the church is facing a laborious task. Much must be strengthened and healed. When this laborious task is completed and that which "in the human area" could hinder progress has been eliminated, "we shall show forth the church in all its splendor." Elsewhere it is stated somewhat more moderately that the church should appear in a form which is "in a wholesome degree modernized and rejuvenated."[3] Sometimes one has the impression that the renewal has to do with a question of church discipline and hence with a regulation of the life and conduct of the clergy as well as the laity. The picture presented by the Roman Synod with its 755 articles comes to mind!

Now we do not intend to say anything against such an understanding of the word "renewal" *as such*. We know that Christian *paranesis* has a necessary place in the life of the church; on our side we know all too well that exhortation on the one hand and earnest acceptance of exhortation are needed and that often there is far too little said about it among us.

We also know how badly needed is a reanimation of the Christian congregational life in worship, in missions, and in works of love. The attitude of ministers toward their work and the faith of the laity which should find expression in their everyday world are in urgent need of deepening and open activity.

What troubles us is not so much what is said as what is *not* said. Does the here described understanding of the word "renewal" really get to the roots or has the most important thing, without which the rest loses its ultimate importance, been forgotten altogether?

Renewal or reform cannot take place without what is often painful remolding, without critical revision of all the church's forms of expression in the light of the Word of God. The church along with all its functions is always being questioned as to *whether* it is really the instrument of the Lord of the church, *whether* it is really *his* work and *his* salvation and therefore also *his* glory which are being expressed here. It is God's ordinance, given with the incarnation itself, that he chooses external means and concrete persons for his work of grace. God has related his saving work to external means. But there is a clear, although invisible, limit between the human and the divine in the church. God has united these two, but he never identifies them. When these limits are transgressed, that is, when the church appropriates to itself what is God's alone as its own authority, then God says *his* NO, which is unmistakable to him who has ears to hear. *No* church, even the "most spiritual," is exempt from painful self-criticism, the purpose of which is to ask ourselves how we are using the Means of Grace entrusted to us by God! Are we willing to subject ourselves to this self-examination?

There is in our churches a human-all-too-human self-assurance, an almost metaphysically grounded self-satisfaction which is nurtured by the experience of the centuries and which has created a mentality which almost nothing can disturb because it turns everything to its own advantage; a kind of spiritual urge to self-preservation which has absolutely nothing to do with faith. It is against this attitude that the words of John the Baptist are spoken: "Do not presume to say to yourselves, 'We have Abraham as our father'; for I tell you, God is able from these stones to raise up children to Abraham." This applies to every church on earth, and certainly also to the Roman Catholic Church.

Renewal begins with *metanoia*, repentance. I am well aware that one should speak of *metanoia* with caution and that the evangelical churches that speak much of repentance and judgment are under the temptation to leave it with mere words. But this cannot alter the fact that renewal and repentance, that is, recognition and confession of sins, including those that occur within the church, in the sanctuary itself, in theology and at the councils belong together. These things affect not *only* "the human area" but go infinitely deeper. There is no area in which renewal would not be necessary. This does not abolish the church; on the contrary. This *metanoia* and the repentance connected with it is a structural element of the true church. He who does not see this is tempted, despite all good intentions, to identify renewal with a vigorous restoration and intensification of moral and religious forces.

A council must necessarily concern itself with the renewal of the church. This is why every council is in the first instance a *dogmatic* council. It is always a matter of the pure doctrine, of the proclamation, of our understanding and use of the Sacraments. It is always a matter of the *whole*, of the unity of faith and life, because faith and life cannot be separated from each other. The coming council will also be a dogmatic council despite the alleged assertion that this time doctrine will occupy only a subordinate place in it. This only appears to be so!

The *real* question which is directed to the church comes, not from the world, but from *God* through his living Word. Wherever this Word is heard renewal takes place. Not mere religious revival but rather return to the source. This return to the source we as the church must learn. For this reason a good fight must always be fought in the church *against* the church *for* the church, a fight against the temptation to identify the church with the kingdom of God, to make it a religious, "supernatural" world, instead of the place where the kingdom of God makes a breakthrough on earth. The church of Jesus Christ is always subject to the threefold temptation in the wilderness. In this temptation it is the purpose of the shrewd and cunning Adversary to let the true church perish in the midst of its own external and inner florescence. The bishops must realize that as fathers of the council they are exposed to this danger and that the most fearful stratagem of the Adversary is to keep them from being aware of this. How will the word renewal be understood by the fathers of the council during the preparations and at the council itself?

A second question is that of what is meant by the *church.* Right here is where the profound divergence between the Roman Catholic and the evangelical view becomes especially apparent. Not in the sense that Roman Catholicism is "the religion of the church" par excellence, and evangelical Lutheran Christians ultimately have

no sense of what the church is, because for them the only thing
that counts is the salvation of the individual. The discerning know
that this is not so. For Reformation faith the church is just as real
a magnitude as it is for the Catholic faith; the difference is that
this magnitude is understood differently. We recall the characteristic statement of Luther: *Ecclesia est creatura Verbi.*[4] When
Luther says "Word," the term has a threefold meaning: (1) God's
almighty, creative Word: "For he spoke, and it came to be"; (2)
Christ himself, the eternal Word of the incarnate, historical Jesus
in his words and deeds, the crucified, risen, and exalted Lord;
(3) The act of the Holy Spirit, who through the witness of the apostles interprets the person and work of Christ and causes the proclamation of the church to "go forth" for salvation. In the Word the
triune God himself is present as "Creator, Savior, and Giver of
Life" (Nicene Creed).

This Word is radically *before* the church and *above* the church.
But it is also *in* the church as its sole life and substance. *"Tota vita
et substantia Ecclesiae est in Verbo Dei."*[5] Through his Word God
has chosen and created for himself a people and in his grace allows
this Word to dwell among his people. Hence Luther could say:
"It is a perilous and dreadful thing to hear or to believe something
which is contrary to the unanimous testimony, faith, and teaching
of the whole holy, Christian church, which has been unanimously
held from the beginning throughout the world for over fifteen
hundred years."[6]

When Luther uses the term "Word" he does so to emphasize unmistakably that the church does not rest upon itself and that it has
no "autonomy" whatsoever, however hidden it may be. For this
Word is and will always remain *God's* Word. The church is the
servant of this Word, and this means that it cannot stand in a relationship of *cooperatio* with the saving work of God. I am aware
that when we use the word "cooperatio" (cooperation) we are using
an extremely difficult term and that in doing so we are touching one
of the sorest points in the relation between both parties. It is the
question of the relation between nature and grace, man and God
in salvation, hence the very thing for which the Reformation
fought. It is charged against us that the Reformation view of the

church exposes the nature of the incarnation to a misunderstanding. We do not think so, but we admit that the words "incarnation" and *cooperatio* are of very special importance in the dialogue between the confessions. *Cooperatio* has often been wrongly interpreted by Protestant theology; nevertheless, there lies here one of the deepest divergences, to which we shall always have to return in our efforts to reach mutual understanding. The last word has not yet been spoken in this matter.

Both confessions have the same elements in their view of the church, but the elements are, so to speak, put together differently. Both represent a "fulness," but this "fulness" has a different structure. Also the evangelical Lutheran faith knows that the church is the mother of the faithful and that as the church of the Word of God it is holy and infallible. It recognizes a genuine apostolic authority, which is given with the clear apostolic witness found in the Holy Scriptures. The exercise of this apostolic authority occurs in proclamation and teaching in the community through the office of bishops, pastors, and teachers.

We have a common concern, but we understand it in different ways. The evangelical Lutheran faith must reject the binding of the Word of God to an episcopal succession, with the bishops as an absolute guarantee of the apostolicity of the church, and being bound to a specific "*sedes apostolica,*" that is, to Rome, with the pope as the head of the church furnished "*jure divino*" with supreme jurisdiction and infallible doctrinal authority. According to evangelical conviction, the Word of God bursts any such bond. Despite a constant awareness of our own weakness, we evangelical Christians cannot fail to say to the Roman Catholic Church that it exercised *too little apostolic* authority. If it had done so it would have had to say No to many "developments" and definitions of faith.

The church possesses its power and its glory as the witness of the triune God. Where the Word of God is at work there is the kingdom of God, the *regnum Dei,* the true church—always in battle against the *regnum diaboli* and against the false church. The church of Christ will always be assailed and threatened by the world and by the false church in its own midst, it is "hidden under the cross" because the kingdom of Christ has not yet been made manifest.[7]

In the pope's addresses concerning the council the church is frequently introduced. And naturally John XXIII speaks as a Roman Catholic theologian and—above all—as a fatherly and responsible shepherd. We shall not go into this here but merely call attention to several points that seem significant to us in this connection.

The pope speaks of the splendor and the glory of the church. In a number of passages, which we have already dealt with, he then goes on to say that after a laborious renewal "the church will be set forth in her full splendor" in order that she may be able to say to the non-Roman Catholic Christians, "Come, come." In one passage the phrase from the Epistle to the Ephesians is used: *"sine macula et ruga"* (without spot or wrinkle).[8] The coming council is to be a "wonderful spectacle of truth, unity, and charity" and thus an invitation to the others to return to the Roman Catholic Church. We must confess that these expressions strike us as being *very* strange. We are confronted with a line of reasoning which it is impossible for us to go along with. Our first question is whether the church is not conceived completely uneschatologically. Is not the ultimate goal anticipated and the earthly church so glorified that one asks oneself whether this is not actually an "overstepping of the bounds"? "The church here on earth is not *'gloriosa'* because it is a church of sinners."[9] We know that Augustine as well as Thomas Aquinas interpreted this passage of Ephesians in another way than does the pope. Here on earth the church is never "without spot or wrinkle." At first Augustine advocated a view in which the kingdom of God will be fully realized on this earth, but later he gave up this view and interpreted Ephesians 5:27 definitely eschatologically. The church "is never without spot or wrinkle here, but through that which it has received here it will be led to that glory and perfection which is not here."[10] "Behold, the whole church says: Forgive us our trespasses. Therefore it has spots and wrinkles. But in the confession of sins the wrinkles are smoothed out, the spots washed away. The church perseveres in prayer in order to be cleansed by the confession, and as long as it lives here it so perseveres."[11]

Why does the Roman Catholic church generally find it so hard to speak of the sins of the church? Does this stem from a fear of succumbing to Protestantism, where sometimes we inadmissibly speak of the "sinful church"? But this ought not to prevent one from speaking of it in the *right* way! Even Thomas Aquinas interprets Ephesians 5:27 eschatologically: "That the church be glorious, without spot and wrinkle, is the final goal to which we are led through the sufferings of Christ. This will therefore be so only in the eternal home, not in the way to it, where, if we said we had no sin, we would be deceiving ourselves, as is said in the First Epistle of John 1:8."[12] Must we not speak of a *hidden,* often painfully hidden, glory of the church, instead of its evident glory, which surely is not convincing and which becomes an easy prey of doubt, because this is to build on the visible instead of the invisible, on that which is of this world rather than of the one that is to come? Are not the Roman Catholic Church and its Christians also familiar with the temptation of faith which no visibility can withstand and in which the cry of the hard-pressed father, "Lord, I believe, *help* my unbelief" (Mark 9:24), acquires its actuality?

It made a strange impression upon me when I read in *Osservatore Romano* the pope's 1960 Christmas address in which he made direct reference to the story of our Lord's walking upon the sea and the sinking Peter without inquiring into something which is very essential to the story, namely, the terror of the high waves and the storm. *Osservatore Romano* quotes the following words of the pope in the headline: "The humble successor of Saint Peter is not aware of any temptation to be afraid. We feel Ourselves strong in faith and together with Jesus we can walk over not only the little Sea of Galilee but all the oceans of the world. The word of Jesus is sufficient for salvation and for victory."[13] There is mention of the strong faith of the pope, but no mention of "little faith," of mortal fear of the depths of the sea. After all, the saving word of Jesus, which was at the same time a reproach, was addressed to the sinking and despairing apostle. This fact is by no means unessential to this story, it is a fact which is indeed not unfamiliar to the church of Jesus Christ. It is inseparable from its situation in the world, "hidden beneath the cross," not only in the "East" but also in the "West." When this is forgotten the glory of the church is falsely understood. We are afraid of expressions like "a wonderful spectacle of truth, unity, and charity," which recur repeatedly. Let it not be *too* hastily said that this is the familiar "Protestant sickness," an almost hysterical "Puritanism" and a quite exaggerated fear of the visibility of the church. I believe that we are facing something more serious that should give us both pause: the danger of a dreadful temptation that lies in wait for both of us, the form of which has features in common with Jesus' struggle in the wilderness!

The language of the council. The council will speak to the whole world. The question is: *What* will be said, and *how* will it be said? Language and understanding belong together, but often they do not coincide at all. We all live under the curse of Babel. We do not understand the speech of others or we understand it only fragmentarily, and often we do not even have the good will to do so. This is the trouble with language and human speech, and a Roman Catholic council is not exempt from it. It can be defeated by a *strange* language which does not promote understanding but rather increases the cleavage between Christians still further. The language of a council—it is said—should be clear and unmistakable; therefore the Latin language is the most suitable. This assertion is very much open to question. The clarity and logical consistency of language can be deceiving. The language of the Christian tradition has a long history in which, through a very complicated and often inscrutable process in interaction with general human and philosophical language, words have acquired their very definite and established meaning. Ecclesiastical and theological language *can* become a prison for living thoughts, so that only with difficulty does the thing itself find expression. We Christians—Roman Catholics as well as evangelical Lutherans—can hardly realize how strange our Christian words have become to other people. And what is more, we ourselves are often quite unable to understand the meaning of Christian terms which we come to take so much for granted. With our words formed by tradition we are shackled men. This is the difficulty of the language of preaching, of theology, and also of a council. The strong words of Dietrich Bonhoeffer, written a few months before his execution, apply also to the coun-

cil: "We are again being thrown back wholly to the beginnings
of understanding. Atonement and redemption, the meaning of re-
generation and Holy Spirit, of love of our enemies, the cross and
resurrection, of life in Christ and Christian discipleship—these are
all so difficult and remote that we hardly dare to speak of them.
In the traditional words and ceremonies we sense that there is
something new and revolutionary without being able to understand
and utter it yet. This is our own fault."[14] The question is whether
the fathers of the council are aware of this difficulty of language
and of this fault. It will do little good to "adapt" our old words
to the new situation or to "modernize" them; one thing is needful:
that we try to think these things through afresh and to express
them anew. This will not happen of itself. The great preparatory
commissions are now at work, and soon the council itself will come.
We can only hope that the council will become aware of and be
disturbed by this altogether great difficulty of our Christian words
and concepts, this struggle with language which is the only way
in which we can arrive at a right understanding and a proper
expression of what is understood. Then the council could become
a sign of Pentecost, but only then. In this respect too we are all
involved, for all of us are facing the same difficulty and the same
task. The prerequisite for a new language is that we must listen
anew to the Bible in order that our thoughts and our way of expressing them may be unshackled.

The language of the council—it is said—will be more biblical,
more patristic than scholastic. Only so, it is said, will the council
have the chance of being understood by the evangelicals and the
Orthodox. Here is where caution is needed. For what does it
mean to speak biblically? It cannot be a matter of using biblical
phrases and words to a larger extent than before. This would be
a purely formal affair. Even the language of the Council of Trent
was largely stamped by biblical language and still it was not understood by others but only further separated the two parties from
each other.

To speak biblically presupposes a very definite "act of seeing,"
which leads to an understanding and a rediscovery of the dimensions of the biblical world. We are all tempted to understand the

biblical words on the basis of our various traditions. Tradition slowly and unconsciously shapes our act of understanding, so that we interpret that which is first and original through what is secondary and subsequent. Certainly there is truth in this, and it dare not be suppressed: that which is not understood at first is later understood. There was much in the life and the utterances of Jesus that was not understood by the disciples at first, but which later they did understand in the light of later events and under the guidance of the Holy Spirit. So there is such a thing as legitimate interpretation of the original on the basis of what happened later. But this dare not mislead us into allowing the original and primary to be absorbed by the secondary. Tradition as the continuing history of the church dare never be made in practice the sole valid hermeneutical principle. The Scripture is not a magnitude which is to be understood on the basis of something else. The Bible has its own voice which can be heard and understood. *Far more* important than to stress the truth inherent in interpretation that "proceeds backward" is to see to it that the "original" remains in its independent power and validity. This original must critically illuminate everything that comes later, the entire historical reality of the church. Later times and places have their important, though secondary, importance for interpretation but must never receive the primacy in relation to the original. But this is exactly what has often happened in the church. To think biblically means thinking by "starting from the beginning," thinking "on the basis of the original," that is to say, the mighty message of the whole Bible, the Old as well as the New Testament, must be unchained and freed from the often stifling embrace of tradition.

We know that the problem of the Holy Scriptures is to be discussed at the council. This undoubtedly means that the hermeneutical questions will also be dealt with. What does it mean to understand the Bible? The Bible and the church belong inseparably together. But this means that the Bible must be *heard* in the church, and heard in all its sovereign independence. The Bible arose in the church, but it is the original prophetic and apostolic witness of the Word of the triune God and as such it stands *before* and *above* the church. The principle that the Bible is to be understood by means of tradition is therefore dangerous, if not untrue, because it can obscure the other principle that the Bible must be *heard* in the church. There it has its authority which is absolutely superior to all other ecclesiastical courts of appeal.

It is the task of the church to proclaim the Bible in such a way that it will find a hearing. This requires that the radical dualism between the old aeon and the new aeon must be held fast and not be allowed to be rendered innocuous by a philosophical line of argument that relativizes this dualism as has often been the case in the history of the church. The institutional church and the way in which all its functions are understood must be shot through with the biblical, eschatological tension between the old world and the new. Genuine eschatology must be introduced also in Roman Catholic theology. The tension between the biblical conception of the kingdom of God and the immanental, philosophical view of religion, which has so often stamped the history of the church and paralyzed its functions, must again come into its own. Only so will our Christian concepts recover today their New Testament originality. To speak biblically is a perilous thing! Much depends upon how the council will understand this expression.

The coming council is not intended to be a reunion council. Considering the relation of the churches to each other, this would be an impossibility. But, according to the intention of the pope, it is to be an important step toward the realization of unity. The third part of his inaugural encyclical, which was quoted in the preceding chapter, deals with the *unity of the church*, which, the pope says, "lies quite specially on Our heart and is most closely bound up with the pastoral office which God has entrusted to us." The pope speaks out of love for all who bear the name of Christian. As early as his first radio address in 1958 he said, "We embrace with cordial paternal love the whole Eastern church just as we do that of the West; also to those who are separated from this Apostolic See we lovingly open heart and arms."[15]

The pope names three aspects of unity: unity of doctrine, of government, and of liturgy. These are the three points that constitute the greatest difficulties for the evangelical Lutheran and other evangelical churches, difficulties which in the present state of things

are insuperable and furnish the very reasons why we can *not* be
members of the Roman Catholic Church.[16] Evidently the pope does
not intend to discuss these three aspects fundamentally and openly
with the other Christians. Further discussion appears to him to be
superfluous and fruitless.[17] What is needed is energetic action, that
is, an inner reform of the Roman Catholic Church through which
"the wonderful spectacle of unity which only the Catholic Church
presents" will show forth even more wonderfully and clearly and
move the other churches.

One asks oneself seriously, however, whether this can be the
right way. If something on the way to a real unity is to happen,
there will have to be something deeper than this. The other side
must be taken seriously precisely at the point of its difficulties.
It would have been good if the pope had said this. Now it looks as
if the dogmatic difficulties are not really being taken seriously. We
understand that it is difficult for the Catholic Church to carry on a
conversation with us concerning these things because we are so
divided in many respects. We also grant that it cannot be done in
one isolated discussion but that many factors must work together.
But we must seriously question the train of thought expressed in
the inaugural encyclical. Is not this a shortsighted judgment that
will be disastrous for both confessions because it does not recognize clearly enough the deepest wounds in our mutual relationship?

It is correct that in the necessary things unity must prevail. But
we are bound to face together the question of what is necessary.
If this question is not understood in all its seriousness, it is futile
to think of unity among us. The road to unity will be full of difficulties, but it is not permitted to us to make it easier. We were
divided by the questions of faith that separated us and we must
come to agreement by way of the questions of faith that are a part
of the necessary. Any union that would evade this dilemma is illusory.

What is of primary importance to evangelical Lutheran Christianity is not so much a church which is purified and "modernized"
in the human area as a church which is constantly going back to
the saving Gospel in order to proclaim it purely and plainly to the
world. The pope says that he wants nothing else but salvation and

eternal happiness for "the separated brethren." If the question of what is necessary for salvation were to be discussed in its full depth at the coming council, and if the result of this were the emergence of the pure Gospel of God's grace and power that redeems sinners, then we would indeed see in it a great invitation. The great difficulty is that we are not at one in the question of what is necessary to salvation, and this confronts us once more with the shocking fact that, despite all our mutual approaches and despite the many gratifying bright spots in our mutual relationships, we are nevertheless "mutually exclusive." It is a bitter but wholesome thing to have to recognize this situation. Only then can we take the next step.

What shall be do? *Ora et labora,* said Benedict of Nursia. The order of these factors is *not* irrelevant in this connection. In prayer we already have a deep unity which is far more necessary and real than we think. In this John XXIII is right. But often we do not know *how* we should pray.

What is the work to consist of? We shall not mention the whole list of possibilities; I should like to refer only to the most difficult points in the questions of faith that separate us. *We* cannot move mountains, but at the foot of the mountains are many stones that we must try to move. But this is laborious work, for we shall find that every stone, even the smallest, coheres to the mountain. Expressed in another way, there are individual questions that both sides must examine afresh in the light of the Holy Scriptures, for example, the question of the incarnation in its relation to the doctrine of the church. Or the hermeneutical question: *How* do we interpret the Scriptures? Or the question of Christian freedom. Where do we separate and where can we walk together? We shall learn to what a large degree every individual question is connected with the totality of our thinking. It would be ungrateful to say that such work is not already going on, and yet there is a long road ahead of us. Perhaps at this moment it is not even *possible* to say the conclusive thing. We are walking through a dark forest where very little can be seen but where a voice is calling us to go on. This is enough.

There are different kinds of unity. In the church of Jesus Christ the question is not one of unity for its own sake but rather of a very definite kind of unity. There is a "fleshly" concept of unity that is remote from the Christian concept, unity as a tangible uniformity visible to all, which is enforced more or less by means of disciplinary power, and there is a pragmatic, utilitarian concept of unity just as there is a politico-ecclesiastical concept of unity. The word "unity" is tainted and must be purified. When in his encyclical the pope speaks of unity he is speaking of "something established, strong, and visible," of a unity which "the other Christian communities lack . . . though it certainly is not lacking in the Catholic Church, as every attentive observer can see."[18] The pope goes on to describe this established, strong, and secure unity of doctrine, government, and liturgy. These are very important points, but when we ask *what* this unity is, we receive no answer. And it seems to me that without an answer to the question of what is the *content* of this unity we can make no progress even in our ecumenical conversation. For then we immediately clash because these three points constitute our chief difficulties. Neverthelss, we should attempt to discover a level that lies deeper than that on which unity is defined as unity of doctrine, government, and liturgy; not that this would be a solution, but perhaps it would open up a new perspective which might be helpful to us. When we try to give an answer to the question: What do the Holy Scriptures say on unity? We are aware that this does not mean we are realizing all the biblical aspects of the concept of unity, but we do believe that this is the determinative factor. The Holy Scriptures are for us the constant reminder of what unity is. It is not a matter of individual Scripture passages nor of something "very important" but rather of that total view without which everything else loses its importance.

God created the world as a unity, that is, as a world of fellowship and brotherliness, without dissension and conflict. Man was created to live in obedience toward God, in trust in him, the Creator and Father, and in fellowship with his brethren. This means that man was created in order to love, for the nature of love is fellowship, unity among those who belong together. The irrational fact of sin consists in the fact that this love and unity have been broken.

The world fell and continues to fall from unity. Differences which in themselves represent a blessing and wealth become separating walls. The nature of man is no longer love and trust, obedience and self-giving but rather self-seeking, which separates men from God and from one another. Thus walls spring up between man and man, between peoples, classes, races, cultures—and between churches. The essence of sin is desire, and thus it destroys unity at its deepest foundation. The world is no longer a world for God but rather a world directed upon itself—*against* God. "Sacred egoism" has taken the place of love. Community has been dissolved by war, by dissension. God continues to be the Creator, but creation has emancipated itself from the Father. The Father is hidden and creation is ruled by an alien power, by the Opponent of God. It is the very nature of the Opponent to divide, to destroy the community. This dualism underlies the whole biblical view of history. The world has grown at odds with itself.

The world's peacelessness evidences itself in the very fact that in the midst of all the discord men have an unquenchable longing for unity. This is the source of the yearning for the great Prince of Peace who gathers the earth together and puts an end to war, the yearning for a *soter*. Hence the most misleading marvel of the Antichrist is that he proposes to create the all-embracing peace and unity for which mankind yearns. He spares no means to create unity without God.

The Bible goes on to tell us that God restores his creation, that he reconciles it to himself and receives it into fellowship. The goal of God's saving history is the reconciliation of all that had fallen into hopeless antagonism: man against God and man against man. God wants to become *Father* once more to the individual and to his universe. Reconciliation means the overcoming of all powers of discord and division, liberation from the devastating power of sin in God's created cosmos and from all the attempts of the Antichrist to erect a false peace and a false unity. God's goal can be expressed in one word: *peace* in the full biblical sense. Therefore Christ is the center of the saving history. "He is our peace" (Eph. 2:14). Reconciliation and redemption occur in Christ. That is what creates *unity* between God and man and between men and men. We call to mind the great association of ideas in the first chapter of Ephesians: "For he has made known to us in all wisdom and insight the mystery of his will, according to his purpose which he set forth in Christ as a plan for the fullness of time, to unite all things in him (ἀνακεφαλαιώσασθαι τὰ πάντα ἐν τῷ χριστῷ), things in heaven and things on earth" (1:9-10). Also important is Eph. 2:14-18, "For he is our peace, who made us both one, and has broken down the dividing wall of hostility, by abolishing in his flesh the law of commandments and ordinances, that he might create in himself one new man in place of the two, so making peace, and might reconcile us both to God in one body through the cross, thereby bringing the hostility to an end. And he came and preached peace to you who were far off and peace to those who were near; for through him we both have access in one Spirit to the Father." In Christ the unity is restored.

The same truth is expressed in the hymn of creation and redemption in the Letter to the Colossians, "In him all things were created . . . in him all things hold together" (1:15ff.). In him occurs the beginning of the new mankind and the redeemed earth. The world was created for fellowship and unity with God. This unity is established through the blood of Christ. This unity is God's deepest purpose for his world, even in its present rebellion, dissension, and destruction. Christ creates this unity, not by fiat, not by any kind of external authority, not by assuming world dominion like a successful Augustus or Alexander, but *solely* through his suffering and his bitter death, through the sacrifice of love. In the generation of Adam, that would be as God and therefore must die, reconciliation and unity can be realized only through the sufferings and the sacrifice of the God-Man. Reconciliation, and with it unity, can take place only in the same depths in which rebellion, presumption, and dreadful self-seeking occur, namely, in the inmost center of man's being. Through the obedience of the God-Man our disobedience and thus our disunion and discord are overcome. Thus Christ becomes the head of a new race. This new race is the people of God, the church of Jesus Christ.

If this is true, then we begin to comprehend that the unity to which the church is called and chosen is not just *any kind* of unity, but rather a mystery of the love of God. Then unity is the very essence of Christianity, *reconciliation* with God and *brotherliness* among men. Then we understand that unity can never be something that is finished but rather something that is always coming into being, always threatened by the powers of destruction. Unity is eschatological in the sense that it will be a complete reality in its fulness only when Jesus comes again and God is all in all.

On the one hand the church is the first fruits of the new world in which reconciliation and unity are established and on the other hand the means through which the new world of reconciliation and unity is carried to the boundaries of all creation. Everything that happens in the church of Jesus Christ should promote this unity, the reconciliation of man with God and the brotherliness of men. In the proclamation of the Word of God this unity is not only described but rather becomes a reality. In the proclamation God's battle against the destroying powers is continued. When the message of reconciliation is made known and heard the people of God are *one* people. Where it is not proclaimed or where it is falsified the people of God are brought to confusion and subjected to the corruption of the Adversary.

Through the sign of the Sacraments the new world of reconciliation and unity breaks into our old world and becomes present among men. In Baptism men are made participants in the reality of the coming kingdom of God. In Baptism the old man dies and the new man rises. What happens in Baptism happens only once, and yet it does not come to its perfection until the kingdom of God brings about the restoration of all things. Baptism is the Sacrament of unity. All are incorporated in Christ, the Crucified and the Risen One. All receive the same Spirit and thus constitute the body of Christ on earth, the kingdom of reconciliation and brotherliness.

In the sign of the Lord's Supper or Eucharist the cross of Christ, reconciliation, and unity become present among us. The wall of separation is torn down, "the two" are united into one. Nowhere else is the message that the unity of the church grows out of the sacrifice of love made so manifest as it is here.

The signs of proclamation and the Sacraments contain within them the present Lord and Savior, and yet in their hiddenness and lowliness they are an expression of the prayer *"Maranatha"* (Come, our Lord), of the everlasting *"Quousque Domine."* Without this eschatological outlook we have not understood either the purpose of preaching or the Sacraments.

The ministry of the church also has only one function: to serve this unity. In order to help the church to fulfill its task, God has given the ministry to the church as a "gift" (Eph. 4): apostles, prophets, pastors, teachers, evangelists to which are added deacons, presbyters, and bishops. The various ministries exist solely for the sake of the people of God as long as they are on their pilgrimage. The ministry is not, or does not constitute, the unity, but it is intended to be a means to true unity in that it constantly proclaims reconciliation and administers the Sacraments of reconciliation and brotherliness. According to the New Testament view this ministry possesses concrete authority, authority to proclaim, to give instruction, admonition, and encouragement, and direction for true prayer and right worship of God. The shepherds belong to the flock, and the shepherds are necessary for the sake of unity, not as a guarantee, but as a help. But this unity must be understood in its depth dimension as the unity of *Christ,* the unity of reconciliation and brotherliness. When the ministry no longer serves this unity it is no longer a true ministry. The Adversary knows precisely what he is doing when he divides as well as when he tempts men to seek false unity. When the ministers of the church succumb to this temptation then the dreadful result is that the sheep are left without a shepherd as happened so often in the Old Covenant and in the New as well! Through God's faithfulness and power new and true shepherds are awakened.

The temptation of the Antichrist appears in two ways in the church: in part through the intrusion of division, pride, and false self-assertion among the brethren in the church and in part through the setting up of a false unity, perhaps even a unity disguised as Christian, that wreathes itself with many Christian words, without being unity "through his blood." God's history with his people is hidden. So it was in the Old Covenant, and so also in the New. The people of God have no external securities but can trust the Word of God and the promise of Jesus that the gates of hell will never prevail against them. When will the people of God be satisfied with the Word of God alone? Why is it so hard for Christians to recognize and accept in faith the hidden and invisible in God's history with his people? This would really mean to follow Jesus.

A unity of the church that is secured through unity in doctrine, government, and liturgy can never be an unequivocal sign of that unity which is intended by the cross of Jesus. Such a unity *can* be a "fleshly" unity. To speak quite concretely: The unity of Christians at the coming world conference of churches in New Delhi, which will not present a visible spectacle of unity because it is clear to all that profound differences separate the participants from one another, *can* become a more genuine and promising unity than the unity at the coming council in Rome, even though the latter has been called in the words of the pope an "established, strong, and secure" unity. In New Delhi the true unity of Christ can be present or come into being just as it can also be destroyed by men and their measures. What is true of New Delhi is equally true of Rome.

These observations may be sufficient as an attempt to make clear the nature and the peculiar character of the unity of Jesus Christ.

The unity of the church is the unity of reconciliation and brotherliness, its signs are unity in faith and unity at the Table of the Lord. This brings us to the point in our presentation at which the greatest distress and difficulty prevail because right here the inexplicable has happened, the fact that the unity has been broken: Something impossible has happened even though this "impossible" is all too explainable historically. When the pope says that this unity which is lacking in the other Christian communities is "certainly not lacking in the Catholic Church, as every attentive observer can see," we are not convinced. Both of us are in this need, and perhaps the Catholic Church should reconsider *its* share in this crucial difficulty. It would be a blessed thing if the coming council, which is so concerned about the unity of the church, would begin right here. We know how many clergymen and laymen are thinking about this; will their voices too be taken into account in the statements of the council? Or will everything go on as before?

In this connection I should like to try to construct a little dialogue.

In the sixteenth century there occurred a break, a painful division of Western Christendom, which had vast consequences.

The question is asked: Was this break a break with the one, holy, catholic, and apostolic church? Was this break a conscious, arrogant rebellion against the true people of God and the unity without which there is no people of God? Did not Luther, with his genuine concern in the midst of a church that truly needed a reformation in head and members, nevertheless sin against the true unity which was realized in the Roman Catholic Church despite all its faults "in the human area"? Was it Luther's fundamental error that he did not see this but in his zeal and his understandable reaction against the many abuses in the Roman church actually contributed to what should not have happened under any circumstances, namely, a break in the church? To the question so stated the Roman Catholic theologian would answer Yes.

It is also asked: Was it not God who took this at once powerful and fragile instrument into his service in order to reform his church? Was not the pure Gospel brought to light again through the voice of Luther in a church which had forgotten the Gospel and replaced it with all kinds of religious practices? Was not the Reformation in the last analysis a necessary break with a development in the people of God which constituted a mortal danger to true unity in faith? Had not that unity become largely a unity of worldly dominion which had largely departed far from the unity of Christ? Was not the Reformation ultimately an affirmation, though a hidden one, of the true unity of reconciliation and brotherhood and therefore a good fight *against* the church *for* the church? To this the evangelical Lutheran theologian would say Yes.

Having asked these questions we are confronted with a decision that dare not be made easy by either one side or the other. In answering these questions we part company.

Here there appears to be a clear Either-Or. Without in any way trying to blunt this Either-Or, I should like to carry the dialogue farther by venturing to let the Roman Catholic theologian speak: "If the unity of the church is what has been briefly described in the preceding, then this unity is also truly hidden in our church, in the Roman Catholic Church. Then it may perhaps not be so 'established, strong, and secure' as we have thought. Then it is not so apparent to the outside observer after all. Then I must admit that the Adversary has often had a hand in it and that the history of the church shows how often he has tried to falsify its true unity. Then perhaps the unity which, according to the pope, will show forth so gloriously and splendidly at the coming council, is not so self-evident and unproblematical as we Catholics think. An external unity in the means of salvation is very little, if the crucial thing, the unity of reconciliation and brotherliness, is forgotten. True, the church is infallible, but there have been mistakes *in* the church, and how often has not its face been disfigured! Yes, it is true that faith in the unity of the church is '*fides non apparentium*,' faith in that which is not seen. So I too, as a Roman Catholic theologian and in faith that God's ways with his people are hidden, can say that the break, even though I cannot understand it, is a part of God's plan for his people."

And the final reply of the evangelical Lutheran theologian would be: "My affirmation of the Reformation stands. In gratitude and appreciation I hear in the Reformation the voice of the Gospel in the midst of the universal church, to which I too belong. My affirmation, however, cannot be quite the exultant affirmation of the Reformers. When I look back I see how since the Reformation first one and then many separate churches have been formed. And if I look at the Lutheran Church itself and its four-hundred-year-old development I see a 'living tradition' in which strong elements of distortion and defection have appeared, just as they have in the Roman Catholic Church—except in quite different forms. And it is small comfort to me that this defection has received no place in the *confessio publica* of the Lutheran Church. Where is there unity of reconciliation and brotherliness among us? Do we not find the curse of disunion and negative nay-saying among us? Among us too the face of the Antichrist can be seen. Therefore the faith of the evangelical Christian must be a faith in the midst of sore need, a faith in that which is hidden."

The Either-Or remains. And yet, would not such a point of view change everything? Would not much be gained even if we were able to do no more than join in a common *Miserere mei* and a common *Te Deum,* not merely as an expression of a mood but rather as a visible and audible sign of a unity which was starting from here? Would not our life together then begin to take on a different shape? For behind, perhaps far behind, our disunion lies the unity of reconciliation and the brotherliness of Christ, the unity which he himself is and for which he gave his life. That unity calls us never to stop half way, never to cease realizing it in smaller and greater ways, until the hour comes when God establishes it fully among us.

Let us sum up what we have said. In about a year the council will take place. All the episcopal fathers of the council, a large number of the most eminent theologians of the Roman Catholic Church, hundreds of journalists, and thousands of pilgrims and tourists will gather in Rome. Gorgeous and impressive processions and services will be enacted before the eyes of the world. Great sessions will be held in St. Peter's Cathedral. Through the newspapers, weeklies, and magazines, by radio and television a large part of the world will be able to follow the course of the council. Behind the splendid exterior there will be energetic work, thought, and deliberation. Theologians on the subcommissions will be working on the proposals for the final decisions, and finally the sessions will be summoned for the solemn proclamation of the definitions of the council. Perhaps the council will direct a message to the whole world. None can predict the results of the council with certainty. We must be prepared for surprises. In the midst of the whole stands the aged pope, who has been an untiring source of inspiration and fatherly authority during the long period of preparation. At the council itself he has the final and deciding voice.

At the council and all around the world there will be fervent prayers offered to God, to Mary, and to all the saints. Roman Catholic Christians are of the deep conviction that their prayers will be heard since for them it is certain that the decisions of the council are the voice of the Holy Spirit, not in some kind of heavenly language, but through the voice of men in this historical situation, just as the church is always a people in a very definite situation.

Once more the question is addressed to us evangelicals: Does this grandly planned, world-embracing council concern us? We are afraid of the great spectacle. And this fear arises from our understanding of the Gospel of Jesus Christ and his church. We are not in a position to see that the bishops of this great assembly are *eo ipso* the legitimate successors of the apostles of Jesus, who have received from God through a sacramental act a sacred power to rule the church of Jesus Christ and maintain the message of salvation in its purity and its development. For us this council is not *eo ipso* an organ furnished with guarantees by the Holy Spirit, whose decisions are infallible, assuming that its canons have received the approval of the bishop of Rome, the heir of the primacy of Peter.

We cannot look upon this council as a "free, Christian, ecumenical council" as long as one half of Christendom is not present and free discussion is not possible. There are reasons for an attitude of rejection.

The foregoing presentation has attempted to show that, despite the above-mentioned points of view, this attitude of rejection cannot be Christian justified. The relation of evangelical Lutheran Christians to their Roman Catholic fellow Christians and to the council cannot be reduced to one denominator. There is in it something paradoxical which results in constant unrest, a riddle which we are unable to solve, a mystery before which we must stop short. When the relation consists only of a flat No, the problem is "solved." The same is true when the No is changed into a Yes. To many people the fact that Yes and No exist *simultaneously*, without the one being annulled by the other, seems like wavering, irresolute vacillation. They would say, what is lacking is the genuinely Protestant, flatly nonaccepting *"Non possumus"!* Only he who has not grasped the depth of this matter would speak in this way. This simultaneous Yes and No, paradoxically held together, is proper and right as long as the mystery of the schism of faith has not been

resolved and because we are both members of the same people of
God. The two churches *cannot* get along without each other today.

With regard to the council evangelical Lutheran Christians
stand between fear and hope. We have spoken about the fear, but
we must not forget that this council has its peculiar character.
This consists in the reality of a new theology, which is nourished
by the Bible and the primitive Christian tradition and has its center
in a concentration upon the crucified and risen Lord. This theology,
which is not merely an academic matter, indicates genuine search-
ing and wrestling in which new ground is being broken. It indicates
a depth-dimension that surprises us and invites us to cooperate.
The peculiar feature of this council consists also in the lively
interest of many priests and laymen with their often clear-sighted
eyes and their critically positive ideas, men who know that the
church is not a power of this world and who, therefore, are against
any political compromise between state and church, men who
grieve that the face of the church is often distorted and who can
no longer keep silent. We know that there are other trends too, but
this does not rule out the fact that these movements exist and cannot be done away with. Evangelical Christians can and must pray
that, despite all the well-nigh invincible hindrances, the Holy Spirit
will perform his work of truth, unity, and love at the coming council. Even here the saying of the apostle applies: "If one member
suffers, all suffer together; if one member is honored, all rejoice
together" (I Cor. 12:26).

A wise and far-seeing Roman Catholic theologian once said to
me that not too much is to be expected of this council. Its significance lies in the fact that it was convoked at all. We must
have patience. The conclusive thing may not, perhaps, take place
until the second, third, or fourth council which will follow this one!
It will be long journey, on which Paul's saying, "In hope he
believed against hope" (Rom. 4:18), will have its validity for both.
Evangelical Lutherans can and must take part in this journey with
their Yes and their No just as they must also be willing to listen to
the Yes and the No of Roman Catholic Christians. This journey
will not be in vain. "After all, we are not the ones who can uphold
the church, nor were our forefathers the ones, nor will it be our

descendants; rather it was, is now, and will be he who says, I am with you all the days until the end of the world, Jesus Christ" (Martin Luther).

Notes

1. Hans Küng, *Konzil und Wiedervereinigung*, p. 19.
2. *H.-K.*, XIII, 1959, p. 514.
3. *H.-K.*, XIII, 1959, p. 515.
4. *W.A.*, 6, 560 f.
5. *W.A.*, 7, 721.
6. *W.A.*, 51, 516.
7. Melanchthon, Apology VII. *Die Bekenntnisschriften der evangelisch-lutherischen Kirche*, Berlin, 1930, p. 237.
8. *H.-K.*, XIV, 1960, p. 9.
9. R. Grosche, *Pilgernde Kirche*, Freiburg, 1938, p. 66.
10. *Retractiones*, 1, 7, 5. Quoted from Grosche, *op. cit.*, p. 66.
11. See Grosche, *op. cit.*, p. 67.
12. *Summa Theologica* III, q.8, a.3, ad 2. Cf. Hans Küng, *op. cit.*, p. 43.
13. *Osservatore Romano*, Dec. 24, 1960.
14. *Widerstand und Ergebung*, München, 1955, p. 206.
15. *Orientierung*, 24, 1960, p. 206.
16. See also the excellent article by Hermann Volk, *"Die Einheit der Christen und die Spaltung der Christenheit"* in *Catholica*, 14, 1960, pp. 241 ff.
17. See the pope's address to the Preparatory Commission, June 30, 1959: "Today it is clear that it would be impossible and futile to enter into endless discussions which would lead nowhere." *H.-K.*, XIII, 1959, p. 515.
18. *H.-K.*, XIII, 1959, p. 543.

Chapter VII

The Mystery of the Division and the Unity of the Church

I

When the pope calls for a council, all of Christendom takes notice. The convening of such a council will most certainly affect the outer and inner conditions of the Christian churches, whatever resolutions the council adopts. Also through the council summoned by Pope John XXIII the state of Christendom will suffer changes in one way or another. One may certainly expect an effect for all of Christendom as a result of any great church convention, whether it be a plenary assembly of the World Council of Churches or the Lambeth Conference of the Anglican churches or a plenary assembly of the Lutheran World Federation or a pan-orthodox council. But the outcome of a council of the Roman Catholic Church would probably carry especial weight for all the churches of Christendom. Two reasons can be mentioned for this.

One reason consists in this that no Christian church keeps the wound of the division in Christendom open as inexorably as does the Roman Catholic Church. This church sees the unity of the church in the light of itself as the only true church. The inner difficulties into which its doctrine of the essence of the church is drawn through this fundamental conviction cannot be indicated here. But

170

it is obvious that the consequences of this opinion which the Roman Catholic Church has of itself work themselves out in history. If the unity of the church is found exclusively in the Roman Catholic Church, then all other Christian churches are not only churches divided among themselves but they are above all separated from the one true church which alone is founded by Jesus Christ. This does not mean that people in a church separated from Rome, according to Roman Catholic doctrine, do not stand in some kind of church relation to the Roman Catholic Church. But the claim of the Roman Catholic Church to be exclusively Una Sancta means that this church by the manner of its existence interposes the sword of division as no other church in Christendom does. From that very church, which with all the means at its command, especially the means of dogma, canon law, and liturgy, essays to demonstrate that the church is one and only one—from that very church issue the forces that have driven the greatest wedge of separation into Christendom.

Since the Roman Catholic Church is the church by which the division of Christendom is caused and maintained in an extraordinary way and with unusual force, its decisions also affect the total situation of Christendom in a marked way and with singular force. Whatever she may be doing: whether she institutes liturgical reforms, sets up new regulations in the area of canon law, or interprets her dogmas or develops them more fully, every one of her steps will touch the wound of divided Christendom with alleviating or aggravating effect, with good or evil result. No other church determines the depth of this wound as does the Roman Catholic Church.

The second reason for our thesis, introduced above, is connected with the first but is rooted still deeper in the history of Christendom. The character of at least four great church bodies of Christendom is determined in part by their relation to the Roman Catholic Church, or, more exactly, by their relation to the bishop of Rome. These four churches are the Orthodox churches of the East, the Lutheran churches, the Reformed churches, and the Anglican churches. The Old Catholic Church could also be included here. These churches cannot disregard the fact that the bishop of Rome lays claim to jurisdictional authority over them and enforces this claim with the strongest emphasis, even making salvation depend on it. When these churches wish to say how they understand the fact that they are churches, they must do so with reference to the bishop of Rome. None of these churches considers itself a "new" church that was newly "founded" at a definite point in the church's history. Every one of these churches claims to be an apostolic church. Every one of them is convinced that its Baptism, its proclamation of the Gospel, its Eucharist, its Absolution, its ministry go back to the institution of Christ. All these churches know that throughout the ages they have been connected with the church of the Apostles in a very definite, uninterrupted manner, though they may have interpreted this connection variously. Every one of them believes that this connection is by no means an imaginary thing but an actual reality. Therefore none of these churches can get away from the fact that there was a time when the continuity of the apostolic church did not include the breach with the bishop of Rome. The anathema which stands as a wall of separation between the church of Rome and these other churches did not always exist but occurred sometime in the history of Christendom. Will this wall of separation remain standing as long as the earth endures? What has come about in the course of history can also be resolved again in the course of history. Also the anathema which stands between the Roman Catholic Church and the other churches is not entitled to ceaseless existence. But according to the convictions of the churches named above, which have been separated from Rome, the duration of this division depends above all on the decisions of the Roman Catholic Church and thus on the decisions of the pope. Every one of these churches is waiting to see whether in the future of Christendom, before the return of Jesus Christ, a situation will arise in which the anathema through which they are separated from the bishop of Rome will become invalid and the fellowship with him which once existed will be restored. Will the council summoned by Pope John XXIII stiffen the wall of separation, or will there be a step, though it be a very small one, to bridge the chasm of separation? Whatever this council may do, its sessions and its resolutions will stand in the spotlight of this question. Therefore the bishops of the Roman Catholic Church can be assured that the churches separated from Rome will observe them very carefully when they will assemble for the council.

These reflections pertain in a special way to the churches whose character is determined by the Reformation of Martin Luther. In all schisms and divisions of the church the so-called non-theological factors have played a role. That also holds for the Reformation of the sixteenth century. But the influence of the non-theological factors can be of varying strength. It is clear that in the separation of the Anglican church from Rome under Henry VIII the non-theological factors carried a decisive weight. Also with regard to the schism between Rome and Byzantium, at its origin, doctrinal reasons played a subordinate part. The Reformation of Luther, however, was the result of a conflict involving the central content of the Gospel. For the Lutheran Reformation the papacy, according to 2 Thess. 2:4, became a manifestation of that which is antichristian in character, because the pope by his doctrines and ecclesiastic statutes, which he carried through by his claim to primacy in the church, hamstrung, corrupted, and persecuted the saving message of the Gospel and so endangered the salvation of souls to an unheard-of degree. It is not constellations of power-politics, nor contests for positions *of church politics or church law,* nor differences regarding ritual that lie at the root of the division between the pope's church and the churches of the Reformation but differences in which deliverance from divine judgment on the last day and purity of the apostolic Word and of the Sacraments instituted by Christ are at stake.

The pope and the other bishops of the Roman Catholic Church will assemble for the council in a situation in the history of the church marked by this that a great part of Christendom is separated from the Roman Catholic Church for the sake of the saving faith and of everlasting salvation. Those who are separated from Rome because of the doctrine of salvation look with especial concern on that which the pope and the bishops will do at the council. Will that on which the true salvation of souls rests be revealed to the council? Will the apostolic Gospel, given to us in Holy Scrip-ture, at the coming council be able, in this or that respect, to break through the manifold fetters and incrustations which the dogma and the statutes of the Roman Catholic Church have laid upon it?

Since the division between the Roman Catholic Church and the churches of Martin Luther's Reformation from its origin until now extends down to the uttermost depths of the issue of salva-tion, every decision of the coming council will be standing on the horizon of this issue and will thereby affect the relation between the two churches in a most delicate fashion.

In addition there is a final point that will cause the Lutheran churches especially to take notice when the pope convokes a coun-cil. From the very beginning Luther's Reformation desired nothing more ardently than a unanimous clarification of the questions raised regarding faith, doctrine, and order in the church. No other means is in sight by which a clarification leading to unity in the Gospel could be reached than an assembly of the churches in a council which is obedient to the only judge appointed for us by divine revelation—namely, God's apostolic Word present in his church through the Holy Scriptures. According to the conviction of the churches of the Reformation, neither the Council of Trent nor the first Vatican Council proved to be such a council. Nor can the approaching council, called by Pope John XXIII to the Vati-can, be the council for which the churches of the Reformation have been waiting since November 18, 1518, the day on which Luther issued his appeal for a general Christian council. Nevertheless, even today, when an "ecumenical council" is announced, the churches of the Reformation hope for a genuine ecumenical council some-time in the future which would bring peace to Christendom. The churches of the Reformation have never desired to exist as separate churches. They stand for the Reformation only for the sake of all Christendom. Wherever a transaction is noted in the area of the churches touching Christendom as a whole, the churches of the Ref-ormation will take note with rapt attention; because they have been waiting from century to century for the turn of affairs which will once more grant to Christendom as a whole unity in the pristine truth of the apostolic Gospel.

II

The expectations of the churches of the Reformation that the anathema which separates them from Rome may be overcome is, of course, of somewhat different character from what it was at the time of the Reformation. The reformers expected the conquest of the papal church through the spiritual power of the Gospel. The last day, to be sure, did not seem to them to be far away; nevertheless they continued to hope for the deliverance of Christendom from the papal captivity endangering the souls of men in the course of history—and that soon. This expectation was anything but the expression of a fanatical conception of history. Before the Counter Reformation began, about nine-tenths of the population of Germany of that day had become evangelicals. The northern part of Europe had almost entirely broken off fellowship with the Roman See. A strong spiritual influence of the Gospel, newly brought to light by the Reformation, extended far beyond the borders of the Romance countries. It cannot be our task here to investigate how the spread of the Reformation was checked or even suffered serious reverses. What we are concerned with in this connection is merely the observation that the churches of the Reformation must see the situation and the future of Christendom in a different light today from the way their fathers did in the sixteenth century. For every soberly thinking critic the expectation that the Roman Catholic Church will break down at any probable future time is out of the question. A visible overthrow of Catholicism in the course of history has been denied the Reformation. A consideration of the course of church history of the last four centuries must lead to the insight that the division of the churches which came about in western Christendom cannot be overcome by the removal of the Roman Catholic form of Christianity through the Gospel with the effect that only the churches of the Reformation would remain.

This is a very sober observation and really quite self-evident. But are we clear with regard to its spiritual and theological range? Do not the course of church history and the church-historical situation of the present demand also an intellectual theological penetration? How does our faith respond to the fact that the churches of the Reformation and the Anglican Church together with other Protestant groups, after a history of over 400 years, have only about half as many members as the Roman Catholic Church? To be sure, matters of majority and minority are not criteria by which the truth, and especially the truth of the Gospel, is judged. Many things even favor the view that the truth of the Gospel, in the long run, in this world will be held by only a suffering minority. But we must not allow this idea to satisfy us. Neither may we be content with the consideration that the truth of the Gospel, wherever it advances, arouses Satan, the prince of this world, and challenges his mighty powers of resistance; because we know that the prince of this world is held in check by God's almighty hand.

From whatever angle we may view our problem, simple faith will have to say to itself that it was not God's will that the Roman Catholic Church, with the pope at its head, should break down. According to God's will the churches of the Reformation, now as before, are to have the pope and the Roman Catholic Church, with their heresies, opposing them, and to exist even with this opposition. Meanwhile, we are convinced that God by no means demands of us that we forfeit the truth of the apostolic Gospel, as it has been brought to light again by Luther's Reformation, or that we affirm the false teachings of the pope and his councils.

But surely it cannot be God's will that Christendom be divided! What is God's real purpose regarding the history of his church? Are we here concerned only with the absolute secrecy of God's will? Does not God unequivocally desire the salvation of men? Does he not desire what is best for his people on earth? Surely, God cannot be in contradiction with himself! Could it perhaps be that in a most paradoxical and mysterious manner the fact that Christendom is to journey toward its eternal goal through long periods of time, suffering under a profound division, may still to be for its good? But wherein could that good consist in the midst of immeasurable harm? Before we try to answer this question, we must unroll the same problem for the Roman Catholic Church.

In consideration of late medieval Catholicism Martin Luther must have appeared to be a rebellious heretic. That God, through the work of Martin Luther, had accomplished something of decisive

worth for the church of Jesus Christ on earth, at that time remained entirely hidden from the pope, the papal court, and practically all the bishops. When large areas under the protection of the
territorial princes accepted the Reformation, papists indeed saw
the dangers of this heretical defection, but they found no trace of
the church in it any more. The heresy of the Augustinian monk of
Wittenberg was not the first one with which Rome had to deal.
There had been great heretical defections in earlier centuries—for
instance, Marcion and his numerous congregations, the communities of the Gnostics, the Arian bishops and their churches, the Albi-
genses, the Cathari, and others. Although these movements had for
a period of time lessened the influence of the Roman Catholic
Church in individual countries, yet, with the exception of the remnants of the Waldensians and the Hussites, they were extinguished
in the course of the church's history. Was the heretical movement
unleashed by the apostate Augustinian monk to have a different
destiny? Let it extend itself for the time being; sooner or later it
will collapse within itself. Has it not already broken up into frag-
ments? Have patience! Soon it will disappear again, save for slight
remnants of practically no importance.

It is not impossible that some leading personalities in the Roman
Catholic Church, who have no concrete conception and no exact
knowledge of the Reformation, still have similar opinions today.
They may, perhaps, think as follows: How many crises has the
Roman Catholic Church survived victoriously in the last 400 years!
What powers were released in her in the very repulse of the Witten-
berg Reformation! What a proud path leading from the Council of
Trent and over the first Vatican Council to the coming second
Vatican Council! In contrast to this, what examples of decadence
in Protestantism! What loss of dogmatical substance since the days
of rationalism! What splintering divisions, especially in the Anglo-
Saxon areas! Why need we be concerned about the so-called
churches of the Reformation? Let us leave them to the forces of
dissolution that are active within them and let us go our own way
unconcerned. Are there not many indications that Protestantism is
already being increasingly absorbed both by the natural increase
of our population and, with reference to the mission fields, by the

concentrated and well-planned employment of forces and resources on the part of the Roman Catholic Church? Has not Protestantism already lost the great influence it enjoyed during the development of modern science, literature, and art? It will now only be a question of time until its decay becomes manifest in all areas. Perhaps the hour is not far away in which the remnants of Protestantism in which some genuine longing for the church is still alive will return home from their prodigal journey into a "far country." Let us prepare for that hour. Let such preparation be one of the tasks of the coming council. All else we can confidently leave to the course of history.

If there are bishops, theologians, and laymen in the Roman Catholic Church who still think like that today, it will not be easy to convince them that they misjudge the nature of the Reformation and the churches of the Reformation and that they fail completely to recognize the meaning of the division of the western churches. We may be thankful that in the realms of the French, the Dutch, and the German languages a different evaluation of the Reformation, of the churches of the Reformation, and of the present hour in history is gaining ground among Roman Catholic theologians—and not only among them. But even one who might still be entertaining the views sketched above should be willing to consider the following: Four hundred years of church history are not a mere episode. As we indicated above, the churches of the Reformation were not able to overthrow the Roman Catholic Church during this period. The same holds true for the Roman Catholic Church. It must admit that the reforms of the Council of Trent and the forces of the Counter Reformation have also not been able to destroy the churches of the Reformation, neither have they been able to eliminate them. While this is being written, the churches federated in the World Council of Churches are preparing for their coming plenary convention at New Delhi. With few exceptions representatives of all the larger churches which directly or indirectly trace their origin to the Reformation will be assembled there. In addition, the Old (Roman) Catholic churches, a large number of Orthodox churches, and other ancient churches of the East will be represented. If we were to try to estimate the number of baptized Christians living in these churches, we would certainly arrive at a figure of over three hundred millions. Anyone who may have followed the almost fifty-year-old ecumenical movement, if only in a literary way, will not get the impression that in this movement he encounters only the decadence of churches banded together in order to maintain bare existence. He would rather be unable to escape the impression that there has been increasing consolidation and strengthening in these churches. Especially the fact that this movement and its agencies have the characteristics of a church has come more distinctly to view in the course of years.

It is still too soon to ask the bishops and theologians of the Roman Catholic Church how they will receive this factual situation spiritually and theologically and how they will treat it dogmatically? Surely, it should be evident that one can no longer do justice to this factual situation by mere tactical deliberations. However the figures concerning conversion may appear in the future, no one can expect any longer that the division which exists between the 430 million Catholics on the one side and the far more than 300 million non-Catholic, properly baptized Christians on the other, will be overcome through the conversion of individuals. One might ponder whether the oriental churches united with Rome do not point to a model for reunion which in the eyes of the Roman Catholic Church offers a chance for the solution of the problem. But such a plan would include that the churches separated from Rome would first unconditionally give up the dogmatical conviction which they have been holding, so far as they contradict the dogmas of the Roman Catholic Church and, wholly accepting the dogmas of the Roman Catholic Church, would place themselves under the jurisdiction and the infallible doctrinal guidance of the pope. Also here a sober evaluation of the situation would arrive at the conclusion that none of the churches belonging to the World Council, nor even a part of any of these churches, could be willing to enter such a corporate union with Rome.

From whatever angle we approach the problem with which we are here engaged, it appears that as far as men can judge there can be no solution either today or tomorrow. It is in the realm of possibility that genuine church fellowship and church union can come about in increasing measure among the churches separated from Rome. But up to the present not the smallest possibility has appeared for ending the division between the Roman Catholic Church and the churches of the Reformation. This division is so insuperable because it is rooted exclusively in the area of the fundamental conception of salvation and therefore doctrine itself. Perhaps it is not entirely impossible that the doctrines of justification by grace alone and of the importance of good works at the last judgment could be clarified on both sides to such an extent that they would no longer necessarily be considered divisive. But a corresponding agreement with regard to the Roman Catholic dogmas of the sacrifice of the mass, of the papacy, and of the Virgin Mary is out of the question. What the Roman Catholic Church teaches on these points is in direct contradiction to the Gospel and is therefore heresy in the strictest sense of the word for evangelical Christians. It is true that in some areas a theological interpretation of doctrines can make for mutual agreement in some respects. But in view of the three areas of dogma mentioned above, even the greatest possible mutual advances cannot close the gap that divides the churches and necessitates mutual exclusion. Here we are up against a wall which, as matters now stand, cannot be breached from either side, either from the direction of Roman Catholic theology or from that of Reformation theology. Neither is able to convince the other. Do we not therefore have to live with the division?

As Christians and as a church we have to reckon with a history that extends into the future. Certainly, this future is circumscribed by the last day. We are already standing in the light of that day. Therefore his future is not simply at our "disposal." All our visions of the future can be overthrown by God's intervention. We have this future as we have the other things that belong under the heading of "daily bread"—that is, we have them as though we had them not. Yet we must take the future seriously because it is within it that we are responsible before God.

In this future the churches of the Reformation have to live as churches separated from the Roman Catholic Church. But the Roman Catholic Christians must say the same thing on their part. Both the Roman Catholic Church and the churches of the Reformation, in the future of which we are speaking here, will have to live under the burden of a division based on this that we must charge each other with heresy.

This, at first glance, seems to be a very simple observation. But the more we think about it, and the more we try to see this observation in the light of our Christian faith, the more mysterious will the fact of the division become and the more extensively will our present theological thinking and the work of the churches be determined by the same. We *have* to live with the division! We have to *live* with the division! Will the responsible groups dealing with the preparations for the coming council of the Roman Catholic bishops have a clear understanding of this situation? Will the council itself consider it? Will the theological reflections and the decisions regarding church law at the council be penetrated by this understanding?

III

We restrict our discussion to the division existing between the churches of the Reformation and the Roman Catholic Church. Each of the two "religious parties," as they were still referred to in the 16th century, has to live with the division. If both have to live with the division, must they not also live *with each other* under the division? Divided in the faith—yet living with each other! Is that possible?

The first answer given to this question in Christendom was for a long time negative. The conviction prevailed that it was impossible for churches which must charge each other with heresies to live with each other. Moreover, the Reformation, as is well known, still held fast to this negative answer in a very incisive manner. For Luther and his time the idea that the papal church and the church of the Reformation could live side by side in a city or principality with equal rights was impracticable. He had indeed come to know that no one can be forced to believe and that no one dare be put to death for his faith. But the public proclamation of a false doctrine and the conducting of a false worship service, according to his conviction, could not be tolerated in a place where the pure Gospel had been brought to light and had been accepted in faith by the

government. Therefore, for people of a different faith there remained only the liberty of emigrating from a Protestant country
to a Catholic country.

In this connection, one must consider that it was not a matter
of emigrating from the German Empire but "only" from a certain
principality. Under the emperor the churches of the Augsburg Confession and the papists remained together as members of the
empire. It is very moving to observe how Luther took his stand
for the same emperor who had declared him an outlaw, when it
came to supporting him in his resistance to the Turks. For the
Anabaptists and the fanatics Luther, to be sure, saw no territory
in which they might be tolerated. But according to the stipulations
of the religious peace of Augsburg in the year 1555, the territories
adhering to the papal church and those in which the Augsburg
Confession prevailed were not only able to exist peaceably side
by side in the empire but were supposed to do so.

We cannot here pursue the question as to how the problem of
tolerance in Europe and in North America progressively developed
since the Reformation. The result of this development can no longer
be abolished. Put into few words it is as follows: Churches of the
Reformation and Roman Catholic churches can and should live
together in every state, enjoying the same rights in civil life and
with regard to the laws of the state. It is high time that the last
remnants of restrictions limiting the free exercise of religion be
removed. In view of the situation in Spain, South America, and
elsewhere, the coming council will have abundant material for its
work if it accepts this principle. Can it really close its heart to the
acceptance of this principle? The weighty problems arising from an
impartial regulation of the civil rights of different faiths in the area
of education are not hidden from us. But these difficulties can be
solved both in principle and in practise. Everything will depend on
this that we not be amenable to such solutions only when they
are advantageous to our own faith or when the secularization of the
conception of the state forces them upon us, but that we, recognizing
the fundamental doctrinal lawfulness of these impartial solutions,
bring them about, not by compulsion, but on account of our own
convictions—not for the sake of outer or ideal advantages, not from

dogmatical indifference, but from a new ethical and doctrinal view of other confessions from which we are divided in the faith. The history of the problem of tolerance and its result demands of the coming council a rethinking of the question regarding the light in which we see those from whom we are divided at the Lord's altar in their relation to the Lord, to the Spirit, to the Gospel, to the truth, to the kingdom of God.

The question as to how Christians and churches that are divided in faith can still live together receives its sharpest edge in the so-called mixed marriage. By "mixed marriage" we mean here a marriage of baptized Christians who belong to divided churches, especially a marriage in which one partner is Protestant and the other Roman Catholic. The Protestant church points out to its members the difficulties and the dangers that are encountered in such a marriage. To the complete fellowship of man and wife this doubtlessly also belongs that both be agreed in the confession of the Gospel and that both together receive the body and blood of Christ. Anyone who becomes a partner to a mixed marriage must forego this fulfillment of conjugal fellowship. Questions as to the form which the common life of faith in the home is to take, in which faith the children are to be brought up, and the like, cause great difficulties. Nevertheless, mixed marriages are numerous. There are reasons to believe that their number will even increase in the future. Experience shows that a mixed marriage does not in every case result from spiritual failure, indifference to truth, or a lack of earnest thinking. Entering into a mixed marriage can also involve a genuine spiritual decision. Light is shed on this question by the way in which the subject of mixed marriages is treated in contemporary literature. Yet, in every case, the mixed marriage provides the heaviest burden by which the relation between the divided churches is put to the test. The relevant regulations imposed by Roman Catholic law in the Codex Juris Canonici (the body of ecclesiastic law) is subject to serious doubts. These doubts also apply to the theological convictions underlying the regulations. There are few points in which theological disregard of the Sacrament of Holy Baptism appears so strongly as in the way the present law of the Roman Catholic Church concerning mixed marriages regards the non-Catholic party to the marriage! Why, he is treated just as if he were not baptized at all. Will the coming council give attention to these problems? History shows that on the basis of the dogma of the Roman Catholic Church other legal solutions of the problem of the mixed marriage are possible than those set forth in the Codex Juris Canonici. If anywhere, reform is urgently required at this point. But also in this connection a fundamental rethinking concerning the baptized Christian belonging to a separated church, and therefore concerning this church itself, is not to be evaded. Should not something commonly held, despite the division with which we have to live, come to view—something in the nature of truly belonging to Christ, something in the nature of actual gifts of the Holy Spirit, something in the nature of present participation in eternal salvation—in short, something held in common which would demand and make possible also a different solution of the problem of mixed marriages?

It will be well if the churches in those countries whose inhabitants, according to denominational statistics, belong, with few exceptions, to the same Christian denomination will become aware of the fact that they are fundamentally and practically drawn into the sphere of the same problems which prevail in the countries where there are various confessions. As a result of the social development which in our century as with the force of destiny affects mankind everywhere, there are no longer any cultural reservations, and there are no confessional ones left either. These are facts which the churches must ponder, too. Humanity is coalescing. In this development there are reverses, but as a whole it cannot be halted. In this development good is found mingled with evil. We shall not be able to say that only evil is at work in it. We shall have to ask whether what is happening in the present history of civilization is not meant to be a challenge to Christians, to which they must find an answer that is good and pleasing to God. We shall have to ask whether the standardization of a technologically fashioned human civilization, though doubtless dangerous, could not perhaps be made to serve a more profound idea of unity—namely, an idea of unity which after all is natural to the one human family.

These questions can only be mentioned here. But it must be clear to us that we are considering the mutual relation of the Roman

Catholic Church and the churches of the Reformation at a very definite point of human history. The historical situation of mankind at the present time not only may but must enter into our thinking concerning the mystery of the division and of the unity of the church. It would of course be entirely wrong if we were to derive our standards for our theological dicisions from the historical situation. Far be it from us to do that! The standard for our theological decisions can only be the will of God revealed in his Word. But the question as to the concrete form our obedience to the revealed will of God must have, if it is really to be obedience to the living God, cannot disregard the historical situation in which it is rendered. It must rather seek to master this situation in a salutary way and thus regard it as something to be rightly molded.

While we are following this principle, we must observe that in the social pattern of present-day humanity the churches of the Reformation and the Roman Catholic Church are no longer territorially and sociologically divided churches, although, as heretofore, they are still ecclesiologically divided. Though it was not the case before 1914, the churches of the Reformation and the Roman Catholic Church today and in the future, whether they like it or not, must live together socially. There is now at least mutual cognizance of one another's existence in many areas, and this will continue to increase in the future. Pet ideas which we form about the nature of the other party can be maintained less and less as time proceeds. Anyone who maintains or even strengthens pet ideas which do not correspond to the facts, in every case hurts the cause of the church to which he belongs. Intellectual contact between the faithful of the different confessions in the areas of literature, art, and science are already a matter of course. The cultural peculiarities which may still remain alive in present and future patterns of human society will necessarily provide fruitful contacts with the contributions of other confessions.

If denominationally divided churches can no longer exist in sociological and cultural isolation from each other, it will doubtless be an incentive for rethinking the fact of denominational divisions. For it could be that a historical situation in the West, and among men in general, which in principle no longer exists, has helped to determine our doctrinal opinion of the other party in a manner which cannot continue to exist in the presence of the truth of the apostolic Gospel. The question: "How do we look upon the ecclesiastical and spiritual state of the Christian and his church who are separated from us?" must be restated and rethought on a new level no less by the Roman Catholic Church than by the Protestant churches. When the bishops of the Roman Catholic Church in the near future assemble for their council, they will certainly also consider the general social situation of mankind. Will they also be conscious of this that this situation demands, with special urgency, an examination of the answers which the Roman Catholic Church, through those authorized to teach, has previously given to the question about the nature of the Christians separated from Rome? Will they sense the weight which this question has in our day—namely, what the churches of the Reformation—aside from the charge of heresy brought against them—in their inner spiritual and ecclesiastic nature really are? Should the dreadful division under which Christendom will have to live in the future not be able to unfold its "mystery" in a positive direction?

The necessity for this achievement of a genuine "togetherness" by the Christian churches in the midst of their denominational division rests especially on the world-spanning phenomenon of a consciously a-religious, not infrequently anti-Christian, secularism. The secularism we have in mind here is something fundamentally different from the purely worldly character of civil and institutional science and economy. Who would deny that there is an abundance of areas of human existence in which reason is correctly and competently the rule for knowledge and action? Moreover, reason has its peculiar depth. The worldly character of the civilization it produces is not superficial. The problem which the secularism of our century poses does not rest in reason's claim for the modeling of its own proper areas of life. The problem is rather a matter of keeping reason within its proper sphere. Reason can and should know about its own limitations. But it can also revolt against this possibility and obligation. Therein lies a fatal threat to human existence. In our day this threat is already present in many forms. It will also obtain in the future. This threat has its roots in a fundamental and radical denial of that reality to which we refer with the words: God, revelation, faith, prayer, eternal life. In such a denial, reason goes beyond its legitimate secular realm and raises a claim that extends into the dimension of an absolute claim regarding salvation. Where this occurs, we are dealing with a secularism which, besides denying the reality of God and of his revelation, sets up a dogmatic principle and therefore also provides active expression for its denial. This secularism, in its dogmatic a-religious and anti-Christian attitude, becomes itself a kind of religion—that is, a pseudo-religion. It therefore hurls its anathema against all genuine religion, especially against Christianity, which cannot but bear witness to the exclusive nature of salvation in Jesus Christ.

Deeper than the divisions among the Christian churches is the chasm gouged out in humanity by the secularism of which we are speaking. The fact that this chasm has burst open will necessarily help to determine the relation of the Christian churches to one another. Moreover, the relation of Christianity to the non-Christian religions will not remain untouched by this world situation. However, we want to confine ourselves here exclusively to the consideration of the relation of the Christian churches to one another. In their ecclesiological division no change has come about because of the chasm that has burst open. And yet something has changed. The denominational division has moved into a new light. Its theological-doctrinal acuteness has in no way been rendered relative. But it has become evident that there is another division in the human family, which puts that which is held in common by the divided churches into a new light with a view to its importance for the well-being of mankind. To be sure, in view of the a-religious anti-Christian secularism facing them, the Christian churches will be all the more painfully conscious of their divided condition. But this sorrow at the same time unfetters a type of oneness suggested by that which they possess in common. In view of the chasm that has burst open through secularism, the recognition of this common possession, which had never been entirely lost in theological thinking, will have to become fruitful in a new way. When the Council of Trent assembled, there was hardly a trace of this secularism in the general cultural consciousness of the West. At the time of the

first Vatican Council it doubtless was already at work. But what incisive changes have come about in this respect since 1870 in the
total spiritual situation of mankind! When the bishops of the Roman
Catholic Church assemble for the Second Vatican Council, they will
doubtless be conscious of the changed world situation. Will they
collectively be aware of the fact that the mutual relation between
the Roman Catholic Church and the churches of the Reformation is
being affected by the cleft which "dogmatic" and totalitarian secularism is drawing through the human family? In view of this cleft
and in the midst of the denominational division should one not be
able to descry a togetherness of the "divided brethren," which should
not only have some practical results in the area of church law but
which, above all, wants to be received and mastered in a theological-doctrinal way?

The solution of this task might be of great importance to the future of mankind in still another respect. It is in connection with the
historical development of the intellectual attitude indicated in the
foregoing that mankind today, in the midst of the process of coalescing, is being torn asunder as never before by ideological, sociological, and political systems. In those areas of life, the solution of whose
problems lies in the province of secular reason, convictions and
ideologies have arisen involving an exclusive, quasi-religious absolute claim that must have a divisive effect. Can the systems of the
West and of the East be really united in the United Nations Organization and, in spite of profound differences, yet be aware of a joint
responsibility for the weal of humanity? We are all perfectly aware
of the fact that the future of mankind in large measure depends on
the answer to this question. However, we probably do not sense
quite so keenly the fact that the Christian churches, on an altogether
different level, are confronted with an analogous problem. The
Christian churches are confronted with the following question: Can
the organizations of baptized Christians that exclude one another
from church fellowship still live together as divided churches in the
one Christendom? Should it not be possible to find such a solution
to this question which, by virtue of the doctrinal clarity achieved,
would be able to transform the concrete historical division of the
churches of the Reformation and the Roman Catholic Church into

a genuine spiritual togetherness, though the denominational division of these churches continue as heretofore?

It is quite evident that the task to be accomplished here is extraordinarily difficult. I do not hesitate to declare this task to be the most difficult one that has been set for the church in her whole previous history. Its solution is more difficult than the solving of the puzzling problems of modern society, business, and politics. The strain which is put on theological-doctrinal thinking cannot as yet be estimated; it is just beginning to appear in rough outline and to be consciously perceived. Hardly less exertion will be required in finding a lawful structure to embody this solution adequately. It will be still more difficult to carry through the practical results of such a solution into the mission fields, with their great temptations to rivalry and displays of power. But if this task which confronts today's Christendom is to find a solution, we may be sure that its power would be felt far beyond the realm of the church in the narrower sense. If the Roman Catholic Church and the churches of the Reformation should be so fortunate as to find such a solution for their mutual relation which, while the present anathema is retained, could give expression to the common sharing of Jesus Christ, of the Holy Spirit, and of the life of God the Father and make this sharing effective in the history of mankind, then this solution would surely prove to be a spiritual force which would cast its beam with the power of a symbol upon the disrupted human family.

We observe the following: On the sociological-political plane and on the spiritual-denominational plane mankind in our day is facing problems of analogous structure. On both planes there are convictions which lay claim to exclusive validity. On both planes, however, there is being traced in the rough the recognition that the claim to exclusive validity must be imbedded in something possessed in common, if its unequivocal demand is not to bring an incalculable misfortune on all mankind. This is excommunication on the basis of a conviction concerning an "absolute" truth, and yet at the same time a sharing on the basis of something that is indestructibly and really a common possession.

Should not the possibility of a solution—of this squaring of the circle—on the sociological-political plane, finally depend on a solution first being found and lived on the spiritual-denominational plane?

IV

It is impossible for us here to give even a mere sketch of the solution of the problem assigned to us. We can, in concluding our discussion, as it were, discharge only a few arrows in the direction in which the solution must be sought. The place from which we look for the solution is the understanding that the division between the churches of the Reformation and the Roman Catholic Church is based on both sides upon the necessity for a spiritual decision demanded by conscience. We should mutually own up to this that the anathema and the damnamus hurled by both sides does not proceed from stubbornness, levity, and contentiousness but from a sense of responsibility for the apostolic Word transmitted to the church.

We Protestant Christians indeed cannot understand how, for instance, the dogma of the bodily assumption of Mary into heaven could be proclaimed with a responsible attitude based on the apostolic tradition given in the New Testament. We cannot understand how Pope Pius XII could declare that we who dispute the truth of this dogma have "entirely fallen away from the divine and catholic faith." We must confess that almost all of the anathemas pronounced against the doctrine of the Protestant church since the Reformation contradict the pure apostolic Word of the Holy Scriptures. It is true, an examination would be in order to determine which anathemas actually concern the doctrine of the evangelical Lutheran church. Much clarification of theological controversy in this matter is no doubt still to be done. But there can be no question that the decisive convictions of all the churches of the Reformation are actually rejected by the Roman Catholic Church. We know about the historical conditions that have led to such rejection. We do not overlook the abundance of non-theological factors which have often unfolded their disastrous power at the very decisive turning points in the history of the church. But we cannot and will not dispute the fact that the Roman Catholic bishops and theologians rendered their decisions because they felt themselves responsible for preserving the apostolic tradition—no matter how incomprehensible and painful the decision may be to us. Nor do we wish to fail to recognize that in their anathemas, care for the welfare of human souls is involved. The churches of the Reformation should be ready to observe that the final and decisive motive for the rejection of reformative doctrine on the part of the Roman Catholic Church is not theological disputatiousness, not a matter of maintaining positions of power in the church, nor irresponsible dealing with divine revelation, but anxiety concerning the truth of apostolic doctrine and care for souls entrusted to her.

When Christians charge Christians with heresy, they are right in doing so only when they are actually convinced that responsibility for the apostolic Word entrusted to them and responsibility for the salvation of souls demand this extreme course. Defense of the pure apostolic Word and care for the salvation of souls are closely connected; because the means are contained within the apostolic Word —namely, the oral proclamation of the Gospel, Baptism, the Lord's Supper, and the declaration of the forgiveness of sins in Absolution, by which sinners receive the gift of salvation which Christ has won. Anyone who corrupts these means at the same time endangers the salvation of man.

A particularly dangerous form of the corruption of the saving Means of Grace making salvation dependent upon something that is not contained in the apostolic Word but is demanded of man as an additional performance, perhaps even as an additional act of faith. Martin Luther's attack on the papacy is not understood at all if this attack is not seen on the level of this question. Luther knew by experience how the Gospel-corrupting statutes of the papal church, prescribed as being necessary for salvation, can thrust the baptized Christian into utter anguish of soul without being able to deliver him from such anguish. The fact that Luther saw in the papacy the power of the Antichrist is, above all, based on his own experience of the extent to which the papacy was hurling the baptized Christian into the deepest torments of soul. It did this, he realized, by no longer binding salvation to belief in the Gospel and to confidence in the promise of the forgiveness of sins for Christ's sake but by making salvation dependent upon the fulfillment of rules imposed by the church, ostensibly necessary to salvation, and upon accomplishments of the Christian himself.

We are not ignorant of the fact that a reform of Roman Catholicism observable since the Council of Trent is spoken of with a certain justice. But in one respect the situation is unchanged. Still in our day the churches of the Reformation have to charge the Roman Catholic Church with failing to keep pure and clean the apostolic Word given to us in Holy Scripture. We are also aware of a danger to the apostolic Word in the churches of the Reformation, where, under the influence of rationalism, historism, and modern philosophical trends, theological doctrines have arisen which question the validity of the apostolic Word—though in a far different way from that obtaining in Roman Catholicism—and which help to promote a message that offers baptized Christians stones instead of bread. The churches of the Reformation suffer severely from this thorn in the flesh. But in this connection we are concerned, not with mutually comparing faulty developments in each other's camps, but with giving attention to normative fundamental confessional principles. The claim of bishop of Rome to jurisdiction over the entire Christian church and the mark of infallibility conceded to his doctrinal decisions rendered ex cathedra is by no means a faulty development within Catholicism which could be corrected any day, but an irrevocable dogma; in short, a foundation stone of the Roman Catholic Church. The cultic veneration of Mary is not a wild shoot on the tree of the spiritual life of this church; it is not a tolerated accommodation to certain ancient Mediterranean pious practices; rather, it is founded on formal dogmas and penetrates the liturgy and the prayer life of this church to the highest hierarchical extremities. The sacrificial body of Jesus Christ, offered up daily to God by the priest consecrated for this holy act as a sacrifice of reconciliation in order to obtain salvation and blessings and manifold kinds of help from God, is not the expression of liturgical exuberance but an unequivocally established dogma determining the very heart of the worship of the Roman Catholic Church. When it is said that man's own preparation for the reception of justification and his willing cooperation are decisive for the measure in which we receive the sanctifying righteousness of God, that is not a theological opinion which we may excuse by pointing to the missionary situation and the educational tasks of the church but, again, a firmly established dogma. From the point of view of this dogma one of the most important repudiating judgments of rejection is hurled at the churches of the Reformation, namely the sentence: "Anyone who maintains that the sinner is justified by faith alone and who understands this in such a way as to think that nothing else is demanded by way of cooperation in obtaining the grace of justification, and that it is in no wise necessary to prepare oneself and make oneself receptive by the exercise of one's own will, falls under the anathema."

These dogmas, as such, must penetrate the entire body of doctrine of the Roman Catholic Church, as well as all its official transactions and its religious life. The churches of the Reformation are convinced that the preaching and the practice determined by these dogmas affects the purity of the apostolic Gospel and therefore, by inner necessity, endangers the salvation of souls. What that saving faith is can hardly become visible in the maze of these dogmas. This saving faith is that which under the judgment of the law Christians actually lay hold of God's forgiveness through the grace assured for us by the proclamation of the Gospel. Is not the danger present in the Roman Catholic Church that the Christian, who through life and death approaches his Judge, *will put his trust in this* that the Virgin Mary will intercede also for his soul's salvation, that also for him the sacrifice of the mass is offered by the priest, that he himself will have put forth a sufficient effort of will to prepare himself for the reception of grace and, in addition, from having cooperated with the grace received, will be able to exhibit meritorious good works of his own on judgment day? He who dies with a misplaced confidence does not die well. A Christian who would base his hope of salvation on a work of Mary of which the Scriptures know nothing, on a sacrifice of reconciliation offered by the church, and on his own effort of will and his own cooperation with divine grace will discover that he has built his house on sand when the storms of temptation break over him and the accusations of divine will confront him with its demands.

Should not the Roman Catholic bishops, who will soon be assembling for a council, be able to understand that what divides Protestant Christians from Rome is still today a question involving salvation? Should it not be possible to find unanimity at the council on this point that the motive which still in our day makes it necessary for the churches of the Reformation to reject some of the central dogmas of the Roman Catholic Church, is their responsibility for the defense of the apostolic Word given in the Scriptures and therefore also their responsibility for keeping open the way of salvation on which men may be saved from the depths of temptation? Could not such an understanding, if it prevailed at the council, put the mutual relation of the divided churches, despite that division, on a new basis, on a spiritual basis, on a basis of mutual respect? If I realize that also the other party, in his way and compared to his knowledge, wants to understand my responsibility concerning the Gospel truth delivered to us by the apostles of Jesus Christ—further, that he also wants to share my responsibility for the salvation of the souls (this means that he regards himself as being placed before God in the same final responsibility, although he sees the awareness of the responsibility in a different light than I do)— would not then such a realization have to show a mutual way in the midst of the ecclesiological division—would it not point out something in common that refers to the very essence of the church?

But with these deliberations we have not yet touched the real mystery of the division of the occidental church. We have seen that the churches of the Reformation and the Roman Catholic Church are divided by their mutual accusation of false doctrine. This directs our attention to the question of the relation of heresy to the church. According to our arguments concerning the connection between the defense of the pure apostolic Gospel and the salvation of souls from the judgment of God, it should be clear that the assembly of baptized Christians, among whom preaching and the administration of the Sacraments are such as to endanger the souls of men, cannot be the place where I can see the marks of the church shining clearly. In that assembly I therefore cannot find the place in which I can confess the one holy catholic and apostolic church and receive the Sacrament of the Altar. But the question is whether or not there is anything left of the church at all in that assembly of

Christians with whom I am not able to realize church fellowship. It is so hard to answer this question because the New Testament evidently does not refer to the form of church division under which we are forced to live today. It is true that the New Testament is aware of the necessity of the anathema against heresy. But what is the heresy of the apostolic age? According to the New Testament, heresy which is excluded from the church by the anathema is a conception of redemption which completely undermines salvation in Christ. As an example we might mention the astronomically* determined judaizing doctrine of Law-piety which Paul anathematizes in the Epistle to the Galatians. Or we might mention the docetic heresy against which the First Epistle of John draws a sharp line because it denies the incarnation of the Son of God, or "what is falsely called knowledge (gnosis)," which is combatted in the Pastoral Epistles. In the churches threatened by such heresies the Christian faith and Christian salvation, in their entirety, were always at stake.

As unequivocally as the line was drawn with reference to heresy in the age of the Apostles, so manifold were the different forms of Christian doctrine and Christian manner of life within the one apostolic church. This multifarious character of religious conviction and doctrinal form was possible only because there was full agreement in the fundamental conception of salvation in Christ and of his message. But within this common possession we often observe differences of considerable depth. We know that between Paul and the church at Jerusalem considerable tension prevailed at times concerning the significance of the Old Testament and its application to the Christian church. The danger of a "division of the church" —humanly speaking—was not beyond the range of possibility. This danger was overcome. Even James, at the apostolic council in Jerusalem, extended his right hand to Paul as a sign of the prevailing church fellowship. But what differences continued to prevail, in spite of this agreement, between the theological convictions of James and Paul! What a difference between the churches of the Jewish Christians in Palestine and the Christian churches of the

---

*Referring to the anxious observance of "days, and months, and seasons, and years" (Gal. 4:10).—The Translator.

one-time heathen peoples in Paul's missionary realms! Nevertheless they held fast to the church fellowship existing between them.

A glimpse of the New Testament Scriptures will show us that under certain circumstances very profound differences in faith and in theological doctrine are matters with which one should and can bear. But the New Testament also impresses upon us that the anathema is necessary when salvation in Christ as a whole or its foundation are at stake. We are convinced that the heresies of a Marcion, of the Gnostics, of an Arius, and of a Pelagius do indeed attack the salvation in Christ as a whole together with its foundation. But how about the divisions of the church in the Reformation of the 16th century? Do they not constitute something new in the history of Christianity as regards the question we are considering here? Did they not include new ecclesiological circumstances which could not be mastered with these directions of the New Testament Scriptures? It is true, as far as the New Testament is concerned, that in the congregations of the heretics who were affected by the ban of the apostolic anathema the reality of the Christian church was obliterated. Can this judgment be upheld in view of the division of churches and their mutual exclusion of each other which came about in the 16th century?

Let us, to begin with, look at the divisions between the Lutheran, the Reformed, and the Anglican churches. These divisions are also based on the rejection of false doctrine. That is especially clear with reference to the division existing between the Lutherans and the Reformed. Nevertheless, none of these churches can say of the others that they call into question salvation in Christ as a whole or its foundation. Nevertheless, for doctrinal reasons, there is no church fellowship between these churches. The error in individual doubtless very important doctrines, as in the doctrine of predestination and that of the Lord's Supper, was felt to be so profound that a sense of responsibility for the preservation of the apostolic Word and for the salvation of souls prevented the establishment of church fellowship. But none of these churches would dare say of the other that nothing of the church is to be found in it. None would dare to say of the other that in it the salvation of Christ is subverted. That is a circumstance which evidently is not foreseen in the New Testament.

The World Council of Churches has come to see that it is one of its most important tasks, in view of its responsibility regarding the apostolic testimony, to clarify this situation with regard to theological dogma and church practice.

May we also give a place to the division which exists between the Roman Catholic Church and the churches of the Reformation in this cycle of questions? Must the churches of the Reformation say to the Roman Catholic Church: "Your heresies completely overthrow Christ's salvation as a whole together with its foundation. With you the church of Christ is simply no longer to be found"? Must the Roman Catholic Church answer with the same charge? We shall see that it actually does. In its official doctrinal pronouncements it applies the New Testament position about those excommunicated by the anathema undiminished and unbroken to the churches of the Reformation. In contrast, the ecclesiological opinion of the churches of the Reformation with regard to the Roman Catholic Church is essentially different.

The churches of the Reformation see in the Roman Catholic Church a high degree of danger for salvation in Christ. Therefore they will not be able to establish church fellowship with it so long as this danger continues. From the beginning they have never disputed that salvation in Christ has not yet been extinguished in the Roman Catholic Church, despite the fact that it is endangered by false doctrine, but have maintained that it is still being proffered effectively. Luther never doubted that also in the papal church, in which he saw the power of the Antichrist at work, "the true old church with its Baptism and the Word of God nevertheless still remains" and that the temple of God is being built through it. He did not dispute that in it there are still the Means of Grace through which men are saved. In this connection he considered the Sacrament of Baptism to be especially important. He never doubted that under the papacy throughout the centuries this Sacrament was preserved in all its salutary effectiveness. He was also convinced that in the Roman Catholic celebration of the Mass, in which the congregation communed, the body and blood of Christ were truly present and were distributed under the bread, in spite of the profound corruption such a celebration exhibited as compared with

its true character as instituted by Christ. To be sure, he considered
it to be extraordinarily difficult—his own experience speaking here—
for an adult person to hear the voice of the saving Gospel in the
papal church of his time, but he was convinced that it actually
did occur here and there. Thus, the churches of the Reformation—
including the Reformed church—never left the matter doubtful that
"traces of the church" remained under the papacy, also after the
division of the church was consummated. Today Protestant doctrine
still teaches that in the Roman Catholic Church salvation in Christ
is actually being offered and received, that men are being saved,
and that they are even now being added as living members to the
body of Christ, which is his church. *Jesus Christ, the head of the
church, has in his body living members who live and die within the
denominational borders of the Roman Catholic Church.* This is an
incontestable dogma of the churches of the Reformation. The
churches of the Reformation therefore have a message somewhat
as follows for the Roman Catholic Church: "Your heresies are a
serious danger for salvation in Christ. Therefore we are separated
from you. But your heresies still do not invalidate everything. Therefore we may still believe the Church of God still really exists within
your boundaries, although we no longer see the pure proclamation
of the Gospel and the administration of the Sacraments according
to their institution, the marks of the true apostolic church, in your
midst. Yet we know that in the Means of Grace, so far as they are
still being preserved in your midst, Jesus Christ is still mighty to
save men from sin and death and even now grants the forgiveness
of sins and eternal life to those who believe in life and in death in
him and in his promises."

What does the Roman Catholic Church say to us, the churches
of the Reformation, with regard to the same matter? When we
examine the official doctrinal pronouncements of the Roman Catholic Church concerning our question, we are most deeply perplexed
with the fact that the Roman Catholic Church does not say of the
churches of the Reformation what we have just said about her,
although she does at least recognize the "validity" of the Baptism
dispensed by the churches of the Reformation. According to the
official doctrinal pronouncements of the Roman Catholic Church,

members on the body of Christ are in reality found only within the visible denominational boundaries of the Roman Catholic Church. The visible church under the pope and the mystical body of Christ are identified to the extent that outside of *this* visibly circumscribed church within the present and future time on earth, there are no living members of the body of Jesus Christ. That, of course, does not mean that human beings who are not members of the Roman Catholic Church are therefore eternally lost. For centuries the doctrine has been accepted that a person who desires salvation in Christ, but is prevented by definite circumstances from receiving Baptism, may receive the grace of Baptism through a desire and a wish for it. The same holds for the Sacraments of Penitence and the Eucharist. The Council of Trent expressly retained this doctrine of the "votum" or desire. It was especially Pope Pius XII who in our own time by doctrinal declarations sought to give an answer to the question concerning the eternal lot of non-Catholics—among whom schismatics, heretics, Jews, and heathens are included—by referring to the ancient doctrine of the desire for the Sacrament. In agreement with formulations of the prominent polemical theologian Bellarmin (1542-1621) Pope Pius XII also granted to the longing and wish for membership in the church a certain amount of significance for the attainment of eternal salvation.

The question concerning the lot of non-Catholics of necessity became especially disturbing for the Roman Catholic Church's understanding of herself as a church. We get an idea of this when we consider, for instance, the following authoritative doctrinal documents. Pope Boniface VIII, in the Bull "Unam Sanctam" (1302), declared that outside the visible boundaries of the Roman Catholic Church no salvation and no forgiveness of sins can be found. The council which in the years 1438-1445 at Ferrara, Florence, and finally in the Lateran sought to bring about a union with the Oriental churches, affirms, in the decree of 1442 (intended for the Syrian Monophysite Church of the Jacobites) and no one can receive eternal life outside of the Roman Catholic Church. If a non-Catholic does not join the Roman Catholic Church before his death, he will be a victim of eternal fire prepared for the Devil and his angels. The shocking thing about these pronouncements, which in their literal reading go back to the north African Bishop Fulgentius (467-533), consists in this that not only Jews and heathen are subject to this excommunication but also heretics. Indeed, even one who is only a schismatic forfeits eternal bliss because he lives in a "church" that is separated from the Roman Catholic Church. In view of this, it already amounted to a certain mitigation of the doctrine when Pope Pius IX, in a declaration of December 9, 1854, stated that those living "in insurmountable ignorance of the true religion" are not on that account guilty of eternal damnation. But he too maintained "that outside of the apostolic, Roman [!] church no one can be saved. She is the only ark of salvation, and everyone who does not enter her, must perish in the flood."

If it is a settled matter that outside of the church there is no salvation and that this church in which salvation is available is contained within the visible boundaries of the Roman church, then doctrinal pronouncements in our day can no longer be satisfied with this declaration alone. An attempt must be made to say something concerning the realm of humanity outside of the Roman Catholic Church which goes beyond that which the medieval church and even Pope Pius IX himself said. An attempt must be made in some way to steer this realm in which there is no salvation toward salvation. Pope Pius XII had clearly recognized this necessity. In his encyclical "Mystici Corporis Christi" (1943) he tried to solve the problem with the help of the doctrine of the efficacy of "longing" or "desiring." If the desire to receive the Sacrament under certain circumstances could take the place of reception itself, the inference is suggested that the desire for membership in the church (votum ecclesiae), which is the epitome of all mediation of salvation, could under certain circumstances achieve something like placing the soul on the way of salvation. What is peculiar about this papal utterance is that such "longing" and "desiring"—contrary to the desire for Baptism on the part of a catechumen—need not consist in thoughts of which one is distinctly conscious. The pope speaks of "a kind of unconscious longing or desire" *(inscium quoddam desiderium ac votum)*. A communication of the Holy Office addressed to the Archbishop of Boston in the year 1949 explains this papal doctrine of the "votum" in such a way that this longing for membership in the church under certain circumstances can be effective also in a person who is held by an insurmountable ignorance. In this case it is sufficient that this person lives with such an inner attitude that he desires his will to conform to the will of God. One may then grant that "longing" for membership in the church is present in such a person.

The details of the doctrine of the desire for membership in the church need not be especially dealt with here. Theologians who attempt to penetrate it dogmatically frequently get into such a jungle of distinctions and conditions that they can hardly find their way through. The efficacy of the desire for membership in the church seems to extend so far that very few are finally threatened with the loss of eternal salvation. On the other hand, it is restricted to so narrow a circle that one is left uncertain as to who those non-Catholics are to whom it is concretely applicable. We are here concerned only with the observation that the doctrinal pronouncements of the Roman Catholic Church have in no case departed from the principle that outside of the visible boundaries of the Roman Catholic Church no living persons are at present members of the body of Jesus Christ and partake of the gift of the new life of grace coming from him. Pope Pius XII, too, in the aforementioned encyclical, "Mystici Corporis Christi," unequivocally affirms that all who are separated from the Roman Catholic Church in faith or in government—therefore also we Protestant Christians—do not live in that one body or out of that one divine Spirit of whom the Apostle Paul speaks when referring to the body whose head is Jesus Christ and which he calls the church. Pope Pius XII expressly rejects the idea that the church as the body of Christ could extend over the visible church separated from the Roman Catholic Church, in such a way that other Christian associations, though separated from one another in faith, would still be united by an invisible spiritual tie.

The conclusion we must draw from this doctrinal encyclical of the Roman Catholic Church is obviously this: Baptized Christians living outside of the boundaries of the Roman Catholic Church, as regards their possible association with the mystical body of Jesus Christ, are in principle, dogmatically speaking, no better situated than unbaptized Jews or heathens who consciously or unconsciously

harbor the longing or desire that their will may be in conformity
with the will of God. According to this papal doctrine, it is out of
the question that in the churches of the Reformation the Holy Spirit
is actually given as a pledge and earnest of the eternal inheritance;
through Word and Sacrament, that the forgiveness of sins is actually bestowed, and that the new birth of water and of the Spirit
by which one becomes a member of the body of Jesus Christ
actually can take place. Outside of the Roman Catholic Church,
according to this official doctrinal utterance of the pope, one cannot
even find traces of the reality of the church but, at best, only a
hardly comprehensible, indistinct longing for membership in the
church, of which the person himself is often unconscious.

It will be a mystery to every Protestant believer how the pope
with this doctrine of his concerning the boundaries of the church
can pass over the salutary power of a valid Baptism as though it
did not exist. We cannot understand how a Baptism can be valid
and yet not be efficacious in the dimension of a real, salutary incorporation of the person into the body of Christ. Is it correct for
those who have received the Sacrament of Baptism merely to be
referred to the doctrine of the "votum" or desire in the matter of
their association with the body of Christ, and thereby, in principle,
placed on a level with unbaptized non-Catholics? Do we not here
have a case of contempt for one of the Sacraments instituted by
Christ? Would it not be a questioning of the salutary power of Jesus
Christ himself, if a true Baptism, rightly dispensed, were thought
to have no salutary effect in the act of dispensation? Is that Baptism
still a Baptism, when the person baptized has received and retained,
trusting in the promises of the Gospel, a genuine Baptism but still
lacks the grace of forgiveness, and lacks the reception of the one
Holy Spirit, by which one is implanted into the one body whose
head is Jesus Christ? Is it anything more than a mere shell, which
is only then filled with the gifts of salvation attributed to it by the
apostolic Word when the person baptized by a heretic is converted to the Roman Catholic Church?

It will furthermore continue to be a mystery to every Protestant
Christian that the pope, through his doctrine concerning the boundaries of the church, so restricts the effective power of the apostolic

Word with regard to the dispensation of salvation and establishment of the congregation of the redeemed that to the Protestant Christian it appears like disputing that power. We must, of course, take into account that what the New Testament has to say about the saving power of God's Word is largely concealed and forgotten in the Roman Catholic Church, in which the saving power of the Sacraments holds the preeminence. But God's Word, which comes to us through the Holy Scriptures and is preached to us on the basis of Scripture, is asserting its claim to be a saving Means of Grace also outside of the churches of the Reformation today. There are indications that also within the Roman Catholic Church the oral preaching of the apostolic Gospel is being recognized more strongly than before as a divinely instituted Means of Grace besides the Sacraments. If the Holy Ghost is truly at work in the Roman Catholic Church, she cannot forego declaring that the living voice of the apostolic Gospel is also a fully valid and indeed fundamental means for the outpouring of the Holy Ghost. "O foolish Galatians!" Paul writes in his epistle to those congregations, ". . . Let me ask you only this: Did you receive the Spirit by works of the law, or *by hearing with faith?*"

Of what importance for the Roman Catholic doctrine of the boundaries of the church is the fact that among the non-Catholics there are baptized Christians who, invoking the triune God, read the Holy Scriptures, hear the Word of the apostles read and preached in the assembled congregation, and who answer to the voice of the apostles with the Credo of the church? In view of this, should not an association of these Christians with the exalted Lord, present with the congregation assembled in his name, be realized that is far different from that which this doctrine of "desiring" and "wishing" would have us believe?

In our discussion on this point we get into a situation somewhat similar to that of the Apostle Paul when he was obliged to defend himself against his opponents at Corinth (Cf. 2 Cor. 11 and 12). We, too, must call attention to the simple fact that the churches of the Reformation, which, according to the doctrine of Pope Pius XII, are denied the grace of living from the one Spirit that runs like a stream through the mystical body of Christ, also can display some-

thing of those operations and gifts of the Spirit which, according to
the doctrine of the Apostle Paul are expressions of this very body.
Paul says, "What I am saying I say not with the Lord's authority
but as a fool, in this boastful confidence. . . ." What are the conversions and the revivals which countless Protestant Christians have
experienced in the churches of the Reformation? What is the zeal
for the spreading of the Gospel which aroused missionaries and
led them to the heathen, many shedding their blood for the name of
Christ? What is that self-sacrificing Christian love for the poor, the
sick, and the crippled which has left its traces also in the history of
the churches of the Reformation? What is that power of resistance
and that ability to suffer for the sake of the Gospel which, to the
astonishment of many, came to life among Protestant Christians
under the antichristian oppression of our own century? Were not
realities experienced here which were wrought by the same Holy
Spirit whom we jointly confess and praise as the third person of the
Holy Trinity? How are these spiritual experiences and gifts to be
reconciled with the papal doctrine concerning the boundaries of
the church, since charismatic gifts exist only in living conditions
with the body of Christ? Has God himself not given an indication
here which plainly shows that, especially in official doctrinal declarations, one should speak differently of baptized "non-Catholics"
than the popes and church law have spoken about them.

The New Testament speaks of a spiritual gift consisting in this
that spiritual songs, psalms, and hymns originate in the church. It
should not be possible to dispute the fact that this charism came
to life anew in an unusual manner, especially in the churches of
the Reformation of the 16th and the 17th centuries, and in Luther
himself. Some bishops of the Roman Catholic Church also recognized this in a practical way by having some of the spiritual songs
which originated in the churches of the Reformation of the 16th and
17th centuries incorporated into the hymnals of their dioceses. We
cannot imagine that these bishops were of the opinion that these
songs did not become true spiritual songs until they were sung from
a Roman Catholic hymnal at a Roman Catholic Mass, while before
this, at the time of their composition, and afterwards, when they
were sung in evangelical worship services, they were empty husks,

stripped of the Holy Spirit—the life-giving stream that flows through the body of Christ. But does not the relation between Jesus Christ, the head of the church, and the visibly circumscribed Roman church, as taught by the popes, demand the proposition that outside of this church there are no real spiritual gifts flowing from the exalted head of the church into his body? The theologians of the churches of the Reformation are profoundly grateful that at least in the realms of the German, Dutch, and French languages there are not a few Roman Catholic theologians who have evidently recognized the fact that the doctrine of the "desire for membership in the church" alone is not sufficient for giving adequate expression to the pneumatological and ecclesiological status of Christendom. We hope that a great deal will come from these beginnings. What will be their lot? Will the coming council relegate them to the bounds of the present ecclesiology governed by the official doctrinal declarations, or will the council be open to the insight that the Word and Sacrament, the Spirit and spiritual gifts, the forgiveness of sins, true membership in the body of Christ, and the present possession of eternal life are realities existing also outside of the Roman Catholic Church— realities bestowed by God the Father himself by virtue of the institutions and the promises of Jesus Christ? Not until we come to understand this do we sense the depth of the mystery of the division of Christendom. To a considerable degree the mystery of this division consists in this that the division of the occidental church, which became necessary for the sake of the apostolic Word and for the sake of the salvation of souls, *is still embraced by the one body of the exalted Lord.* The division of the occidental churches can neither divide this body of Christ nor restrict it to the visible boundaries of any one church.

Here we have in outline the solution of that "squaring of the circle" of which we spoke above. A proper dogmatical evaluation of the ecclesiological import of the division of the occidental churches in the 16th century will make clear to us *how the exclusiveness of the dogma on which the necessity of excommunication is based is to be reconciled with the willingness to recognize something essential held in common in which the possibility of genuine communication in the midst of ecclesiological division is offered.*

It should have become plain that the solution to which our deliberations point is not touched by the charge of indifferentism, about which the draft of the constitution prepared at the First Vatican Council, speaks concerning the church. It is indeed not a matter of indifference to us whether a baptized person lives in a church in which the encounter with the saving apostolic Gospel is seriously endangered by heresies that have crept in or whether he lives in a church in which the Gospel is preached in conformity with the Holy Scriptures and the Sacraments are administered in accord with their institution by the Lord Jesus Christ. We cannot help the fact that the Roman Catholic Church, in view of her responsibility, brands the churches of the Reformation with the blemish of heresy. The churches of the Reformation are also compelled to reject as heresies some doctrines which are essential to the Roman Catholic Church. The differences in faith and in doctrine do indeed reach such a depth that we cannot celebrate the Lord's supper at the same altar. In this there will be no change as far as our view extends. But much would be changed if churches which are compelled to excommunicate each other because of heresies would not lose sight of the fact that the body of the Lord actually exists in the midst of the other "church." It would certainly be of far-reaching importance if the council of the Roman Catholic Church could understand that it has pleased the triune God in his mercy and his saving acts to breach the visible boundaries of the Roman Catholic Church in quite another way than that which is expressed by the doctrine of the "desire" for membership in the church. We are not able to estimate what particular changes would be wrought by this insight. But we are certain that there would be some fundamental change in the mutual relation of the separated churches if in our spiritual life—and no less in our theological thinking—the understanding would gain ground that the reality of the body of Christ, already here on earth and in this hour, extends farther than the visible boundaries of the church of which one is a member. Between correctly rejected indifferentism on the one hand and the identification of a visibly circumscribed church with the body of the exalted Lord as espoused by the papal documents on the doctrine of the Church on the other, there must be a third position that goes far beyond the papal doctrine of the "votum." *Of this third position we expect more for the future of divided Christendom and also a stronger spiritual power for the future of the divided human race than we do of our present anathemas.*

If the *mystery* of the division under which Christendom is living has unveiled itself to us to such an extent that we can see the *third position*, we may venture a step still farther and say: We not only bear with the person separated from us and esteem him, but we also *need* him. We need him in order that he, being different, by virtue of the very fact that he is different, may help us to keep the Word of truth and to understand it better. The truth, by inner necessity, is opposed to error. In the division under which we are living we are concerned with truth and error in the faith with regard to doctrine and preaching. When truth is polemically engaged with error, it must be sharpened to a point like an arrow so that it can hit its mark. While it is in the process of becoming pointed, it must of necessity temporarily neglect some of its own essential content. There is the danger that this neglected content be lost because of the necessary sharpening procedure. Therefore we have need of the other person, whose truth, pointed against us, can draw our attention to matters which have not only been temporarily neglected by us but which perhaps may already have been suppressed among us.

Among his people God himself brings about such sharpening of his Word, in certain situations, in order that it may, like an arrow, pierce our hard hearts, which try to frustrate its activity. We are convinced that in the Reformation of Martin Luther such a sharpening of the truth of God's Word was brought about by God the Holy Spirit. We are convinced that this pointed arrow must render its service in Christendom in our day also. But we are beginning to understand that the necessary *sharpening* of the truth dare not becloud our vision of the *whole* truth. However, keeping our eye on the whole truth by no means requires that its point be dulled. But it does keep us from seeking the truth only in the form of its sharpened polemical point. Sharpening the truth must not lead us to forget the truth itself. One who would break the head off the arrow and would think that in the arrowhead alone he had the entire arrow, would be deceiving himself. As certainly as the fullness of the truth

in a given situation of God's people must be sharpened, in order
to bring about the right decision, so certainly does sharpening the
truth require the awareness of that which could not enter into the
"polemical arrowhead."

It would be wrong if we from the point of view of these reflections would see in the churches of the Reformation only the "polemical arrowhead" of the truth of God's Word and on the other
hand would want to pass off the manifold strange additions to the
truth in Catholicism for the fullness of the truth. In the churches
of the Reformation, too, we are concerned with the one truth of
God's revelation in its entirety! On the other hand, the Roman Catholic Church has dogmas which appear to us to be "polemical arrowheads" broken from the truth. The identification of the denominationally circumscribed papal church with the mystical body of
Jesus Christ present on earth, is such an arrowhead. It is broken
from the shaft and therefore is no longer suitable for hitting the
mark. Such broken arrowheads are found also in Protestant theology.
An understanding of faith in which everything is made dependent
upon a personally rendered decision, no room being left for the
steadfast existence of the new creature brought into being by the
new birth, is an understanding, in truth, which is likewise nothing
more than a severed arrowhead but no longer an arrowhead of the
truth. It might correspond to the will of God, who has ordained
the division under which we live, if we were to give attention to
recognizing the dangers connected with the sharpening of "polemical arrowheads" and in so doing would listen to the "brethren"
separated from us. Might it not be that God has kept us separated
for the very reason that we might not lose the truth of his Word?
"The spirit is willing, but the flesh is weak." If we were left to ourselves without any opposition, drowsiness of the flesh might easily
overcome the watchfulness of the spirit. What would have become
of Christendom without the polemical sharpening of the truth of
the Gospel by the Reformation? What would have become of the
sharpening of the truth in the Reformation without the opposition
of the Roman Catholic Church? Could it not correspond to the will
of God, who is at work also in the division under which we live,
that we look upon the church separated from us not only with the

question as to the extent to which we are right but also with the question whether in the polemical arrowhead of truth offered to us by it, something might have been overlooked which belongs to the truth itself—something which possibly is still alive in the church separated from us? Could it not be that through the heresy against which our anathema must be directed a question might come to us which we had not yet heard before? Should not our recognition and liberation of the truth disguised in heresy constitute our most effective defense against it? If we concern ourselves about this, then we shall actually begin to take the division upon ourselves, and to bear with the churches separated from us by the division. If we begin to understand that, because of our flesh, God did not want to preserve his truth on earth—the truth in its richness and sharpening form—in any other way than in opposing the separated churches, then we shall on the basis of such conclusion make the first step into the future. If it is God's will and we have faith, then in this future not only that church will be one which is being built into the body of Jesus Christ through the Word and Sacrament, but also that church which delivers the means of salvation to the world and in this delivery is now divided. Not until those who are separated in the administration of the Means of Grace are *one* in this activity and are permitted to stand at the same altar—not until then will that be fulfilled which the Lord of the church promised when he prayed for it:

> *. . . that they may all be one; even as thou,*
> *Father, art in me, and I in thee, that*
> *they also may be in us, so that the world*
> *may believe that thou hast sent me.*

BIBLIOGRAPHY

Prepared by GERHARD PEDERSEN

Note: The following bibliography is merely a selection of the literature on the coming Council. The items marked by an asterisk are of non-catholic origin.

1. *Newspapers and periodicals which regularly bring out information on the Council.*

America (New York)

American Ecclesiastical Review (Washington, D.C.)

Catholica

Commonweal (New York)

The Ecumenical Review (Geneva)

Herder Korrespondenz (Freiburg i. Br.)

Irenikon (Chevetogne, Belgium)

Istina (Paris)

Materialdienst des Konfessionskundlichen Instituts (Bensheim)

Ökumenische Rundschau (Stuttgart)

Osservatore Romano (Vatikan)

The Tablet (London)

Una Sancta (Augsburg)

Unitas (Engl. ed. Rom/French ed. Paris)

2. *Books and articles.*

*) *Alivisatos,* Kamilcar S., The proposed Ecumenical Council and Reunion (in: The Ecumenical Review 12, 1959, p. 1-10).

*) *Asmussen,* Hans, Das kommende Konzil nach dem Stande vom lo. November 1959. Meitingen 1960.

Bacht, H., Das Vaticanum II—ein Unionskonzil (in: Catholica 14 1960, p. 197-205).

Bea, Augustin, Kardinal, Die Kirche und die Begegnung mit den getrennten Christen (in: Una Sancta 16, 1961, pp. 28-34).

Brandenburg, A., Evangelische Christenheit vor dem Konzil. Osnabrück 1961 (Fromms Taschenbücher Nr. 11.)

*) *Calogirou,* J., The character of the Orthodox church according to the soteriological principles of the N. T. Athens 1961. (ed. in Greek.)

211

*) Bischof *Cassian,* Concile Romain et unité chrétienne (in: Le Messager orthodoxe 13, 1961, p. 2 ff).

Le *Concile* et les conciles. Contribution a l'histoire de la vie conciliaire de l'Eglise. (With contributions by B. Botte, H. Marot, P.-Th. Camelot, Y. Congar, H. Alivisatos, G. Fransen, P. de Vooght, J. Gill, A. Dupront und R. Aubert.) Paris/ Chevetogne 1960.

Le *concile* oecuménique. Lumiēre et vie. (Lyon) 45, 1959. (With contributions by P.Th. Camelot, M.-B. Carra de Vaux Saint-Cyr, J. Hamer, Y, Congar, R.-C. Gerest, G. Racoveanu, J. Bosc.)

Congar, Yves M. J., Die Konzilien im Leben der Kirche (in: Una Sancta 14, 1959, pp. 156-171).

Cornelis, Jerome, The General Council: The Hope of Unity (in: Unitas 11. 1959. p. 85 ff.).

Daniel-Rops, H., Vatican II. Le concile de Jean XXIII. Paris, Coll. Le Signe, 1961.

*) *Dietzfelbinger,* Hermann, Die eine Kirche und die Reformation. München 1961.

*) *Dulac,* R., The catholic's preparation for the council (in: American Ecclesiastical Review 141, 1959, pp. 145-154).

Dumont, C. J., Le prochain Concile et l'unité chrétienne (in: Vers L' unité chrétienne 12, 1960, p. 1 ff.). German translation: Das bevorstehende Konzil und die christliche Einheit. In: Ökumenische Rundschau, 8, 1959, p. 76 ff.

Duprey, P., Orthodoxe reacties op het pontificaat van Paus Joannes XXIII (in: Het Christelijk Oosten en Hereniging, Nijmegen, 13, 1960, pp. 3-21).

Fenton, J. C., The Ecumenical Council and Christian reunion (in: American Ecclesiastical Review 141, 1959, pp. 45-57).

――――. The forthcoming council of the Roman Church (in: Life of the Spirit, 14, 1960, pp. 300-306).

Fedin, Hubert, Ecumenical Councils in the Catholic Church. An Historical Survey. Edinburgh and London 1960.

Johannes XXIII, Acta et documenta concilio oecumenico vaticano II apparando. Series I. (antepraeparatoria) Vol. 1. Acta Summi Pontificis Joannis XXIII. Romae, 1960.

Anregungen und Hoffnungen für das zweite Vatikanische *Konzil* (in: Wort und Wahrheit 15, 1960, 1. Die Kirche auf dem Weg zur Einen Welt. pp. 245-262. 2. Glaube und Leben im Zeitalter der Technik. pp. 325-346. 3. Erneuerung in Verkündigung un und kanonischem Recht. pp. 405-422).

Fragen an das *Konzil.* Herder Bücherie 95, Freiburg 1961.

Küng, Hans, Konzil und Wiedervereinigung. Erneuerung als Ruf in die Einheit. Herder, 1960.

――――. The Forthcoming Ecumenical Council as seen by three Russian Theologians (in: Unitas 11, 1959, p. 107 ff.).

*) *Leuba,* Jean Louis, Was erwarten evangelische Christen vom Ökumenischen Konzil? (in: Ökumenische Rundschau 9, 1960, pp. 77-90).

McQuade, James J., What you should know about the Ecumenical Council, in questions and answers with discussion topics. St. Louis (Missouri, USA) 1960.

Matzerath, R., The Ecumenical Council and the Ecumenical Movement (in: American Ecclesiastical Review 140, 1959, pp. 392-398).

*) *Meinhold,* Peter, Der evangelische Christ und das Konzil (in: Wort und Wahrheit 14, 1959, pp. 489-501).

———. Was erwarten evangelische Christen vom angekündigten Ökumenischen Konzil (in: Una Sancta 15, 1960, pp. 30-40).

———. Die christliche Ökumene. Evangelische Besinnung auf die Weltkirchenkonferenz in Neu-Delhi und das Zweite Vatikanische Konzil (in: Wort und Wahrheit 16, 1961, pp. 101-116).

———. The Protestant and the Council (in: Cross Currents 10, 1960, pp. 125-137).

*) *Opinions orthodoxes* sur le prochain concile romain. Le Messager orthodoxe, 6, 1959.

Saint John, H., Ecumenical survey: prospects of the coming council (in: Blackfriars 41, 1960, pp. 128-132).

Sartory, Thomas, Das Konzil—eine innerkatholische Angelegenheit? (in: Ökumenische Rundschau 9, 1960, pp. 62-76).

*) *Schmemann,* Alexander, Rom, das ökumenische Konzil und die orthodoxe Kirche (in: Una Sancta 14, 1959, p. 283 ff.).

Sheering, J. B., How Ecumenical will the Council be? (in: Catholic World 188, 1959, pp. 445-448).

	DATE DUE	